HUMANS ARE NOT ROBOTS

HUMANS ARE NOT ROBOTS

Why We *All* Need Work Flexibility
and What Company Leaders
Can Do About It

Robert Hawkins

MAVEN HOUSE

Published by Maven House Press, 17 Church St., 2nd Floor, Lambertville, NJ 08530; 610.883.7988; www.mavenhousepress.com.

Special discounts on bulk quantities of Maven House Press books are available to corporations, professional associations, and other organizations. For details contact the publisher.

Library of Congress Control Number: 2020939038

Hardcover ISBN: 9781947540040
Paperback ISBN: 9781947540156
E-book ISBN: 9781947540057

CONTENTS

To Andi,
Forever my muse

robot noun

1: a machine with a human appearance or functioning like a human.

2: a machine capable of carrying out a complex series of actions automatically.

3. a person who works mechanically and efficiently but insensitively.

[Czech, 1920, from *robota* "forced labour"]

— Australian Concise Oxford Dictionary, fifth edition (2017)

CHAPTER 1

Introduction

Forget the old concept of retirement and saving for the future – there is no need to wait and every reason not to. Whether your dream is escaping the rat race, experiencing first-class world travel, earning a monthly five-figure income with no management, or just living more and working less, this book is the blueprint.

— Marketing Blurb, *The 4-Hour Workweek* (2007)[1]

Why *This* Book?

THE 4-HOUR WORKWEEK, written by Tim Ferriss in 2007 as a guide for people who want to escape their normal jobs and have "more life," tapped into something big.

Whenever I had my copy out in public, a stranger would often give me a sly, sideways smile to show that they too were discovering the secret recipe to freedom. Or sometimes, if they were a little braver, they would walk up, interrupt my lunch, and ask me if I had found my *muse* – a side hustle designed to create a passive income allowing this escape from the normal working world. Not a lot of books create this bridge between strangers. Not a lot of books tap into a shared feeling, a shared desire, a shared pain. Not to this extent.

Over 2.1 million people in the United States alone bought *The 4-Hour Workweek*,[2] hoping that they too could each find a niche product for a niche audience, test the market, start selling the product, and then automate and outsource the entire process so all they had to do was sit on a beach in Rio and check their ever-growing bank accounts (once a week, on Monday mornings). The premise of the book was not to help people become billionaires, or even millionaires, it was to help them make enough money to replace a traditional salary so they could free themselves from the traditional workplace.

I was one of those people. But it wasn't until years later that I started to wonder why we felt like we needed to free ourselves in the first place. Why were people's normal jobs and normal workplaces so painful that the idea of escaping them warranted interrupting a stranger's lunch just to check the progress of their muse? No one ever comes up to me when I'm reading *The Lord of the Rings* to see if Frodo has finally destroyed the One Ring. No, there's something much more real about this pain. There's a collective knowledge that something is fundamentally wrong with our lives and the way we work.

Some of us did manage to escape our normal jobs. I'm sure thousands of ex-accountants and ex-plumbers produced wonderful side businesses that mostly look after themselves – with online sales funnels and virtual assistants in Mumbai – and now they're sitting back at a café in Madrid, sipping sangria, laughing at the old ways.

But many of us are still trapped. Many read the recipe, tried, and failed (me included – it's called The Spectacular Men's Underwear Failure of 2014; you get the picture). Many scanned the book, scoffed, and put it back on the shelf, thinking it was a bit far-fetched. Many never saw the book and are not aware of mini-retirements or muses and still work their usual jobs because it's all they know. And some – most – are those normal people who just want to make as much money as they can, in an ordinary and secure way, to provide food, a place to live, financial security, and the occasional holiday to Bali for their family without the stress of wondering when or from where their next paycheck is going to arrive. Most of us have always depended on normal jobs, and most of us will always depend on normal jobs.

But, again, these normal jobs are painful.

We are all bound in friendship through this universal foe. We work hard and long weeks, and easily connect with strangers by merely saying "TGIF!" With our normal job, we sell our lives, our freedom, our humanity, to make a living and survive. This way of existing is unsustainable and damaging to our world, and, as we'll find out later, completely unnecessary and not even profitable for the businesses that we work for.

But things are changing.

Globally, a social revolution – specifically regarding work: the way we work, the amount of control businesses have over us, and the realization that the way a business is managed impacts our lives and the world outside the sliding doors – is slowly getting louder.

The drums of discontent are uniting in a chorus that's saying it's not enough for a few lucky individuals to have a life of quality, that this life should be available to us all.

Women, for the most part, are beating those drums. This half of the population, who have fought so hard for so many years to be taken seriously in the working world, are now saying, "Something is still not right. I should be able to pick my kids up from school *and* eventually be the CEO or a director. Why the hell not? And why am I still doing all the housework?!"

They're seeing that even though they have increased access to flexibility at work, they're still doing the majority of the housework, still hurting their careers because they're being perceived as uncommitted slackers (and being called *working mothers* when no man in the history of the universe has been called a *working father*), and still feeling guilty for using flexibility when everyone else is stuck in the office.

More women than ever before are starting businesses, partly because when they're their own boss they aren't constrained by rubbish traditions. They find that they really can have and do it all when they have the power to manage their lives – work, kids, sleep, and everything in between – in a holistic way.

And it's not just women. *Millennials* (and the upcoming *Gen Zs*), in typical millennial fashion, are demanding more of life and their bosses and the people around them by asking that simple yet often demonized question: "Why?" As in, "Why am I forced to sit here till five? I finished everything I had to do two hours ago." Or, "Why do you do it this way? I can write a program that could do it in a fraction of that time." Or, "Why should I care? How does this job impact the planet?"

This well-informed and broad-minded generation knows, in their heart of hearts, that work is more than just about making money and retiring at seventy. They want to live now. They want to experience the world now. They want to contribute, to make a difference, now. And then go home. There's no reason they shouldn't be able to.

And it's not just women and millennials. *Men* around the world are having existential crises. They're angry and stressed and dying early and they don't know why. They want to spend time with their kids, the way their dads never did with them. They want to create and rest and play rather than toil endlessly before some stress-related condition puts them in the grave. Many don't even realize what they want because they're too tired to think about what they want; they just know something is missing, and it damages them and the people around them.

The traditional workplace, with its long and rigid hours, has created a stunted version of men, men who "win bread" but have limited abilities in household management and caregiving and other important parts of life. And men are facing an unusual type of discrimination that hurts both them and their partners – flexism:[3] requesting flexibility but being refused at much higher rates than women because "they don't really need it."*

Humans are voting with their feet. Freelancing – the *gig economy* – and its close cousin entrepreneurship are growing rapidly. Millions of people all over the world are leaving their secure, well-paying jobs to journey into the Wild West – finding their own customers, making their own money, looking after their own taxes, not having sick or parental leave, and, for those in the United States, not having health insurance – with nothing but caffeine and hope.[4] The lack of social security and unpredictability of income are small costs for that taste of freedom, to be in control of their own lives. These people are fighting for their chance to have flexibility.[5]

Not everyone will truly make it as freelancers or entrepreneurs, though. What about those who don't? And what about those who can't work for themselves, either because their skills or profession don't enable them to, or they're just not entrepreneurially inclined? There's a lot more to running a business than just doing the work itself. And what about those who don't even want to be freelancers or entrepreneurs? Should the many people around the world with normal jobs continue to cope with non-freedom and rigid, low-quality lives?

The 4-Hour Workweek and countless other self-escape and self-flexibility books were a great start to help some individuals escape rigid workplaces, and to get many to question their place in the world and what they want from life. But the next questions are overdue: Why can't we *all* have freedom? Do we really need to escape our normal jobs to get it? Or

---

* *Flexism*, defined as "prejudice or discrimination on the basis of a person's working status," also applies to people who have access to flexibility but are discriminated against for using it (mostly women).

could our normal jobs be more accommodating to life so we can have both security *and* freedom? And if this is possible, what's stopping it?

This book answers those questions. This is *The 4-Hour Workweek* for everyone else. I'm not trying to help individuals escape the rat race, but to challenge the existence of the rat race, and to argue that work itself adds incredible value to people's lives beyond money; it just needs to change.

This book was written to guide current and future leaders into changing whole organizations – to free hundreds, thousands, millions of people from a way of working that doesn't meet our expectations for modern life. It's one thing to be an individual who is finding out how to personally escape and work flexibly, and something very different to be a manager or owner of a business who

1. feels compelled to provide flexibility for their workers (or even themselves) in the face of a thousand other pressures, and

2. is trying to put in place sustainable and successful flexibility practices for all employees and managers while still operating a business.

This book helps leaders by providing theory and evidence for the urgent need for flexibility *for all* and then provides practical guidance on rolling out successful (and profitable) flexibility campaigns.

Who the Hell Am I?

Anyone who claims to possess expertise in an area should probably have some credibility to back up their words. There should be a reason someone would listen to me over anyone else who is also writing on the same topic, or even take notice of the topic itself. Do I have a doctorate in flexibility? Or business? Or workology?* Have I built a multi-national company that leads the way in flexible work practices? Do I have the fifteen to twenty years of business or consulting experience generally required to be a thought leader in the area? *Have I ever even visited Harvard?* Well, no.

First and foremost, I am me – a person; a human; Robert. I learned the hard and ugly way, roughly after my second or third retrenchment during my "normal" career, that attaching my identity to my profession is a restrictive and dangerous way to perceive myself. "What do you do?"

---

* May or may not be a made-up discipline.

"Oh, I'm an engineer." "Cool [I've secretly now judged you to be a worthy person to talk to and be associated with because you're educated and have a respectable job]."

Although I have worked as an engineer, a process improvement manager, a casual laborer in a bread factory, a lifeguard at a swimming pool, a duty manager at Subway, and a freelance editor and writer and consultant, I don't refer to myself by any of these titles. No. I am a unique arrangement of universe-energy. I'm a team of thirty-seven trillion cells, each one refined through billions of years of evolution (and each one agreeing with you that this paragraph is starting to sound like pretentious crapola).

A million different things make me who I am: likes and dislikes and loves and hates; things that make me happy, things that make me wildly upset; a missing toe on my right foot. I care about certain things and certain people; I couldn't give a shit about others. I'm good at some things, bad at more. I eat; I have sex; I sleep; I write; I make things; I look at clouds; I read news on the toilet; I watch Netflix; I learn; I have dreams and goals. But mostly, I'm a human.

What I have, in relevance to this topic, is enough experience in enough workplaces in the right positions to see that the whole "work" thing, in its current form, is bullshit; and I have enough passion and desire and knowledge to do something about it.

It only took a couple of years of working the normal nine to five to know that something was wrong, to know that it's not right to feel terrible and exhausted on a daily basis, to crave weekends, and to turn a desperate shade of blue every time Sunday night arrives.

It only took a certain number of coworkers and friends with dead eyes and poor health, who were also craving the weekends or upcoming holidays, to know that something was very wrong.

This was when I was in the trenches as a manufacturing engineer and starting down the route of process improvement (increasing efficiency of machines and people, ultimately to make more money by reducing wasted time and resources). I could already see some terrible flaws in the way we manage others, the biggest being why we need to "manage" others at all.

The feeling of injustice got caught in my throat when I saw grown adults being treated like school children, but with less trust. They were being controlled and coerced into doing the "right" things at work; and this was killing their desire to do their best work, creating an us-versus-them scenario where there was always opposition between the two. In so many ways, businesses were stifling the very productivity that they were paying specialists (like me) so much money to achieve. Why was this happening?

I started to develop and test my own theories about productivity and management, both on myself and on unsuspecting people above and below me on the ladder. These theories mainly focused on energy. Most of us didn't have enough energy to truly give a fuck, or even to think properly. People already had great ideas and a desire to change and do better, but management pressure and long hours didn't leave space (time and energy) for these qualities to be fostered.

I broadened my focus to include waste, and I realized that the way business operates is wasteful, not only to business itself, but a waste of life bordering on criminal. To see adults sitting at a desk trying to look busy because they're "not allowed to go home yet" makes me want to cry.

No one gains anything from these practices; or rather, we – individuals, business, society, the environment, and everything in between – all lose because of them.

During my experiments in different work environments (office, home, factory, etc.) I found that the human side and the work side of a person are inseparable, and they influence each other (sometimes for good, sometimes for bad). I discovered that using up less time and energy improves productivity. Yet the way people are managed doesn't take into account this phenomenon. Instead, people are used as though they're machines, expected to be constantly productive, day in and day out, and the importance of their lives outside of work is rarely considered until something extreme happens (a death, the flu, childbirth). It's all wrong.

Parallel to these slowly developing ideas about energy and productivity, traffic was bugging me.

Growing up in a small town in the middle of Australia, I found traffic congestion completely foreign and, well, shocking when I finally experienced it – every morning and every evening – as a professional working in one of Australia's capital cities, Brisbane. It was surreal: a weird nightmare as I crawled forward in my car behind an infinite line of other crawling cars for a reason that would never reveal itself, while listening to someone on the radio talk about how bad the traffic was.

Day after day the traffic reporter listed streets and highways that were suffering from congestion. Every morning and afternoon it was the same list. It didn't change. There was never any mention of how it could change or anything being done to improve it. A helicopter was burning copious amounts of fuel to tell us what we all knew. Its purpose, I guessed, was to remind people who were stuck in traffic that they were stuck in traffic. I also guessed that I was already in hell.

The engineer in me had to do something. I read about traffic congestion: Why does it exist? What are the different types? How do you reduce it or eliminate it? It was fascinating, and the answers were exactly the opposite of human nature.

To get rid of a traffic jam, you either need to get some cars off the road (more on that later) or you need to drive more slowly and leave a large gap between yourself and the car in front. That erases those sudden stops and starts that propagate a jam, and eventually it disappears.

Japanese jamologist (traffic researcher) Professor Katsuhiro Nishinari recommends a forty-meter gap or more to disperse traffic – a theory tested with great success on Tokyo's Shuto Expressway:

> At 4:00 pm there was always about a ten-kilometer traffic jam. We asked eight cars to keep headway; we asked them to move more slowly than other cars and it was amazing. With just eight cars the jam didn't appear for forty minutes. If you continuously had all cars (keeping headway) maybe you can shift the onset again and have no traffic jam. It's counter-intuitive but if we slow down it makes the flow faster. Slower is faster.[6]

There was one problem with this revolutionary find: people aren't patient at the best of times, and behind the wheel they turn into monsters who need to get where they're trying to get, *now*! I literally ended up on several kill lists (including my then-partner's) by testing this slow, constant-speed driving with large gaps.

In trying to address the problem on a larger scale, and avoid being murdered, I came up with other solutions: a phone app that would help drivers regulate their speed well before they reached an area of congestion, or a leave-your-car-at-home day to encourage people to try public transport or find other ways to avoid driving. I learned about autonomous vehicles and what they could eventually do for congestion. But in my digging for information about traffic, an obvious question came to mind: Why are people driving at the same time in the same direction every day anyway? And this is when I discovered telecommuting – working away from the normal workplace by using technology.

This concept of not going to the office every day was something I must have heard of before, but I didn't take it seriously, or maybe I didn't see the point. The Protestant ethic, "work hard all week, at work, doing whatever is asked of you by your boss, and then relax and drink away your pain on the weekend," was seared into my psyche at an early age. But here was this thing – working from a different location, even home of all places – that suddenly and loudly answered the question, How do we get cars off the road?

And while I was digging for information, I fell down a rabbit hole. I realized that telecommuting was just one form of flexible work, and that these different forms could not only help with traffic congestion but also ticked the boxes for the energy and productivity theories I had been playing with: they answered the questions of how to help people feel happier and more engaged and productive at work, consistently. Eureka! These two parallel roads that I had been putting so much of myself into converged into one superhighway of goodness.

Flexibility also turned out to be a boon for sustainability as well as other challenges the world is facing, such as gender inequality, poor physical and mental health, aging workforces and disability, wealth inequality, skills shortages, job loss due to automation, and more. Double and triple eureka!

From connections I've made in the world of diversity and inclusion and sustainability, from research I've done for consulting and writing on the subject, and from learning about health as I go through my own journeys with depression and chronic pain, I've discovered that there exists such an intricate web between life and work and the world around us that it's impossible for any of these elements to exist separate from the others. Pull one strand and the whole web moves, for good or for bad.

For example, work-induced stress produces adverse physical responses (such as inflammation) that can lead to depression, the leading cause of disability in the world.[7] Governments can reduce traffic congestion and pollution by incentivizing flexible work practices much faster and more cheaply than by building new roads or expanding public transport. Rates of domestic violence can be reduced by allowing for more job control and autonomy for both men and women.

For me, over the course of the last several years, the concept of work flexibility has grown from "telecommuting would be a cool way to reduce congestion" to the premise and driver behind the book you hold:

> We, as humans, expect more. We need more. We deserve more. To be treated like a human and to be free to be human is a basic right, and one that cannot and should not be taken away by fear, arbitrary rules of the workplace, and outdated and controlling management styles. *Flexibility is a human right.*

Being human is a major theme of this book, so I aim to bring my real, authentic self into the words – anger and happiness and imperfections and all. So there will be a bad word here and there; there will be references to topics we balk at in the workplace, such as sex, and mental health, and boredom, and love, and lying, and joy, and, heaven forbid, other passions besides our jobs; there will be (at least an attempt of) vulnerability and humor, mostly in the form of personal stories and dry, rhetorical sarcasm; and there will be hand-drawn stick figures and graphs. This is not by chance. With this book I want to step away from the needlessly sterile, inhuman places many of us call work, and encourage a dirty, truthful, productive, real space where we can be our true selves, and be human all the time, not just after five.

And that's who the hell I am.

Guiding Principles
Flexibility Is for All People

Flexibility is usually only considered important for the working mothers mentioned earlier, or those with some other caring responsibilities. And there are swathes of our population working in industries where *flexibility* would not be uttered for fear of being laughed out of the building, such as healthcare, manufacturing, trades and construction, retail, hospitality, and transport – basically any industry that isn't "knowledge" work and that can't easily be done at any time from any location.

Another major theme of this book is that flexibility is for all people, regardless of their reasons, the industry in which they work, the level or type of job they have, their gender, their age, or any other boxes they fit in. It's entirely necessary *and* possible for all people to have flexible work, and I will show you why and how.

Humans Don't Want to Escape Work

The driving assumption of *The 4-Hour Workweek* and similar books is that people want to escape work itself, but I will argue that we need work for many reasons beyond earning money.

Work fulfills extremely important human requirements for a full life, such as connecting and participating with other people pursuing shared goals, opportunities for us to understand and create and learn, having purpose and mastering skills (even flipping a burger or picking up rubbish can provide that purpose and mastery), as well as maintaining a healthy contrast to the other parts of our lives. The thing that we want to escape is long, rigid, unnecessarily stressful work.

Work, in its current form, is a belligerent, voracious monster, crashing around and devouring all of our resources, while our health, relationships, leisure, discovery and adventure, freedom, higher thought and consciousness, and other passions and interests are all huddled in the corner and under rocks, emaciated and starving, waiting for a precious weekend or holiday so they can finally be taken care of (Figure 1.1). We don't need to destroy the monster, we just need to tame it and feed it less. There just needs to be a better balance so that *all* our needs, including those provided by work, can be fulfilled in a sustainable way (Figure 1.2).

I do call for less time at work throughout the book as a general goal because our current standard is damaging in so many ways, but the aim is not to get down to zero hours, which is harmful in its own way, or a Keynesian fifteen-hour workweek, which is just another arbitrary number. The aim is to focus on the value of work, both to the employee and the employer, and the amount of control someone has over their own work and life.

The Productivity of a Human Is Non-Linear

Unlike a robot, which produces the same number of things all day every day (linear productivity), humans have peaks and troughs of productivity (non-linear productivity), and this needs to be decoupled from

Work for Most People

Figure 1.1. For most people work is currently a belligerent being that demands all our time and effort and energy and forces all other parts of the human experience into the tired margins of the day, starving them (and us) in the process.

time and place constraints for people to fully realize their productive potential.

The value that a person can provide a company is so much more than physical presence and unending toil, and it varies from minute to minute, day to day, week to week. People are capable of improving their work and that of their coworkers, and they have the ability to innovate in abstract and astonishing ways. But that capability can only be unleashed when they are able to fill their *energy buckets* (the balanced source of human energy, fully described in Chapter 5) by regularly fulfilling *all* of their human needs, and it's heavily suppressed by the level of toil and control that are inflicted by traditional work structures. Flexibility allows us to move away from this scarcity of human capital and toward abundance.

Humans Can Look After Themselves

There is this weird assumption that employees need perks and awards and lifestyle training to feel "well" and engaged at work and to make better personal choices about exercise, sleep, and diet. It's all very creepy, and not only disregards the fact that we're living, breathing individuals who can make good decisions for ourselves but also ignores the fact that

What Work Could Be

discovery and adventure | work | rest | freedom | other interests | relationships | health | higher thought and consciousness

Figure 1.2. What work could be: part of the team! With flex, work becomes one of the parts of our humanity and helps the others flourish rather than hindering them (and flourishes itself too, with greater energy, motivation, and creativity).

work itself is often a root cause for our poor lifestyle choices in the first place.

Businesses don't need to educate employees on the benefits of sleep or give them financial rewards to get at least six hours of sleep a night, as some companies in Japan are doing for their employees. They just need to give them the opportunity to sleep more by ensuring that they're not working ridiculously long hours.

They don't need to convince employees to exercise by tracking and rewarding or punishing them based on their Fitbit stats, as the state of West Virginia in the United States tried to do to their teachers, with proposed $500 fines for individuals not tracking their health data.[8] They need to question why their current work practices are sucking up their employees' time and energy to the point where it becomes a Herculean task to choose exercise over collapsing in front of the TV.

I'm very much against a business inflicting itself onto an employee's life with patronizing "we're going to *help* you make better decisions" rubbish, offering free fruit and step challenges and sleep tracking. A main aspect of flexibility is that it gives people the space (time and energy) to make their own choices; what they do with that space is not their business's business.

The Biggest Barrier to Flexibility Is Polite Skepticism

The most common argument against flexibility, the one that I hear more often than any other, is not the absolute and angry rejection of the idea. It's not, "That sounds friggin' terrible; get the hell out of my office." It's much friendlier and more casual – "It sounds fantastic, but it's just not for my business," or "It's just not feasible right now." This argument is known as *polite skepticism.*[9]

And although seemingly supportive and harmless, it is the biggest hurdle to freedom and sustainable lives for millions. Its subtext is, "Well, in a perfect world, sure, I'd love to give more flexibility to all my staff. I'd also love to give them each Lamborghinis and fly them to Nepal for yoga and team-bonding sessions; but it's not really practical, is it? It'd be nice to have; but no, not for us. Thank you! [Big smile.]"

Facebook, a company whose mission is "to build community and bring the world closer together,"[10] recently lost one of its employees because it rejected her request for a simple type of flexibility: working part time. Eliza Khuner, a data scientist, wanted less time at work so she could spend more time with her young children. After being denied she decided to leave loudly.

She publicly challenged both Mark Zuckerberg and Sheryl Sandberg, the CEO and COO, asking for their support for flexibility: "Would you lead this company and the U.S. in supporting working parents; would you give us the chance to show you how kick-ass and loyal we can be with fewer hours at the desk?"

Both were politely skeptical.

Sandberg, a proclaimed feminist and author of the book *Lean In*, explained that "while management wanted to move in that direction at some point in the future, they couldn't right now. Allowing part-time options to all parents would strain the rest of the team."

And Zuckerberg? Khuner wrote that "he was sorry I was leaving, but echoed Sheryl. He said he'd like to offer more options for parents, but the trade-offs in serving the greater community were too great. Maybe later."[11]

Maybe later.

Not right now.

Not for us.

It's just not feasible at the moment.

Sorry.

[Big smile.]

The urgency for flexibility is not clear to everyone. It's a nice-to-have instead of a house on fire, or a *burning platform* in corporate lingo. (Also notice both Sandberg's and Zuckerberg's assumption that flexibility is only needed by parents.)

But it *is* urgent; the urgency is just not obvious. The link between the traditional, rigid workplace and many severe and immediate issues we face as individuals and as a society is not easily seen with the naked eye, in the same way that the link between smoking and lung cancer wasn't easily seen until doctors and statisticians looked deeper in the 1940s and 1950s; and even they were confronted by polite skeptics (and orchestrated propaganda) for decades.[12]

The first part of this book shows the polite skeptics that the platform for flexibility is indeed on fire; the rest of the book shows that it's possible and profitable to put that fire out.

Small Changes Can Make Big Differences

What often lies beneath the polite skepticism is the assumption that flexibility is extreme – a radical change that gets in the way of everyone's work, costs millions, and kills collaboration and teamwork. There's a belief that it's unsustainable – an overinflated bubble due to burst at any moment, at which point everyone can *just get back to damn work!*

But flexibility is not extreme or radical. What's extreme is doing the same thing in the same place at the same time every day, forty to sixty hours a week, and then squeezing everything else in life into the remaining gaps. Flexibility brings work and life back to something more sensible.

And because of the extreme nature of our normal workplaces, and because of the complexities of human nature, small workplace improvements can have profound impacts on people's lives and their productivity. Reducing the workday by one hour can have a huge effect on life sustainability, or working from home one day a week can boost engagement and productivity while making a real difference to traffic and pollution.

Even just taking the time to *listen* to what your employees want, and then giving them some feeling of control and autonomy over their daily activities, can have benefits that far exceed any corporate wellness program.

The Fundamentals Are Universal . . .

Although this book is contextually aimed at countries such as Australia, the United Kingdom, the United States, and New Zealand – because they have the biggest similarities in work and life cultures, having originated from the same British industrial roots – it's written in a way that has universal relevance to any country inhabited by people who work.

For instance, France has been at the forefront of protecting workers' rights since . . . forever, exemplified by their thirty-five-hour
workweeks and their willingness to protest any hint of oppression.
But with proponents of hard work and capitalism pushing for increased workweeks,[13] even France needs a reminder that flexibility is
critically important for sustainable lives *and* good business, and that
focusing on the number of hours worked is making the assumption
that humans are robots.

And at the other extreme, in South Korea – known to be one of the
most overworked countries on the planet – the message of flexibility is
a savage fight for people to have any semblance of life outside of work.
Their government has started on the journey to address the country's
inhumanely long and rigid workweeks by reducing the maximum
workweek from sixty eight hours to fifty two,[14] but they still have a long
way to go. There's a company that literally locks people up in a faux
prison (at the prisoner's request and on their dime) for a day or two
so they can have some respite from busyness and clocks and mobile
phones.[15] The belligerent beast of work is flourishing in South Korea,
and it's sucking lives dry, and it needs to be beaten back with a whip
and a chair.

No matter where on Earth we are, we are humans, and we have fundamental needs that must be considered when structuring how we work.
And the issues addressed by increasing flexibility are global. Traffic jams,
gender inequality, stress-related health problems, and wealth inequality
afflict every country that has people (and roads).

The fundamentals in this book can be applied worldwide.

. . . But Their Application Can Always Be Improved

It would be the height of foolishness if I thought I knew exactly what flexibility should look like for every company, and it would be arrogant to
think that others won't be able to vastly improve on what I've written in
this book.

I give the science for why flexibility is so powerful, at a fundamental level, and I give several examples of what has worked and what could work
better. And I ask why companies exist at all: Is it just to make money? Or
is it to boost the quality of life, improve the world, *and* make money?

In other words, what follows are the fundamentals of why and how
we can improve work, from my point of view and experience, backed

up by evidence; now let's go and together test and improve on the ideas discussed in this book.

Structure

Humans Are Not Robots combines theory and practical methods. Some of the ideas are discussed in great depth to illustrate their power and to challenge conventional thought, which is essential when questioning management and control methods that have been normal for hundreds or thousands of years. But it's also designed to be read and used by any business leader, current or future, to make a real and practical difference to any workplace. This is achieved by dividing the book into four parts:

Part One: For Humans and the World looks at how the traditional workplace starves us of our fundamental human needs and causes significant harm with its long and rigid structures and how flexibility enables a more sustainable way of living that helps employees feel whole and more human. It also challenges the assumption that people want to escape work, by arguing that work fulfills many of our human needs – it just needs to be tamed.

Part One also looks at the broader connection between today's management practices and critical problems the world faces, and how, with some simple changes, organizations can directly impact our crowded roads, the fragile environment, gender inequality, domestic violence, mental and physical health problems, and the negative effects of aging populations.

Part Two: Definitely Not Robots introduces the concepts of *energy buckets* and *non-linear productivity* to explain why flexibility is important from a business perspective, and that to maximize results and profits we should consider employees as whole humans rather than automatons with infinite energy (robots).

It considers how flexibility reduces the wasted effort and energy found in normal work structures, and how it multiplies productivity. Instead of being a cost, flexibility is an investment with significant and measurable returns.

Part Two deep-dives into real cases of a special type of flexibility – reduced hours with full pay (the four-day workweek and the five-hour workday) – as well as remote work, to demonstrate how having the freedom to look after human needs is great for business.

Part Three: How to Flex is a practical guide for rolling flexibility out to an entire organization. It lays out the 3Ts of Flexibility: The Talk, Training, and Trial. These are the critical elements needed to get it right. Although a step-by-step guide for implementation is provided, every business is unique, so this part is really about creating an understanding of why these different elements are important and what needs to be covered when a flexibility strategy is being created and rolled out.

Part Three also deals with the forgotten industries: those that many would consider impossible to implement flexibility because of the need for workers to be present at certain times and the apparent difficulty in automating tasks. They include the healthcare, manufacturing, retail, construction, airline, and legal industries. They require slightly different and more innovative pathways to flexibility, and because of the intensity and rigidity of jobs in these industries, flexibility is arguably more essential than in other knowledge-based industries.

Part Four: Work Revolution looks at a world where flexibility is normal and rigidity is the exception. It considers various changes and adaptions in the workplace, recruitment, management, holidays, language around flexibility, how people connect and collaborate, and, ultimately, what the future might look like when work adds to a full life rather than subtracts from it.

CHAPTER 2

Flexibility 101

So that we're all on the same page (book pun, oh yeah!) I'm going to start with a rundown of what flexibility is, and then describe several of the main types of flexibility, including some that aren't well known yet have great importance.

I'm also introducing the *Flex Scale*, which can help you start to think about your organization's current level of flexibility and show what you can aspire toward. There is a link to an online quiz at the end of the chapter that can show you where your organization sits.

What Is Flexibility?

To define *flexibility*, it's easier to first define *non-flexibility*: **rigidity**. I refer to *traditional* or *normal* workplaces as non-flexible or rigid throughout the book. This applies to most of our jobs, what most of us have grown up thinking *is* normal. These are the jobs with concrete start and finish times, a set location that you must inhabit between those start and finish times, and usually a minimum number of hours in which you must be at the working location. There are a set number of days per week you must be at work. And there are a set number of weeks you must be at work, except on the allocated number of days or weeks during which you can leave – holidays or vacations – and those hallowed public holidays.

Society has dictated, rather arbitrarily, that normal usually looks like this: from Monday to Friday, from eight thirty or nine until five, for forty-eight (or more) weeks a year, you must be at your working location, working (hopefully) the entire time except for one or two meal breaks during the day. Any exceptions need to be requested and then approved by a manager.

Many of us have different start and finish times (shift workers, for instance), but those times are usually still set in stone, and employees are frowned upon (or punished or fired) if they arrive late or leave early.

There is a strict line between what is considered full-time and part-time work. The former usually consists of forty or more hours per week at work, and the latter is anything less than that (and is often not considered as valuable or important as full time).

Flexibility is anything that looks different from the above, such as being able to move your start and/or finish times; working from another location, such as your home or a café; varying the number of hours you work day-to-day and week-to-week; taking more than the regular two to four weeks of leave in a year. Ultimately, flexibility enables you to manage your own life and your own work with less conflict between the two.

Flexibility has commonly been provided to people for caregiving purposes (caring for young children or elderly family members), but as the concept matures, flexibility is being seen as important to *all* people, regardless of caregiving needs. It allows for the changing and moving nature of life and the mutability of human capability and energy.

Here is a formal definition of *flexibility* from the Workplace Gender Equality Agency (WGEA) in Australia:

> Workplace flexibility is where a business and one or more of its employees agree on changes to standard working arrangements to better accommodate employees' commitments away from work. Flexible working arrangements usually encompass changes to the hours (when), location (where) and pattern (how) of work. Flexibility is becoming increasingly important as employees and managers balance competing priorities in life. Flexibility in work can be a number of different things, including:
>
> - Telework or working from home
> - Flexible hours
> - Compressed working weeks
> - Job sharing[1]

Types of Flexibility

(defined on page noted)

Remote work (21)	Flextime or flexitime (23)
Part time (24)	Time in lieu (26)
Purchased leave (27)	Compressed workweek (28)
Reduced hours with full pay (29)	Annualized hours (31)
More or unlimited annual leave (32)	Greater and equal parental leave (33)
Flexible careers (35)	Results-only work environment (36)
Job sharing (37)	Return-to-work internships (39)
Flex for all (40)	

Table 2.1. Quick look-up table for definitions of various flexibility types.

I've added another, more-holistic description of flexibility at the end of the next chapter. It's a little deeper and more abstract and takes into account what it is to be human, what we need as humans to be our best at work and outside of work, and how flexibility provides for that.

Types of Flexibility

There can be a lot of confusion about the different types of flexibility – what they're called, what they look like, their benefits and drawbacks – so here are some new and improved definitions for the most important and common types, along with pros and cons and my personal rating of each (see Table 2.1).

Remote Work

This is also known as *work anywhere, work from home* (WFH), *telecommuting*, and a range of other interchangeable terms. But they all mean (roughly) the same thing: purposely working from somewhere that is not the central or regular workplace, usually at home or a location nearer to home than the regular workplace, either some or all of the time.

If you work at a library near home one day a week, that's remote work. If you work in your home office every day, that's remote work. If you work on a beach in Fiji for two months because you're working while traveling around the world, that's remote work.

This type of flexibility offers many benefits including reducing the time and stress of commuting, getting away from distractions in the office for deep and concentrated work, and having more of a feeling of control over your day.

What *isn't* remote work is when you take work home at the end of the day because there are things that need to be finished. This is not the purposeful avoidance of the commute and the office, and it doesn't save any trips. I would refer to it simply as overtime, but it's unfortunately counted as remote work or telework in many census results, and it skews the data on how often people work remotely since it's not true remote work. My tests for the definition of *remote work* are: Is it done on purpose? Did you save a trip or two, or reduce travel drastically?

Back in the 1980s and 1990s, remote work was just for writers and call center operators; now the term can be used for just about any job that uses a computer and a phone (most of them), and is extending to jobs that people considered impossible and impractical to do when not in the office: lawyers, doctors, business analysts, psychiatrists, engineers, team leaders, etc.; and this list will continue to expand as technology continues to make it more seamless to work with other people who aren't physically in the same space.

Telehealth, for instance, where doctors or nurses can work with patients from thousands of miles away, is a rapidly growing field.

I've devoted Chapter 7 to this important form of flexibility to really get our teeth into the reasons why it's so good and how best to use it to avoid the issues listed below.

The pros:

- Avoid or reduce commute, thereby reducing costs, stress, wasted time, and pollution.
- More time and energy for exercise, sleep, relationships, and hobbies.
- Fewer distractions and less time in meetings, resulting in increased productivity.
- More meaningful connections with coworkers and people outside of work.

- Work in undies or shorts instead of using the air-conditioner, which is good for the environment. (Making sure to remember to put on a shirt for videoconferences . . .)

- Avoid inclement weather and other unforeseen (or foreseen) events that make travel difficult or dangerous; to continue being productive despite those events.

The cons:

- Potential feeling of isolation and loneliness.

- Magnification of any issues with self-discipline (including addictions). It can take time to get used to the extra freedom.

- If only a select few in the company can use it, those people might feel guilty and overcompensate by working long hours; and it can potentially get in the way of promotions, because people in this situation, where the practice isn't normalized, will still likely be measured on their presence in the office.

- Any issues with management styles will come to the fore. For example, if a manager measures a worker's value by seeing them working, they will find managing a remote workforce challenging and may end up stifling productivity by checking on workers too often, tracking their computer usage, etc. This con might also turn into a huge pro because managers might learn to measure actual productivity and value to the business.

★ Rob's Rating: 10/10

Flextime or Flexitime

This refers to varying the start and/or finish times of the day (or break times). For instance, someone might start work at nine thirty every day because they need to drop their kid at school; or someone might leave at three every Tuesday for ice-hockey training; or someone might take two hours for lunch every second day because that's the best time for them to go to the gym.

Normally, with flextime the total number of hours worked for the week would remain the same – still forty or more hours for full-time work, or whatever number of hours for part-time work. Workers would just start earlier if they need to leave early or put in more hours on a different day to make up for missed time.

Or, the total hours worked could be less if a company has a culture of flextime, where people could just arrive when they arrive and leave when they've finished their work for the day; this requires less focus on hours worked and more focus on results and productivity.

The pros:

- Enables people to meet personal commitments outside of work, thereby reducing work-life conflict.

- Provides more of a feeling of autonomy and trust – very important themes regarding flexibility.

- Can help to place more emphasis on results and productivity rather than on time spent at work, which has many advantages for both the business and individuals.

The cons:

- Could result in office politicking, with people tracking coworkers' use of flextime and assuming they are uncommitted or not hard working.

- Potential for upsetting clients or customers if not enough people are present when required to deal with clients. This sort of environment would need more communication and/or structure to make it work.

★ **Rob's Rating: 8/10** if tracked and policed, **10/10** if people have freedom to use as they choose.

Part Time

This is defined as anything less than forty hours per week and is paid on a pro-rata basis. It takes various forms: working two, three, or even four days a week; or working five days, but less than the normal eight hours per day (half days, for instance).

Part-time work has been an important way for people to remain connected to their workplace and continue their career even if they have commitments or lifestyle choices that get in the way of being able to work full time, such as caring for young children.

But it has also had somewhat negative connotations compared to full-time work. It has been perceived as low value compared to full-time work. Rarely would part-time work be a high-paying, senior role – you don't see many CEOs working part time. This is an unfortunate result of the bias of valuing long hours, normal in rigid workplaces. This bias can be reduced by increasing overall flexibility across organizations.

Indeed, as I'll discuss later in this book, the terms *part time* and *full time* become meaningless when we begin to decouple time worked from actual productive output, much to the joy of those who currently work four days per week in their "part-time" roles and know they do exactly the same amount of work (or more) as their "full-time" counterparts.

The pros:

- Enables people to continue working even if they can't or don't want to work the standard forty-hour week.

- Can reduce the gender pay gap by allowing women to continue working while they have caregiving commitments.

- Allows more flexibility with life in general (more time for other passions, missions, leisure, etc.).

- Increases energy and motivation of employees to give their best to their job; they're less tired and exhausted because they have fewer hours at work and less commuting during the week.

The cons:

- Can be seen as low-value or unprofessional work, even if a worker is highly experienced and/or educated.

- Can hinder career progress and promotions (due to first con).

- Can increase the gender pay gap when it's a woman working part time, which it normally is, which is especially heinous when the part-time worker is providing the same (or more) value to an employer as a full-time worker.

- Full-time workers who attempt to move to part-time work usually find the workload doesn't change, and they have to work harder and/or longer to keep up.

- Can have fewer benefits than full time; for example, where health insurance is linked to employment, as in the United States.

★ **Rob's Rating: 8/10**

Time in Lieu

This is also known as accrued time off – earning (paid) time away from work to make up for equivalent overtime worked. For instance, if someone works an hour late today, they can choose a day later in the week where they can leave an hour early. Or someone accumulates half a day of overtime, and then leaves at midday on Friday. The total number of work hours for a week or period remains constant.

Time in lieu has its place as a basic starting point for flexibility because a company is recognizing and paying back extra time worked by the employee, and it provides somewhat more freedom to attend to life's commitments. But it has its drawbacks, and I don't consider it to be one of the better types of flexibility.

For one thing, time in lieu generally needs to be administered, tracked, and approved, requiring extra work from both the employee and the manager that doesn't add any value to the business. It also demonstrates a lack of trust from the manager that an employee can manage their own time based on what needs to be done. Focus is shifted away from productivity and instead it's put on the clock.

Also, the employee needs to "earn" their flexibility; that is, the flexibility comes only after the time off has been earned through overtime. This means that it's not guaranteed or regular, and so it's not actually that flexible in practice. Flextime wins out over this type of flexibility because the time off can be used when it's needed without having to be earned.

Lastly, there is an incentive to game the system, which can result in lower productivity and motivation. Imagine there's a football game next Monday afternoon at three that you really want to go to. What's to stop you from working a couple of hours of overtime this week to earn that time off – *even if you need to decrease your pace of work as an excuse to stay longer, or you simply do nothing for two hours but look busy?* I don't mean to say that many people are dishonest enough to purposely do this, but, again, time in lieu increases the incentive to do so compared to a system in which someone is trusted to dictate their own needs. The drive to game the system may be more subtle and subconscious than actively finding ways to work longer to earn time off. (I delve into Parkinson's Law – how work magically expands to fill the time available – in Chapter 6.)

The pros:

- Employees are compensated and acknowledged for overtime.
- Allows more flexibility between life and work (but can only be used after being earned through overtime).

The cons:

- Demonstrates mistrust of employees by the manager (unless employees are free to administer themselves).
- Could cause employees to game the system by simply staying at work longer one day to earn time off on another day.
- Keeps the focus on time worked instead of value provided to the business.
- Needs to be earned, so it's not regular and there's less freedom (than in flextime, for example) to use it effectively for work-life balance.

★ Rob's Rating: 4/10

Purchased Leave

This is leave without pay (for those on hourly wages) or a reduction in salary according to how long the leave will be (for those on a yearly salary). For example, someone on a salary may purchase 25 percent of the year off by reducing their yearly pay by 25 percent. Or someone who is paid an hourly wage may purchase a day off simply by not being paid for that day.

Purchased leave is a fairly basic type of flexibility that enables more freedom than a fully rigid work environment – any ability to increase the amount of leave is beneficial because the amount of time we normally work is extreme. But the major drawback, obviously, is that we lose pay.

That being said, the ability to, say, go traveling in Spain for three months and have a guaranteed job waiting for you is a great advantage over having to quit and then find a new job upon returning. This is a form of long-term flexibility.

The pros:

- The ability to decrease the number of weeks worked in a year is great for overall health and well-being, as well as for motivation, energy, and creativity when the person returns to work.

The cons:

- Not being paid during the time away. Even though employees' time away may allow them to contribute more value to the company that if they worked the hours, businesses still measure value by measuring time.

★ **Rob's Rating: 4.5/10**

Compressed Workweek[*]

This refers to maintaining the same number of weekly work hours by squeezing them into a reduced number of days. For example, using a standard forty-hour workweek, instead of having five eight-hour workdays, you could have four ten-hour workdays, followed by three days off; or three thirteen-plus-hour workdays, followed by four days off (pretty extreme, but often shift work in mines or manufacturing plants looks similar to this). Another popular example, often used in government, is four nine-hour workdays, then half a day on Friday (or a whole Friday off every two weeks).

This has been a popular way of introducing flexibility without compromising the number of hours worked in a week, so employers are still getting the "same amount of work" out of their employees, but the employees have a whole extra day to go and live life. The gift is a three- or four-day weekend, but it's paid for with long days.

The compressed workweek is a rather silly type of flexibility, and by the time you finish Chapters 5 and 6 you'll understand why. In a nutshell, people often aren't highly productive in a normal eight-hour workday, so

---

[*] Occasionally this is called the four-day workweek, but in this book, the four-day workweek refers to when the total work hours are decreased by leaving four days as they are and cutting the fifth day, with no cramming of those missing hours into the other workdays.

expecting them to be productive for ten or twelve hours is like throwing money into the wind. And those three or four days of long labor create terribly unsustainable lives.

I recommend that, if you want the benefits of an extra day off for your staff, reduce their hours and/or days without adding the time on elsewhere (see the next section). It's better for the individual and for your business, and you'll be showing that you don't think of humans as robots.

The pros:

- Fewer days mean less commuting.
- Increasing the weekend by one or two days allows for greater rest and recovery from the workweek.

The cons:

- Long days of work are needed to "earn" the longer weekend. A ten- or twelve-hour day plus commuting doesn't leave much time or energy to do anything else, so the longer weekend is used mostly to recover from working unsustainable hours.
- Terrible for productivity. Again, humans aren't capable of being fully productive for long days, so this is wasted money and effort.

★ Rob's Rating: 3/10

Reduced Hours with Full Pay

This one doesn't show up on many flexible work lists just yet because it's a more advanced and seemingly radical concept. But it's pretty groovy, and perfectly illustrates how the productivities of a human and a robot are very different.

Reduced hours with full pay is a structural change to the workplace that reduces the expected or minimum weekly hours for everyone *without reducing their overall pay*. This is done either by reducing daily hours or by keeping daily hours the same and removing a whole day or two from the week. It's different from the compressed workweek because there's an overall reduction in hours for the week, not merely a transfer of those hours to other days.

This method can be as informal as having a culture of "When you've finished your work, get outta here," or it can be a formal "We only work six-hour days here – that's the company-wide target, and we're all doing this together." Both are good, because both take into consideration the human side of employees and managers, and they allow for greater freedom to live life outside of work while not punishing with reduced pay. And it pushes the focus onto productivity and the value of work. Also, because this method is company-wide, there's no opportunity for anyone to be stigmatized because they work fewer hours than others.

An example of reduced hours with full pay is the four-day week implemented by Perpetual Guardian in New Zealand in 2018. Everyone in the company reduced their workweek to four days, but they were paid the same amount as they were before the change. Their total hours were not compressed into those fewer days; instead their total hours were reduced from 37.5 to 30.0 per week.

The resulting *amount* of work they produced – clients served, hours billed, etc. – didn't drop. In fact, their creativity and collaboration increased, as did their level of customer service, along with a bunch of other good things. Overall, business profits increased, and the company has permanently adopted the practice. I explore how this happened later in the book to show why human-centered work practices are awesome.

It's with this sort of flexibility that we start to see a blurring of the line between full-time and part-time work, and it illustrates that the value an individual can provide to a business is not as time-related as most would assume.

The pros:

- Lower stress.
- Greater productivity.
- Greater collaboration.
- People actively search for improvements to their work and the business (with more of a focus on value than time worked).
- Increased feeling of work-life balance.
- And more! See Chapters 5 and 6, where the effects of reducing hours are investigated.

The cons:

- Can create some confusion and issues around legislative requirements for the amount of leave accrued by the worker.

- Employees spend less time on Facebook, so there's a potential decrease in advertising revenue for "The Bergs."

- Less time for meetings at work (only a con for those who love Power-Point and ice breakers).

★ **Rob's Rating: 9/10** (loses a point because there is still a high focus on time in the office).

Annualized Hours

This means working a certain number of hours per week, month, or year, but the employee has the freedom to choose when those hours are worked; the employee is paid a regular salary based on the total hours for the week, month, or year.

For example, someone may have a sales job and agree to work eighteen-hundred hours per year, but they have the freedom to decide what time they start and finish and which days they work, and they may increase or decrease their weekly hours based on seasonal fluctuations or their personal requirements. They may choose to work twenty hours one week, because they have some other commitments (or just feel unproductive), and then the next week they may work fifty hours because they're on a roll and their energy is through the roof.

This is quite a good form of flexibility, because even though it still measures time worked, it allows people to fit work into the ebbs and flows of their lives and their own productive energy.

This method also allows for seasonal variation. For example, accountants might have very busy periods around tax time, when they might need to work longer hours, but during the quieter months they could decrease their time at work.

This type of flexibility usually fits well with remote work, where someone has the freedom to decide when and where they work.

The pros:

- Enables great flexibility on a daily and weekly basis.

- Provides variation in workload throughout the year, allowing for recovery during quieter periods.

The cons:

- Focuses on the number of hours worked, taking focus away from true productivity and value for the business.
- Requires tracking and administration of hours worked.
- Successive long days can be detrimental to the individual and productivity.

★ **Rob's Rating: 8/10**

More or Unlimited Annual Leave

This is any amount of paid leave above the legislated amount. For example, in Australia, companies are required to provide twenty days (four weeks) of paid leave to full-time employees, so if a company provides twenty five days (five weeks), that counts as more leave and is a good form of long-term flexibility.

There are also companies that allow "unlimited" leave, which is fully paid (i.e., the employee's yearly salary remains unchanged). In this instance, the employee can choose how much leave they want to take during the year, and it's their responsibility to ensure that their work is complete in the amount of time they give themselves to complete it.

The employee can use their own discretion and can create beneficial patterns of work and rest for themselves throughout the year. But this creates the potential for people to abuse the system by taking too much time off and leaving others to do their work (especially if there isn't a clear way to measure deliverables from each employee). There's also the potential for people to take even less time off than they would if they had a normal amount of leave, out of fear of using the unlimited leave.

One of the overlooked benefits of more or unlimited leave is the ability to just take a day or two off when you need a break to recharge. In the normal system, when someone needs some time to recharge, they call their boss and pretend to be sick. It's estimated that almost half of sick days are just people wanting – needing – a break, needing a breath, needing respite from the traffic, and interruptions by coworkers, and stress, and the inability to choose where and what they do on a daily basis and when they do it.[2]

"Sickies," as we call them in Australia, are a symptom of something much bigger and much worse: unsustainable lives. Because of the limited amount of annual leave businesses normally provide, employees often choose to lie and pretend to be sick instead of just asking for a day off, thus preserving their precious annual leave for actual holidays.

With more leave, people would no longer need to lie when they need a day off. They could simply let everyone know the day before, or even schedule it a week in advance, allowing time to find a replacement. This has enormous ramifications for mental health, physical health, and productivity for the business. A day off to recover, guilt free, could be the difference between life and death; or at the very least it could result in fewer people sitting and staring at their monitors when they should be recharging at the beach or with friends, and thus increasing their productivity when they return to work.

The pros:

- More time during the year for people to properly recover and recharge, which is beneficial for the individual and for business.
- A greater feeling of autonomy and freedom for the employee.
- Greater openness and honesty about just needing a day off.
- Helps shift focus to results rather than number of hours worked.

The cons:

- Could create confusion over coverage of work or increase the workload of coworkers if it's not adequately planned.
- People could end up taking no leave at all, or less than they would normally take, because they're afraid of using that freedom.

★ Rob's Rating: 10/10

Greater and Equal Parental Leave

Paid parental leave is one of those wonderful things that allows new parents to bond with and nurture their new kids (and recover from the birthing process, which I've heard is pretty rough) while keeping a job. It's normally mandated by a country's government, and it can come in all sorts of lengths, with different amounts of compensation, depending on the country and the company. Some are more adequate than others.

At the bare minimum, the International Labour Organization (ILO), an agency of the UN, calls for at least "fourteen weeks of maternity benefit to women" while being paid "no less than two-thirds her previous earnings."[3] The United States falls embarrassingly below this recommendation by providing twelve weeks at zero pay.

At the other end of the spectrum, Sweden has decided the bare minimum is nowhere near enough and provides 390 days of leave at 80 percent of a mother's wages. This allows the mother and child time to bond and experience those crucial early months together, without the stress of rushing back to work.

What's ideal? Well, I think employers and governments should at least be hitting that ILO minimum. But if we consider our employees as humans, and if we consider the gift of giving life to be part of the human experience, perhaps we can take the lead of the more progressive countries and companies and allow people to really savor the process without the pressure of getting straight back to the office.

What about dads? As a cruel result of our traditional work culture, which divides parents into primary caregivers (usually mothers) and secondary caregivers (usually fathers), paternity leave for fathers is often neglected completely or is pretty dismal compared to its maternal counterpart.

Dads get to be there for the birth, then maybe they can spend a couple of days or a week or two at home to help mum and bub settle in, then it's off to work. With this structure the workplace has *created* this primary- and secondary-caregiver dichotomy, and with that comes a wealth of issues, especially regarding gender equality, both at home and in the workplace. I'll address this further in Chapter 4, but for the moment it's enough to know that providing longer, or even equal, paternity leave is fantastic, for dad, mum, and bub.

Dads can connect more with their children and become proficient in household and caregiving responsibilities, effects that last well beyond the time spent on leave; and mums can transition back to work more easily while dad takes over caregiving. And they both have a much more helpful and capable partner for years following the initial leave periods.

It's been shown that to best encourage men to take paternity leave, it should be a use-it-or-lose-it policy that can't be transferred to the primary caregiver. This serves to incentivize its use and reduce the stigma surrounding men taking extended leave. Iceland is a great example, where, because of its non-transferrable paternity leave, about 90 percent of fathers spend an extended amount of time at home – 101 days on average. This has resulted in closer father-child relationships and greater workplace equality between men and women.[4]

The pros:

- Increased gender equality at home and the workplace (when greater paternity leave is available and incentivized).

- Better connection to children (with both longer maternity and paternity leave).

- Increased well-being and physical, mental, and sexual health.[5]

The cons:

- Increased costs to cover extended leave of either parent. But this seems worthwhile, and companies will be rewarded with an employee who has a close bond with their family.

★ **Rob's Rating: 10/10**

Flexible Careers

I can't do much better than the definition from Australia's Workplace Gender Equality Agency for this one, which is:

> The ability to exit and re-enter employment with the same company, or to increase or decrease your workload or career pace to suit different life stages. This may be particularly relevant for employees transitioning to retirement. It can also include employees who are able to take a "gap year" early in their careers and return to work for the same employer afterwards.[6]

In a nutshell, this method looks at flexibility from a long-term point of view, allowing for those ebbs and flows and changing needs in life while still providing the security and stability of employment with one employer (as with purchased leave, but broader and all-encompassing).

The pros:

- Long-term flexibility for workers, such as allowing for breaks to go travelling or pursue other interests, with the security of a job to return to (even if the break is unpaid, similar to purchased leave).

- People closer to retirement age have a greater chance of continuing work if they can reduce their hours, which benefits them (not just financially, but more on that in the next chapter), their employer, and society in general (lower demand on social support).

- A business has a higher chance of retaining employees over the long-term, thus reducing the risk of losing valuable experience and the need to recruit and retrain new employees.

The cons:

- Might require some planning to implement, as with any flexibility.

★ **Rob's Rating: 10/10**

Results-Only Work Environment (ROWE)

This isn't specifically a type of flexibility, but it enables flexibility, since it decouples work from "time at desk" and instead puts the focus on employee outputs, a focus that's critical for flexibility to work effectively.

I've already mentioned the importance of measuring results and productivity rather than time spent at work; well, this is the ultimate example. In a results-only work environment, results are literally all that matters. Workers can work whenever and wherever and however they choose, as long as they're producing what's expected of them. This makes it much easier to have the types of flexibility already introduced, such as remote work and flextime.

Obviously not all businesses can use ROWE – doctors need to be present in the emergency room of a hospital for a certain amount of time – but certainly every workforce should be able to measure the value someone provides. And better measurements of productivity and value increase the ability to implement flexibility, in any business.

The pros:

- Shifts focus on value and productivity and away from location and time worked.

- Freedom and flexibility for someone to structure their own way of working (and living).

- Less surveillance and managing by managers; more coaching, training, and collaborating because the focus is on creating value.

The cons:

- Increases pressure to produce results when that's the only thing being measured. Busywork or just being at work no longer hold value. (There can be growing pains during this change.)

- People could work too long and/or too hard in an effort to produce results, or to pay back the generosity of moving to this work style. There needs to be a team effort to ensure that deadlines are realistic and communication is open.

★ **Rob's Rating: 10/10**

Job Sharing

In job sharing, two or more people share one full-time job and split the pay proportionally according to the time each works, or in whatever way is agreed to. This is a valuable and underused work structure.

A big issue with part-time or casual work is that it's often low-level, low-paid work that doesn't contribute much to someone's career path, or it comes with the part-time-work stigma. Often when women return to work after the arrival of a child, if they choose to work part time or casually, their career, as well as their pay bracket and job quality, stagnates.

This is a big factor in the dreaded gender pay gap. Women and men are usually on the same pay and career trajectory in their early to mid-twenties, but when those late twenties to early thirties arrive (on average, women in OECD countries become mothers for the first time at the age of 30.4 years)[7] the picture changes. Women, traditionally the primary caregivers, tend to drop down to part-time work so they can balance work with caregiving responsibilities. And because of the stigma placed on part-time work, their career progression can take a big hit compared to the working fathers, who continue to work full time.[8]

Job sharing is a brilliant way for someone, regardless of gender, to have the benefits of part-time work (more time with children, more energy, and less stress) *and* the benefits of a high-quality senior role. They can still develop their career because with the job-share partner or team, they can provide the same coverage and agility as a full-time worker. And since the job sharers can combine their minds, efforts, and strengths, and have time to rest and recover from work, the job share team is like a superhuman in the workplace.

Job sharing can involve micro-sharing – splitting a week, so that one person works two days and another works three, or they have an overlapping day when they work together – or macro-sharing, with each person working full time for part of the year (six months each, leaving half the year to travel, start a business, write a book, or whatever).

Melissa Nicholson, founder and CEO of Work Muse, a company that connects people to job-share partners and positions around the world, had this to say (via email):

> Although one of the least-known flexible work practices, it's one of the most innovative for the changing face of work. The structure allows employees to rest, recharge, and return to work engaged, and create better, solution-driven results with the combined skill sets of both – so important in the 24/7 work environment where nine-to-five work boundaries have disappeared due to increases in globalization and technology.
>
> People job share at senior levels, even CEOs. There's even a job share in parliament in the United Kingdom. In fact, the majority of job-share teams are mid- to senior-level, and 71 percent of job-share teams are promoted together. I would say the resistance to job sharing is due to the lack of awareness, education, and training for job sharing. It's a major reason I started Work Muse.

The pros:

- Has the pros of part-time work while decreasing the cons – greater opportunities for decent work and career progression.

- The job-share team can use each other's strengths while ameliorating each other's weaknesses.

- A great way of reducing the gender pay gap since more women can progress to senior positions.

The cons:

- Potential for communication breakdowns if the team doesn't communicate openly and often.

- Potential for conflict within the team if their personalities, methods, or aspirations clash.

★ Rob's Rating: 10/10

Return-to-Work Internships

This is a structured program to support people returning to work after an extended break in their career, usually two years or more. The returning worker might have shorter working weeks to get used to the routine of work again; they would often have a mentor who can provide support and answer questions (but not about how to use the photocopier – an impossible task regardless of how much experience someone has!); there might be other interns whom they can share the experience with; and the program has an end date, so the worker can have a taste without committing to permanent employment.

As with job sharing, caregivers, who are more often than not women, will benefit from this type of flexibility and will be able to keep their professional careers on track. This kind of flexibility alleviates the dreaded gap in employment and its (abhorrent) associated stigma.

The pros:

- It's a way to purposefully reduce prejudice against people with career gaps.

- Decreases the fear of returning to the workforce after a long departure.

- Increases workforce participation of women, to the benefit of women and business by increasing the available talent pool.

The cons:

- Validates the concept that people forget how to work after being away from the workplace for a while.

★ **Rob's Rating: 9/10** (Loses a point because bias makes me grumpy.)

Flex for All

Again, this isn't specifically a type of flexibility, but more of an approach to flexibility, and a bloody good one at that. The ultimate aim of this book and my work in the field is to enable all people to have flexibility with work, regardless of their reason for needing it. They should have job flexibility because they're human.

A business that has this philosophy of providing flexibility for every worker and manager, regardless of their reason or level of desperation, is much more likely to have a successful flexibility program. I'll delve into why this is so when I talk about the Flex Scale in the next section, but in a nutshell, with flex for all flexibility becomes purposeful and normal instead of a seemingly painful and costly accommodation. And with that, a plethora of issues are resolved and the true benefits of flexibility can be uncovered.

The pros:

- Too many to list. Read on!

The cons:

- Requires commitment and work to create the systems and ensure that they work, but if you're reading this book you're already on your way!

★ **Rob's Rating: 11/10**

We'll go further into some of these different types of flexibility, how best to use them, and how to avoid their issues later in the book. I'll be expanding on two types, remote work and reduced hours with full pay, to demonstrate the fundamentals of why flexibility is so powerful. That will make all the other types easier to accept and understand.

People can get caught up in the details of the different types of flexibility, but the important thing to remember is that real flexibility just means having the freedom to choose when, where, and how to do your best work. That said, the types *are* still relevant in a world where flexibility isn't yet normal, because change takes baby steps and those steps need names. But the types lose their importance as we go up through the levels in the Flex Scale.

The Flex Scale

Many employers claim to have a flexible workplace as soon as they have a piece of paper, a policy, that says that employees are allowed to ask for a flexible working arrangement, even if few people are actually using it and the policy is sitting in a cupboard gathering dust and feeling lonely. I've set out to define some levels of organizational flexibility in the Flex Scale so that we can start to identify whether businesses are truly flexible, or if it's just a façade, or if they fall somewhere in between.

This objective measurement tool can be used for recruitment, obtaining grants, or funding for inclusion or sustainable practices. It can give companies a baseline and a guide for where to improve their practices and can be used to measure progress in meeting the United Nations Sustainable Development Goals or goals developed by various gender equality organizations.

This scale will evolve and change as it's used, and some of the concepts will be expanded throughout this book. And I'm sure that others can use it as a starting point to develop more detailed and practical tools. What's important isn't the name of the measurement tool, but *what* is being measured: leadership and involvement from executives, the level of trust shown to employees and managers, the results, financial and otherwise, of flexibility (ROI), communication, how much input staff and management had in deciding what flexibility should look like, whether people feel capable of looking after their own well-being, and so on.

The levels on the Flex Scale, from worst to best, are:

- Level 0: Rigid
- Level 1: Policy
- Level 2: Basic Program
- Level 3: Good Program
- Level 4: Ascended Program (Fluidity)

Figure 2.1. On the Rigid Level, work is hard and immovable. Life must exist and flow around it. This and the figures for the following levels are conceptual images of the relative rigidity or flexibility of work, and to what extent life must give or flow around it. They're not illustrating any particular type of flexibility.

Qualitatively, the Flex Scale levels look something like the following:

Level 0: Rigid

A company that's rigid has no flexible work policy or program. It has a standard nine-to-five, Monday-to-Friday (or whatever) schedule that can only be broken if someone (or a member of their family) is sick or dying. Employees must be present during all work hours and days unless leave is granted. And that leave is only the standard annual, sick, or caregiver's leave required by law.

This (and the next) level is the situation most of us are used to and have adapted to, even though we have a deep understanding that something isn't quite right. Figure 2.1 conceptualizes work, at this level, as rigid and immovable, like a brick wall. The rest of life – our relationships, exercise, hobbies, other passions, leisure and rest, sleep, developing other skills, and everything else – exists only in the remaining gaps, and must flow around the wall of work, being attended to only on the weekends or holidays, when we're less tired.

The issues associated with work rigidity, for individuals and for society, are detailed in Part One of this book. The more rigid our work life, the bigger the issues.

Level 1: Policy

Having a policy means meeting minimum legislative requirements of granting flexibility to those individuals who have requested it and "need it." It's usually only granted for exceptional circumstances, such as a

Policy Level on the Flex Scale

Figure 2.2. On the Policy Level, some allowance is made for the movements of life (for a few people). But flexibility is seen as a costly accommodation, and it's taken back when it's no longer "needed."

mother needing flexible start and finish times to do school pick-ups and drop-offs.

Flexibility is seen as a costly and wasteful accommodation that should be avoided if possible and rescinded as soon as it's no longer "needed." This attitude adds to the professional gap between women and men: when only primary caregivers are afforded flexibility, it's seen as something that benefits only women, and it perpetuates the idea that women need to be treated differently from men. Along with this perception, many men miss out on the opportunity to work flexibly because they don't "need it."

There are risks involved for anyone requesting or using flexibility at this level because they're perceived as caring more about themselves than the organization or their career. And they can be stigmatized by all the other employees and managers who are still coping with rigid work.

When the business has no more than a policy, the benefits of flexibility for the individual, the organization, and the world aren't measured or maximized. The assumption is that the only benefits to the policy are that legal requirements are being met and that individual employees receive help to cope with added responsibilities. In this situation, people have limited abilities to fulfill their human needs (explained in Chapter 3) and live sustainably.

The mindset is still that the business owns its employees' time and energy. Anyone afforded flexibility is done so because, in the mind of the manager, they deserve some respite and flexibility because their time and energy are already low, but no one else deserves flexibility because they've still got enough time and energy to be fully devoted to their work.

Level 2: Basic Program

This is usually the ad hoc implementation of one or more types of flexibility for most people, or certain departments or levels of an organization. Flexibility is seen as a privilege or a gift, not a business strategy; hence, there's no overall method or vision for the program. And there's often little or no flexibility training, or preparation, or trials.

Distrust and control feature heavily in this program, and it has limited use by managers and little support by senior executives. This usually plays out as an us-versus-them scenario, with the managers using their privilege to police the employees. Only the human resources department is truly interested in the program.

Time spent working is still the main measurement of value, rather than results and productivity, and the idea that the company owns the employees' time is still prevalent, demonstrated by surveillance and tracking methods such as keylogging.

There are *some* benefits for individuals; for example, workers might be avoiding a stressful commute on one or more days of the week if the program involves working remotely. But there is little or no measurement of productivity increases or reductions in business cost, because the program isn't considered an investment with measurable returns. Only 3 percent of companies in the United States who have implemented flexibility programs measured the returns on this investment.[9]

The poorer types of flexibility are the ones most commonly used. These are the ones that rated poorly in the descriptions of flexibility types above, such as time in lieu, compressed workweek, and purchased leave – those that display distrust and treat humans as robots with an infinite capacity for work.

Basic programs have a high chance of being repealed because they "fail." This is usually a self-fulfilled prophecy: managers don't believe in the program from the start, their behaviors mirror their belief, and then they look for anything wrong to confirm this belief. Instead of looking for solutions to issues, they choose to end the program.

A well-known example of this is IBM. The company repealed its remote work program in 2017, and they brought thousands of staff and managers back to set office locations, or sent them packing if they couldn't come back to an office. The reason given by the CEO, Ginni Rometty, was that IBM wanted to increase collaboration and innovation by having people in the same physical space.[10]

Basic Program Level on the Flex Scale

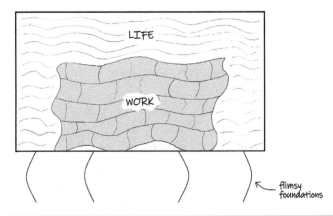

Figure 2.3. On the Basic Program Level, more people are allowed flexibility than in the previous level, but the structure has weak foundations (poor support from senior management, no training or collaborative discussions around implementation, ad hoc, not guided by strong principles and previous learnings). This is risky and can result in failure.

But there are many ways to increase collaboration without forcing people to be in the same space every day, and innovation happens just as readily (if not more so) in a home office as it does in a noisy, open-plan office (see Chapter 7). If IBM truly wanted to keep its remote work program, it could have worked with its staff to find solutions to any problems. No doubt.

Level 3: Good Program

This could be one or more types of flexibility, but it's supported, implemented, *and role-modelled* by senior management with a purposeful goal of getting everyone to use it. The senior executives are not only supportive, they're influential in rolling out the program. All staff are heavily involved with planning and implementation of the program.

Training, trust, and communication are big aspects of the program. Issues are dealt with as they arise, with continuous improvement at the heart of the program.

The types of flexibility used are developed through collaboration and discussion with managers and all staff. There's less use of the poor flexibility types (compressed workweek, time in lieu, purchased leave) and greater use of better, more mature types (flextime, remote work, reduced hours with full pay, etc.).

Good Program Level on the Flex Scale

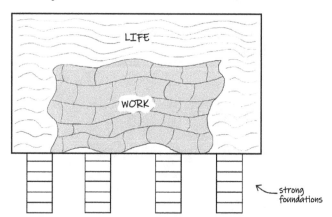

Figure 2.4. On the Good Program Level, the flexibility program is purposeful and is supported by senior management and a good strategy.

The return on investment of the program is measured. Here is where it has ascended to a business strategy rather than the nice-to-have of the previous level. Benefits for the company, for the individual, for energy use, for traffic, and for society in general are measured and communicated internally and externally.

People might still have time and/or place constraints, but they have more time and freedom overall to be more human and aren't driven to exhaustion. The big goal is to help people have energy at the start *and* end of the workday and workweek, however that might need to happen, which has benefits for health, well-being, family, diversity, and a whole host of other goodies.

This level also includes broader, general good practices: letting people have a day off when they need it without subtracting it from their vacation time (you could call it a "low-energy day"), and not tracking time in lieu or making people earn flexibility. The philosophy of humans being human runs deep in a good program.

Even a manufacturing plant or a construction company might aspire toward this level. People need to be present during production because they physically need to move, fix, or produce things, but small changes can have huge effects on the lives of the employees and the managers.

For example, reducing a laborer's hours from ten hours a day to seven, or reducing the number of working days (without compressing them), or using job-share teams with the gain in brain power and engagement to maintain or increase overall output and quality, are innovative ways to have flexibility in industries where you wouldn't normally consider it possible. (More on this particular witchcraft in later chapters.)

Level 4: Ascended Program (Fluidity)

As with Level 3: Good Program, senior management, including the CEO, are responsible for and supportive of this program. Training regarding flexibility is provided to employees and management. There's a planned roll-out, with measurement of results and continuous improvement to solve any problems. Trust is built between managers and employees, which makes for adult relationships. All staff are heavily involved with planning and implementation of the program.

Leaders promote and role-model flexibility; individual workers don't have to ask for it. Key performance indicators (KPIs) are set to show when teams and departments are working toward greater flexibility so that middle and senior managers are held accountable; this won't be as critical when flexibility is a normal practice.

There are no, or fewer, constraints on when and where people work at this level. The business is moving toward, or has reached, a results-only work environment, so that the concept of owning another person's time is gone. Now work is a transaction of value for value. Work and life are no longer in opposition; they exist synergistically. People can choose to mix and match and use whatever types of flexibility are required.

This level results in fluidity rather than flexibility, because it's the complete absorption of work into life, and the two exist around and within each other. Work becomes a normal, non-restrictive part of life that we look forward to.

Another term used to describe this level of flexibility is *work-life integration*. In talking about the flexibility provided for its staff, the University of California at Berkeley website states:

> We use the term work–life integration instead of work-life balance because the latter evokes a binary opposition between work and life. In fact, the traditional image of a scale associated with work-life balance creates a sense of competition between the two elements. Work-life integration instead is an approach that

Ascended Program Level on the Flex Scale

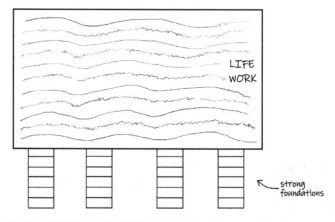

Figure 2.5. On the Ascended Program (Fluidity) Level, work is represented by the squiggly lines and has become just another part of life (the smooth lines), and the two flow around each other as required. This is an example of fluidity or work-life integration. As with the previous level, this program has strong foundations of support from leadership, technology, training, and collaboration.

creates more synergies between all areas that define "life": work, home/family, community, personal well-being, and health.[11]

A special note is that even though work is displayed in Figure 2.5 as fluid and structureless, it's good practice for employees and managers to have consistent working patterns. For example, a person can reserve four hours in the morning for intense, productive work (rather than alternating five minutes of work with five minutes of computer games). But these blocks of work are moveable and resizable as required.

It's also necessary to have times when work should *not* be done or expected. Employees and managers must be allowed and encouraged to switch off during designated times of the day and week to ensure that there is proper disconnection. Technology creep – emails coming in while you're eating dinner at seven, phone calls at all times, and other invasions of work into personal time – can cause people to feel constantly stressed and burdened by work. Don't let this happen.

Levels 0 and 1 are typically where most companies are sitting at the moment, but more and more are moving from Level 0 to Level 1 (motivated by increased legislation), which allows flexibility to be accessed with special permission.

Level 2 is where we have an attempt at flexibility programs for all or most employees, but they haven't quite got it right, and they're either doomed to fail or they aren't getting the most out of the practice.

Levels 3 and 4 are, at the moment, rare. Level 4 may be difficult for those industries where it's more difficult to have complete freedom of activities (such as healthcare, the trades, and manufacturing), but Level 3 is certainly possible for any organization.

Anyone who is serious about flexibility should be using this or similar measurement scales, combining them with audits and surveys designed to capture information about flexibility's effects, and determining at which level their organization sits. My hope is that soon we'll have accreditation bodies that will develop standards, as we do for quality, safety, or air pollution. Perhaps they'll augment a human sustainability or societal pollution measure to determine how companies provide their workers with the freedom to live. But for the moment this scale will be a useful guide for consultants and managers.

> ## Check Out
>
> **www.humansarenotrobots.com** for a short quiz to determine your company's level on the Flex Scale. It's not all-encompassing but it will give you an idea of where you are and what you can aim for.

The types of flexibility a business uses aren't as important as getting the fundamentals right and keeping in mind why you're implementing flexibility in the first place. Which brings us to . . .

Part One

FOR HUMANS AND THE WORLD

CHAPTER 3

Being Human

Life is a banquet, and most poor suckers are starving to death!

— Mame Dennis (*Aunty Mame*, 1958)

NOW THAT WE'VE GOT THE FORMALITIES OUT OF THE WAY we can get into the fun stuff! I'll start by launching into some existentialism: What makes us human anyway? And how does, and should, work fit into that picture?

The Lottery

My mum buys a lottery ticket every week. She has for as long as I can remember. She's probably spent, in present value, about $24,000 on tickets over the course of her life.[1] This money, given gains in the stock market over the last thirty years, could be worth over $120,000 if it was invested rather than gambled.[2] And because I don't recall being driven to school in a Ferrari, I'm pretty sure she never took home the jackpot. (Sorry, Mum, this does have a point!)

She's not alone. In the United States, for example, people spent $80 billion on lottery tickets in 2016.[3] About 49 percent of Americans actively play the lottery,[4] so on average that works out to be $511 spent per person each year. This is a lot of money, and it's basically an extra tax. The government gets whatever is left after paying winnings and expenses, which it uses to fund various public services such as schools, parks, and juvenile detention centers, things that tax money already pays for, or should anyway.[5]

The people who buy lottery tickets give the government this voluntary and inefficient tax for a one-in-three-hundred-million chance of winning the jackpot. That's the same likelihood as picking up a coin and flipping twenty-eight heads (or twenty-eight tails) in a row,[6] not something we would normally bet money on.

But even though most people *know* their chance of hitting the jackpot is next to zero, there *is* that chance. O! that chance . . .

Anyone who has bought a ticket has had that fantasy. Your numbers start coming up, one by one. You jump out of your chair and keep watching and checking as they keep dropping. Your heart races. One more to go. It's yours! You've got *all* of them! You check them. Once. Twice. Three times. You get your partner to check them. You check them in reverse order. You check them slowly. You check them upside-down. They're all there!

You scream. You cry. You've won! You've never won anything in your life! You don't even remember how big the pool is this week, but it was at least forty or fifty million dollars. You've just won enough for everything you will ever want or need. All those debts are gone! You *never* have to worry about money again.

Then comes the most thrilling part of the fantasy.

Your alarm wakes you up the next morning at seven. You iron your shirt or dress, for the last time ever. You drive through the start-stop-start, fifty-minute commute to work, for the last time ever. You walk through the sliding glass doors of your office, for the last time ever. Your smile is so big your face almost breaks in half. Your colleagues have already heard the news; they're hugging you, crying, high-fiving, asking why you even came in. Your cheeks glow and you just keep riding the wave, hoping not to wake up again.

Now the fantasy splits, depending on how much you love or loathe your boss. It will range from either trashing their desk and leaving with an "I'm outta here!" to sitting down and crafting an especially elegant letter of resignation along the lines of "*I will sadly yet gleefully be pursuing sunsets and sunrises instead of paychecks. . . . But thank you for being such an incredible person to work for. . . . XOX.*"

After you deliver this message to your boss, you walk out the front door and drive home (which is much quicker than the drive in, because it's nine thirty in the morning and no one's on the road), for the last time, and begin planning what to do with all that money. You might even go to the beach or the cinema to gain your composure.

It almost feels wrong, but you are free.

Free.

Whenever I ask someone why they buy lottery tickets, I usually get a response along the lines of: "For that chance of financial freedom."

This thing, financial freedom, has a few different meanings.

The first is usually the ability to pay debts. Many of us have debts of various types and sizes, and they all create a feeling of non-freedom. We feel trapped, burdened, weighed down, by those negative dollar signs and reminders to pay.

Part of the reason we work as much as we do is to keep up with payments, and we feel immeasurably stressed at the prospect of not being able to pay the minimum balances. We belong, in the back of our minds, to whomever we owe money to (usually the bank). Being able to finally get out of the bank's pocket, either by gradually paying down debts or annihilating them with a glorious lump sum from a lottery jackpot, leaves us feeling that we've escaped.

Another meaning of financial freedom is the ability to live out our wildest fantasies: buying a yacht and sailing around the world; living in a mansion with a movie room and a popcorn machine; moving to a cabin on a lake in Finland to write that sci-fi novel; buying an Aston Martin and painting a fire-pterodactyl on the bonnet. Many lottery winners do indeed live their dreams of upgrading real estate, buying new cars, and travelling.[7] This is the fun part of financial freedom – ticking off the bucket list.

But the last and most crucial meaning of financial freedom is right there in the name: *freedom*. In its purest sense, it means waking up in the morning and being able to choose exactly how you'll spend your day. Having full ownership and agency of your own body and mind. It's something many of us can't even imagine unless it's the weekend (and we somehow have no other obligations) or the holidays (which are too short).

Now, follow me down a somewhat obvious chain of logic:

1. Having a lot of money, as in the case of lottery winnings, gives us the freedom to do the things we want to do each day (check).

2. Which means that, conversely, *without* a lot of money, we *don't* have the freedom to do the things we want to do each day (check).

3. Which means that, without a lot of money, we're constrained to do something that takes away from our freedom (check).

4. And that thing we must do, to live, if we don't already have a lot of money, is work (check).

5. *So*, work, in its current form, must take away from our freedom by getting in the way of our ability to do the things we want to do (check).

6. And the only way to gain freedom is to get a lot of money so we can escape work (double-check).

Hence the lottery.

This thing exists because we don't feel free. We waste billions of dollars collectively on lottery tickets for a fraction of a chance to escape work, because it's only when we escape that we can be free to do all the things we want to do. When people launch into the Wild West of freelancing, they're also chasing an opportunity to do these things.

More importantly, this deep desire to escape demonstrates that the things we're missing out on aren't just nice-to-haves. They're more fundamental than wanting a yacht or a mansion or a fancy car. In fact, these things are built into our DNA. They're the things that make us human. And we crave them. Because, in the current system, with our current, normal jobs, we're not getting enough – not even close.

Poverties

The World Bank defines *poverty* in purely economic terms: *extreme poverty* is living on less than $1.90 a day (based on 2011 prices). According to this metric, about 736 million people in the world, over half of whom reside in sub-Saharan Africa, live in extreme poverty.[8]

To take into account a more complex nature of poverty beyond mere income, the United Nations introduced the Multidimensional Poverty Index (MPI) in a 2010 report. This measurement includes health (e.g., nutrition, child mortality), education (e.g., years of schooling, number of children enrolled), and standard of living (e.g., cooking fuel, access to toilets, water, electricity, assets). Using this measure, about 1.3 billion people worldwide live in multidimensional poverty.[9]

In either case, millions of people around the world go to bed hungry, live from day to day without knowing what the immediate future holds, and are often too tired and overcome with helplessness to improve their outlook. But – and I'm setting myself up for extreme eye-rolls and comments about First World problems – poverty extends beyond these measures, and it's much more pervasive in developed countries than we might think, afflicting even those with well-paying work and roofs over their heads.

When the United Nations defines poverty as a "severe deprivation of basic human needs, [including] food, safe drinking water, sanitation facilities, health, shelter, education and information," they acknowledge that, as humans, we need more than just food and water to live. Or, in essence, there's a difference between surviving and living, and things such as education and information, although not required for survival, are critical for living.

But humans require even more than these basic needs.

Imagine that you're locked in a box. It's big enough for you to stand up and move around in, and wide enough to lie down in comfortably. In that box is a constant supply of clean water and nutritious food. Purified air is pumped in through a tube. You have a working toilet and shower, and a special light provides for your vitamin D. New books appear weekly through a hole in the wall for you to read. You have a comfortable bed to sleep in. You have a couple of bars on which you can do pull-ups and push-ups. And you also have a stash of cash under your mattress (not that you need it, but your financial security is assured nonetheless).

Essentially you have, according to the World Bank's and United Nations' definitions, everything you need to *not* be living in poverty. You could stay alive for many, many years in this box. The question is this: would you *feel alive* in this box? Would you consider this existence to be living?

Probably not. You would have enough food and water and fresh air, but you would be deprived of other extremely important human needs. Not having any form of human contact, not having freedom to leave the box, not being able to see the sun or the sky, not having any newness or novelty, and not being able to pursue some sort of higher mission or meaning wouldn't just leave you feeling unhappy, it would make you prefer death, and within weeks you would desperately try to escape head-first through the book-hole.

Indeed, in a similar and very real situation, prison inmates who are locked in solitary confinement "often describe feelings of extreme mental duress after only a couple of days. . . . Some researchers have even compared confined inmates to victims of torture or trauma because many of the acute effects produced by solitary confinement mimic the symptoms associated with post-traumatic stress disorder."[10]

These people have food, they have water, they have a working toilet, somewhere to sleep, a roof over their head, room to move around, but they're suffering in many other ways.

The Chilean economist Manfred Max-Neef, in his work on Human Scale Development, asserted:

> The traditional concept of poverty is limited and restricted, since it refers exclusively to the predicaments of people who may be classified below a certain income threshold. This concept is strictly economistic. . . . [W]e should speak not of poverty, but of poverties. In fact, any fundamental human need that is not adequately satisfied, reveals a human poverty.[11]

Fundamental Needs

Humans have many other needs besides those that keep us from physically dying, and when we're lacking in *any* of them, not just food and water and sanitation, we feel it to our core.

These needs have been labeled and categorized throughout the years by various researchers. They usually include basic survival (food, water, health, medicine), shelter and security, connection to and belonging with other humans, understanding and curiosity, identity, freedom, discovery and creation, leisure and fun, and transcendence or greater meaning.

Probably the most famous categorization of needs was Abraham Maslow's hierarchy. Anyone who has attended a management course will have seen Maslow's pyramid of needs, and how these needs can be used as motivators in the workplace.

Maslow himself didn't construct a fancy pyramid infographic in PowerPoint (because it wasn't invented yet), but he did propose an order of importance for human needs, starting with physiological (survival) as the most important, and moving down, in order, to safety, love and belonging, esteem (mastery, achievement, being respected by oneself and others), cognition (understanding and intellectual stimulation), aesthetics (appreciation for beauty and nature), self-actualization (reaching one's highest and true potential), and lastly, self-transcendence (spirituality, a higher purpose beyond the self).[12]

In other words, humans have to fulfill their immediate needs before we can concern ourselves with our more esoteric desires. Someone who's starving to death won't be concerned with whether they're fulfilling their higher purpose in life; or at least that was the initial premise.

This hierarchical approach to human needs isn't overly useful, especially regarding the connection between work and our lives. Maslow himself proposed that the hierarchy "is not nearly so rigid as we may have implied," noting examples of people who perceive self-esteem to be more important than love, or who pursue creative fulfilment over even the basic survival needs.[13]

And there are countless instances of humans over the ages sacrificing the basic needs of survival to fight for liberty, love, gender identity, political and religious ideals, and the fulfillment of many other so-called higher-level needs, thus throwing the hierarchy to the grinder.

Other categorizations for human needs have been proposed over the years, including Three Needs Theory by David McClelland, Human Givens by Joe Griffin and Ivan Tyrrell, and ERG theory by Clayton Alderfer, to name a few.

For this book we'll be using Manfred Max-Neef's list of fundamental human needs, a comprehensive and easy-to-understand classification system. Max-Neef understood the importance of each need independent of the others. To repeat his earlier quote: "Any fundamental human need that is not adequately satisfied reveals a human poverty." He added that *"each poverty generates pathologies,"* meaning that we suffer when any need is unfulfilled, regardless of its place in the order of need fulfillment.

Max-Neef also captured crucial needs that Maslow and others didn't, such as freedom and leisure. The unfulfillment of these has an immense bearing on modern life.

He used his list in the context of national development, arguing that we must take every human need into account when seeking to increase well-being and life satisfaction, and hence the economic participation, of a population. With that understanding, developers, such as governments, can focus on creating or encouraging satisfiers of multiple needs, and ensure that they're not inhibiting or destroying people's abilities to satisfy some needs in favor of fulfilling others.

Max-Neef developed a human-centered approach to economic development, and that's extremely relevant for our approach to the workplace.

Max-Neef's (Modified) List of Fundamental Human Needs

Below are basic descriptions of Max-Neef's list of needs and examples of how these needs can be satisfied. They include examples of what happens when the needs are not fulfilled, providing strong evidence that they are indeed fundamentally important.

The satisfiers provided are not exhaustive because, as Max-Neef postulated, the "fundamental human needs are finite, few and classifiable," but the ways in which those needs are satisfied change over time, from culture to culture, and from person to person.[14]

I've taken some liberty and added a tenth need, nature, to the original list because it's clearly more than just a nice-to-have, or merely a satisfier of other needs, as I'll describe further.*

Subsistence (survival)

This is basic survival, satisfied by having food, clean water, sanitation, medicine, shelter from the elements, and other things that keep us alive and at a comfortable distance from death. It means having enough food to be at a healthy weight, not just enough to avoid starvation.

And even though you can't eat or drink it, money is also a major satisfier of this need, because in most cases we can't survive without it.

The importance of not dying probably doesn't need to be expanded on. Although, as mentioned previously, its importance can be superseded by a poverty of any other need.

Protection (security)

This refers to the ability to continue surviving, and it's satisfied by having a job or some other secure source of income, being mentally and physically healthy, and having social security, health systems, insurance, legal

---

* While reading an early draft of this book, a friend suggested that the list could be further enhanced by including eyeliner and free Wi-Fi; but I questioned the *fundamental* nature of these needs.

Fundamental Human Needs

- Subsistence (survival)
- Affection
- Participation
- Creation
- Freedom

- Protection (security)
- Understanding
- Leisure
- Identity
- Nature (author's addition)

Figure 3.1. List of fundamental human needs devised by Manfred Max-Neef (with one addition by the author).

systems, military, home ownership or rental agreements, support from others (family and friends), savings, infrastructure, access to markets, a functional government and good economy, and so on.

Apart from the practical elements of these satisfiers regarding our continued existence, a deprivation related to this need causes uncertainty and stress long before our survival is truly threatened. An example of this is in the next chapter, where we discuss how even the *perception* of job insecurity can result in physical and mental health problems.

Affection

Affection means love, intimacy, and connection, mainly with other humans, but also, importantly, with the self, and with animals and the natural world. It's satisfied by physical touch, sex, friendship, partnership or marriage, parenting, sharing, caring, laughing, talking, giving gifts, and merely being in the presence of others.

A poverty of this need presents in astounding ways. The brain of a child who is emotionally neglected by its parents won't develop properly. One study found that "globally neglected" children (e.g., minimal exposure to language, touch, and social interactions) had abnormally small brains. And this lack of brain development resulted in a range of developmental problems: "language, fine and large motor delays, impulsivity, disorganized attachment, dysphoria, attention and hyperactivity."[15]

Other (also pretty dark) examples of poverty of affection can be found in the Catholic Church and prisons. Catholic priests, who in general must remain celibate (if not already married before becoming a priest), and prisoners, who have limited access to normal avenues for affection, both often end up fulfilling this human need through abhorrent means:

sexually assaulting children in the clergy[16] or raping other prisoners.[17,18] These people are starving, and as Dr. Malcolm said in *Jurassic Park* when talking about other creatures fulfilling their fundamental needs, "Life . . . uh . . . finds a way."

Understanding

This involves using our brain to figure things out and learn. Mastery. Curiosity. Discovery. Teaching. Finding patterns and connections.

This need is satisfied not so much by the end result of knowing things but more by the *process* of understanding, of figuring something out for ourselves. It's less about *having* mastery and more about *gaining* mastery.

For example, if a friend saved you the effort of watching a murder mystery by telling you who the killer was and why they did it while the opening credits were still rolling, would you feel any sense of satisfaction from having that knowledge? Or would you feel that you needed a new friend because this one deprived you of the reason for watching the movie?

If you've ever been micromanaged in a work environment you will have felt that same deprivation of understanding, of working something out for yourself, of developing your own sense of mastery or skill. It sucks, on a fundamental level.

Participation

A single human in isolation is soft, slow, and highly visible prey. We don't have protective armor, sharp teeth, poison in our skin, or the ability to leap into a high branch at the first sign of danger. But many humans, working together, have become the most indomitable species on the planet.

We know, on a genetic level, that we need to be part of a group to survive, so we crave cooperation with other humans. We know that combining our efforts and knowledge produces greater results than any one individual could achieve. It's why we have a strong feeling of satisfaction when we help others, through charity or volunteering, even when we're helping complete strangers.

Being part of a group, and feeling included, accepted, and respected by others, is strongly ingrained in our psyches. If you've ever experienced those sometimes-crippling feelings of shame or embarrassment (and would rather die than speak in public), which stem from the fear of being ridiculed or rejected by others, you'll know just how important this need is. We want and need to belong to the group.

Leisure

Some might see leisure as a nice-to-have, especially if they work in Silicon Valley and hustle sixteen hours a day. But the ability to rest, relax, play, shut down, daydream, and sit in idleness doing absolutely nothing is as necessary to our lives as night is to day.

To be able to achieve to our full capacity, we must have periods of doing nothing. Constantly doing without adequate periods of not doing has done untold injury to many people. It results in burnout, low productivity, health problems, errors and accidents, suicide, and a lack of enjoyment of life.

Rest, recovery, and play enable our brains and bodies to rebuild damage, consolidate and order information (learn and remember), build strength, increase creativity, and all sorts of other good stuff. And merely enjoying the world is important to a full life.

Creation

Creation is the need to use our imagination, knowledge, and unique self to produce something that wasn't there before, whether it's an idea, music, a story, a new machine, or a better process for picking strawberries.

This is where we have an appreciation for beauty, chaos, variety, and novelty. Boredom from doing the same things with the same people for an extended period of time reveals a poverty of this need. For instance, marriage or staying in an uninspiring job for many years can deprive people of newness and novelty, and they end up leaving or searching for ways to spice things up.

Identity

Because humans are highly self-aware, we're not content with merely considering ourselves one of the many living, breathing organisms with two arms and two legs and opposable thumbs. We have a need to answer two questions in great detail:

1. Who am *I*?

2. How does the puzzle piece of *me* fit into some bigger picture?

The first is answered in an enormous number of ways, including, but not limited to, our name, physical appearance, age, gender, race, country of origin, profession, skills, likes and dislikes, language(s) spoken and accent, sexuality, level of education, relationship status, the car we drive, the clothes we wear, the sports or games we play or watch, the clubs we're a part of, our life history, symbols like tattoos and rings and body modification, how and if we're growing and developing, achievements and failures, dreams and goals and aspirations, favorite music, and so on.

The second question has been bugging philosophers (and every other human) since, like, forever: In the grand scheme of things, what is the point of *me*? Why am I here? What is the meaning of (my) life? And we answer that in a million different ways as well.

Spirituality and religion are ready-made answers that have made many of us content. That is, our purpose in the big picture is to serve a deity, and if we follow all the rules we're rewarded with a glorious afterlife.*

The many other ways we seek this transcendence of the self include helping other people (volunteering, protesting, donating), helping the natural world around us through sustainable acts and practices, pushing for ideals and beliefs, having and raising children, connecting with nature and animals, sharing in rituals and stories with cultural groups and families, looking to the stars or deep under the ocean to try to find new life, entertaining others, or advancing technology and science.

More and more often our jobs and professions need to correspond to some higher meaning beyond making money. (One could argue that work has become a kind of religion in many countries.)

And others seek to just live a good life and enjoy the moment, and their purpose is that they have no purpose other than to live. This forms part of their identity and is something they value and hold on to.

Freedom

Freedom means having autonomy and control over oneself. Choice. Independence. The ability to speak, to vote, to think freely, to have privacy.

As we find our way as a species, we have taken away many freedoms from many individuals and groups. Slavery and the oppression of women are blatant examples of the theft of freedom. These thefts, along with more-subtle poverties of freedom, such as injustice and unfairness, are deeply felt. Even hearing about injustices faced by strangers on the other

---

* Religion is a ready-made satisfier of many *other* needs on this list, if you'll notice, such as affection, participation, understanding, protection, and for some, subsistence. There's no wonder it's played such an important role, for better or worse, in human history. The same could also be said for sport; just replace *glorious afterlife* with *premiership cup* or *Olympic medal*.

side of the planet creates a vicarious deprivation of freedom, and may stir people to action.

Less-obvious non-freedoms include those most relevant to this book: bosses owning an employee's time in the modern workplace by dictating when they must be at the workplace, or making workers feel they have little autonomy, both of which contribute to a strong desire to escape.

Nature (my addition)

Max-Neef saw the importance of nature to people, but only in that it satisfied other needs, such as affection and leisure. But the importance of nature to our physical and mental well-being can't be overstated – especially as we tend toward urbanization.

Just *seeing* (or not seeing) nature has profound effects on our existence. One study involving a prison in Southern Michigan found that prisoners who had a view of rolling farmland and trees were 24 percent less likely to get physically or mentally sick than their poor comrades whose cells looked out onto bare brick walls.[19] The poverty of nature generated pathologies. Thus it fits within Max-Neef's description of a fundamental need.

Being immersed in every part of nature affects us: the sun, the water, the land, and what we put into and on our bodies. The more closely linked we are to nature, the more we benefit. And conversely, when we're deprived of the natural world, we suffer immense harm.

This list qualitatively states what we need as humans, but the importance of our needs can be measured. A study by Louis Tay and Ed Diener, which used a Gallup survey of 60,865 people from 123 countries, quantified the effects of each of our needs on our subjective well-being (SWB), which comprises *life evaluation*, *positive emotions*, and *negative emotions*.[20]

Tay and Diener (and Gallup) used a list of needs similar to Max-Neef's, which I've put in parentheses:

- Basic needs for food and shelter (subsistence)
- Safety and security (protection)
- Social support and love (affection, participation)
- Feeling respected and pride in activities (participation, identity, creation)

- Mastery (understanding, creation, identity)
- Self-direction and autonomy (freedom)*

Table 3.1 shows the relative importance of each of these human needs, across the world, for the three components of SWB. The numbers outside the brackets are basically the percentage of relative importance for each need (e.g., for the world, basic needs account for 63 percent of the variance of life evaluation, whereas for positive emotions they only account for 3 percent of the variance).

The first significant result of the survey was that our needs seem universal across cultures and countries, thus affirming their fundamental nature. The highlighted rows show consistent patterns across different cultural regions for life evaluation, positive emotions, and negative emotions, illustrating that regardless of whether we live in Africa or Northern Europe or the Middle East, our needs are quantifiably similar.†

And following that, you'll notice that different needs hold different relative importance for each of the three SWB components. For life evaluation, basic needs were generally the most important. For positive emotions, social and respect needs were most important. And for negative emotions, basic, respect, and autonomy needs held the most influence.

Tay and Diener concluded that "balance in life is desirable; this follows from the fact that each of the needs makes separable contributions to SWB. . . . Thus, because people need to fulfill a variety of needs, it is likely that a mix of daily activities that includes mastery, social relationships, and the meeting of physical needs is required for optimal SWB."[22]

It may seem crude to place the infinite complexity and wonder of humans into a grocery list of ten or fewer items, but to the contrary, these lists demonstrate how varied and numerous our needs are *at a fundamental level.*

---

* The effects of leisure and nature weren't measured in this study, but I'm sure some interesting results would have arisen if they were.

† There *are* differences between regions regarding the importance of specific needs; this may be due to the relative lack of fulfillment in each region, which heightens their perceived importance. For example, basic needs are significantly more important in South East Asia, Latin America, and Africa, where they would be less fulfilled than in the more developed regions of Southern and Northern Europe and the Middle East.

The Relative Importance of Needs worldwide

Measure	World	East Africa	Former South Asia	Latin Soviet Union	Middle America	Northern East	South Europe/Anglo	Southern East Asia	Europe
Life evaluation									
Basic	**.63 [.24]**	**.62 [.34]**	**.44 [.16]**	**.46 [.23]**	**.61 [.43]**	**.23 [.23]**	**.27 [.18]**	**.88 [.30]**	**.30 [.11]**
Safety	.03 [.01]	.01 [.01]	.00 [.00]	.01 [.02]	.00 [.00]	.14 [.05]	.08 [.07]	.04 [.01]	.02 [.02]
Social	.16 [.08]	.16 [.12]	.12 [.06]	.21 [.11]	.15 [.10]	.19 [.30]	.23 [.17]	.02 [.06]	.28 [.11]
Respect	.04 [.02]	.07 [.04]	.08 [.04]	.06 [.04]	.04 [.04]	.05 [.08]	.13 [.08]	.00 [.00]	.09 [.03]
Mastery	.09 [.05]	.11 [.07]	.16 [.07]	.15 [.08]	.14 [.10]	.16 [.18]	.20 [.14]	.04 [.04]	.18 [.09]
Autonomy	.06 [.04]	.03 [.04]	.20 [.10]	.11 [.09]	.06 [.05]	.23 [.09]	.09 [.11]	.01 [.07]	.13 [.06]
Log income	[.55]	[.38]	[.58]	[.43]	[.27]	[.08]	[.24]	[.52]	[.59]
Total R2	.13 [.22]	.09 [.12]	.13 [.24]	.09 [.14]	.08 [.09]	.10 [.08]	.07 [.11]	.07 [.10]	.06 [.14]
Positive emotions									
Basic	.03 [.03]	.03 [.04]	.08 [.08]	.03 [.03]	.03 [.04]	.05 [.04]	.00 [.00]	.00 [.04]	.03 [.02]
Safety	.01 [.01]	.01 [.01]	.00 [.00]	.01 [.01]	.01 [.01]	.02 [.02]	.01 [.01]	.00 [.01]	.01 [.03]
Social	**.24 [.23]**	**.25 [.23]**	**.25 [.24]**	**.27 [.27]**	**.16 [.14]**	**.19 [.17]**	**.40 [.36]**	**.23 [.26]**	**.30 [.26]**
Respect	**.36 [.37]**	**.44 [.45]**	**.23 [.20]**	**.35 [.34]**	**.44 [.44]**	**.37 [.42]**	**.26 [.25]**	**.34 [.38]**	**.32 [.29]**
Mastery	.18 [.19]	.15 [.16]	.16 [.13]	.17 [.17]	.19 [.20]	.21 [.22]	.17 [.18]	.22 [.20]	.18 [.17]
Autonomy	.17 [.16]	.12 [.11]	.27 [.27]	.18 [.17]	.17 [.18]	.16 [.11]	.16 [.19]	.20 [.10]	.17 [.18]
Log income	[.02]	[.01]	[.07]	[.02]	[.00]	[.03]	[.01]	[.00]	[.05]
Total R2	.23 [.23]	.24 [.25]	.21 [.20]	.24 [.24]	.22 [.21]	.21 [.19]	.12 [.13]	.18 [.13]	.20 [.21]
Negative emotions									
Basic	**.23 [.21]**	**.14 [.14]**	**.34 [.31]**	**.13 [.10]**	**.30 [.28]**	**.22 [.23]**	**.21 [.14]**	**.48 [.53]**	**.25 [.25]**
Safety	.09 [.08]	.04 [.04]	.04 [.02]	.06 [.04]	.06 [.07]	.17 [.19]	.24 [.22]	.16 [.07]	.19 [.20]
Social	.11 [.12]	.25 [.23]	.12 [.13]	.07 [.05]	.10 [.11]	.13 [.10]	.01 [.01]	.00 [.00]	.03 [.04]
Respect	**.25 [.27]**	**.31 [.33]**	**.11 [.09]**	**.38 [.41]**	**.26 [.24]**	**.19 [.21]**	**.13 [.14]**	**.18 [.19]**	**.16 [.19]**
Mastery	.09 [.10]	.12 [.12]	.05 [.02]	.12 [.13]	.11 [.12]	.11 [.09]	.04 [.03]	.06 [.03]	.06 [.07]
Autonomy	**.22 [.21]**	**.14 [.12]**	**.35 [.34]**	**.25 [.26]**	**.16 [.14]**	**.17 [.15]**	**.38 [.37]**	**.12 [.12]**	**.31 [.24]**
Log income	[.02]	[.03]	[.08]	[.00]	[.04]	[.03]	[.10]	[.05]	[.01]
Total R2	.10 [.10]	.15 [.16]	.08 [.08]	.09 [.09]	.11 [.11]	.16 [.14]	.06 [.06]	.06 [.06]	.11 [.12]

Table 3.1. A study by Louis Tay and Ed Diener shows the relative Importance of needs worldwide for three components of subjective well-being.[21] *Note: Total R2 represents the total amount of variance accounted for in the dependent SWB. Relative importance is calculated such that all values sum to 1.00, representing the proportional contribution. Bolded values show consistently large relative importance values across world regions. Numbers without brackets show the relative importance of needs alone. Numbers in brackets show the relative importance of both needs and income.*

These are not optional extras; they are necessities for life:

- Creative outlets
- Rest, leisure, and fun
- Learning and testing new and varied concepts
- Spending affectionate time with friends and family
- Having a sense of freedom and autonomy over one's life
- Feeling part of a broader community
- Being in and around nature
- Having a strong feeling of identity and purpose

A deprivation of any of our needs reduces our humanity – it takes away from our feeling of being alive and harms us and the world around us. Conversely, a balanced fulfillment of every need creates contentment, good physical and mental health, and lives that we don't need to escape from.

These human needs, specifically Max-Neef's modified list, will form the foundations of what we're trying to achieve in this book. Work flexibility is so much more than parents being able to pick their kids up from school. Work flexibility helps us to take care of what makes us *us*.

Twenty-Thousand Years Ago

Meet June.

June is a member of the species *Homo sapiens*. She is a fifty-year-old matriarch of a tribe of about fifty people who live in the Vézère Valley in southwestern France, near what is now the town of Montignac. It's a softly sloping, green landscape with plentiful fauna, flora, and river systems, surrounded by mountainous, rugged terrain.

Sunrise. June opens her eyes and two small, cheeky faces grin down at her. "Are we fishing today, Gramma?" one of the small faces asks.

"Yeah!" cries the other, "We haven't been fishing for soooo long. And you said we would!"

June did promise her two granddaughters, aged five and seven, that she would take them to the river today. They've been helping her weave a new net for the last week out of rope brought to their village by a neighboring tribe; and it's time to test it before the yearly salmon run.

They gather the long net and head toward the river.

June teaches the girls a song about the salmon on their way, a song taught to her by her own grandmother many years ago. She also tests the girls' knowledge of which berries they can and can't eat as they pass different bushes and trees. (The younger, Fi, has developed a habit of eating anything colorful.)

Ryle, the older sister, tests her slingshot skills on a rabbit sitting in the open. She misses and it hops away. "You're getting closer," June tells her as she rubs the top of her head. "Next time remember: two eyes."

Back in the village, some of the men are trying out a new paint pigment on stones. It's an ochre chalk one of them found several kilometers away in a dry riverbed, and they're impressed with the rich red it leaves on the rocks after being mixed with water and lard. They try out various mixtures with different ratios of water and animal fat before settling on the right amounts. Tomorrow they'll go down to the nearby cave and add this to the illustrations of animals they've already begun – pictures to glorify their spirit guides, such as the powerful bison, the proud stag, and the majestic horse.

One of the men is especially excited about going to the cave. Last week his name was Si. But after killing his first bison he is now considered a man and can choose his own name, so he is now called Fasu, meaning *patient*. It's taken many months for him to feel courageous enough to go on the hunt, and he feels proud to have taken his time. He will paint his bison at the cave and join their spirits forever.

A teenage couple sit nearby under a tree, whispering to each other their dreams of journeying far from the valley, to see what's on the other side of the surrounding limestone cliffs. They've spent their whole lives in the same land with the same people, and they're sure there must be something else, something more, on the other side.

June and the girls return in the late afternoon with a bounty of salmon, and Fi has brought back a pouchful of probably edible berries. They're just in time to meet members of their neighboring tribe, who have arrived with their own supply of food for tonight's Moon Feast. They greet each other with gleeful hugs and nose kisses and begin to prepare the food, face paint, and costumes.

After the feast the full moon rises over the craggy hills in the distance, and a full and content elder, June's uncle Dilé, stands in front of the fire and begins to tell the story of Hyena, who was born laughing at all the strange creatures in the world, especially humans, who walk on their back legs and lost their tails. But he finishes by saying that even Hyena has respect for all who walk or swim or fly and the land that birthed them, and that's the way of the world.

One of the visitors sings a song, and the people dance with each other under the bright moon and share stories of their lives since the last feast.

These people are doing many of the things their ancestors have been doing since *Homo sapiens* arrived on the scene over two-hundred-thousand years ago. Some of these things were done by *Homo habilis* and *Homo erectus*, the parents of modern humans, millions of years ago.

That's where our needs come from. They were imprinted on our genes as we were growing up as a species. Through complex evolutionary processes (beyond the scope of this book) humans developed certain adaptations based on what enabled us to survive, both as individuals and as a group, and these things have become part of who we are.

For instance, our ability and will to cooperate and socialize with other humans increased our fitness for survival by providing protection and enabling us to share knowledge about food and water sources, new technologies, and other information that gave us a survival advantage. Those who didn't cooperate with other humans were more likely to die before handing down their lone-wolf genetic information to the next generation; hence, that need to participate and build affectionate relationships was written onto our genes.[23]

The more curious and creative of our ancestors would have found ingenious ways to survive and thrive, identifying patterns such as seasons, the weather, star and moon movements, herd migrations, and growth in different edible plants, and they found ways to keep warm during cold periods after we lost our protective covering of fur.[24] Through using our minds, our brains grew in size and complexity, and now we crave understanding, learning, and higher reasoning.

An important physical adaptation also shaped our cognitive needs. When our ancient ancestors decided to stand up and walk on two legs, our hands became freer to make tools and weapons, carry, throw, draw, build, feel and investigate, and sew clothes and shoes. We developed finely tuned motor skills and opposable thumbs, and the number of nerves in our palms and fingers increased dramatically. Those developments, which we once used to fashion spearheads, can now be used to play

"Flight of the Bumblebee" on a piano.[25] We have a deep sense of satisfaction when we use our hands, in concert with our minds, to visualize something that doesn't exist and then turn it into reality. This is why creation is such a fundamental part of who we are.

Leisure is important to us because leisure was the way we lived. Instead of working forty or more hours a week, ancient humans would have spent most of their time relaxing, chatting, grooming, or playing with members of the tribe, or sitting alone and looking at rocks or stars.[26] In today's world we're overwhelmed by information and stimuli, and when we meditate or switch off from technology, we improve our mental health. This works because the world we evolved in was much quieter than today, with only a bit of talking and singing, and the trickle of a creek (and the occasional volcanic eruption).

We have an affinity with nature because that has always been our home. We're a part of nature. We may have left it, with the rigid squares and rectangles in which we live and work, but it didn't leave us. We grew up under the stars, in branches, surrounded by grass and rocks and hills and creeks. When we're out there again, in the woods, or by the sea, or around other animals, we're home, and our minds and bodies thank us.

And having the freedom to choose what we do when we wake up and how we do it has been part of our DNA for over four billion years. It developed when we were single-celled organisms floating around in whichever direction we damn-well pleased!

I'm not saying that life for June and her tribe was perfect twenty thousand years ago.

A small wound from a cut could spell doom without antibiotics.[27] Food and water scarcity may have been a problem during ice ages and droughts. We were at the mercy of tigers and snakes and cannibals. Infant and child mortality – without modern medical technology and knowledge, and because of infanticide and other causes that we don't see as acceptable now[28] – were extremely high compared to the present.[29] But we could certainly argue from the point of view of needs-fulfillment that June and her tribe had a pretty sweet existence.

It's likely that ancient humans had the capability to fulfill their needs in a balanced and sustainable way that we in the modern world achieve only when we retire or win the lottery. These people had abundant time with family and other social connections, rest and leisure, varied and adventurous days, freedom to choose how to spend their time, exposure to nature, consistent and involved learning and teaching, healthy diets, and active lifestyles.[30]

The Devolution

About twelve-thousand years ago humans were domesticated by wheat. For a fascinating read about humans giving up the beautiful hunter-gatherer existence to toil in fields for rich masters I recommend *Sapiens* (2011) by Yuval Noah Harari.

This domestication would have started small. Abundant wet seasons provided high growth of grasses and grains, leading to semi-permanent settlements where humans could take advantage of this food source until it was depleted. Carrying the grains back to camp for grinding and cooking would have spread the seeds, and experimenting with storing food for leaner periods and cultivating for improved growth lured humans into larger, more permanent settlements.

We became dependent on these crops and on other types of farming and industry arising from permanent towns and cities. Slowly, without noticing much of a change, we left our old ways of living and could never go back. Wrote Harari:

> Rather than heralding a new era of easy living, the Agricultural Revolution left farmers with lives generally more difficult and less satisfying than those of foragers. Hunter-gatherers spent their time in more stimulating and varied ways, and were less in danger of starvation and disease. The Agricultural Revolution certainly enlarged the sum total of food at the disposal of human-kind, but the extra food did not translate into a better diet or more leisure. Rather, it translated into population explosions and pampered elites. The average farmer worked harder than the average forager, and got a worse diet in return. The Agricultural Revolution was history's biggest fraud.[31]

It (obviously) didn't stop there. The larger, permanent towns and cities enabled huge leaps in our cooperative abilities and specializations, mirrored by leaps in science and technology, language and writing, government and laws, medicine, travel and discovery, and all the other things we take for granted in our modern lives.

The Scientific Revolution, starting in 1543 with the publishing of Nicolaus Copernicus's *De revolutionibus orbium coelestium* (*On the Revolutions of the Heavenly Spheres*), and ending in the early 1700s with Isaac Newton (either with the publishing of *Opticks* in 1704, or his death in 1727),[32] opened our minds further to the workings of the world and the universe, formed modern experimental methods, and subsequently produced technology that would look like magic to someone from a few hundred years prior (e.g., telescopes, mechanical calculators, steam engines).

From these developments emerged industrial machines capable of producing more materials and products than any human could make by hand; thus, on the back of mass textile manufacturing in the United Kingdom from around 1760, the Industrial Revolution began.[33]

GDP per capita increased dramatically due to growth in markets, populations took off, and the "standard of living" arguably increased due to advances in technology and life expectancy, greater access to consumable goods, and higher average wages to buy said goods.[34]

Without these Revolutions – the Agricultural, Scientific, and Industrial – I wouldn't be typing this sentence on a computer, I wouldn't be able to drive to the shop to buy food for a whole week, I wouldn't have an understanding that the earth travels around the sun. We wouldn't have achieved any of the current greatness and dominance over the planet that we have so far without these significant periods in history.

But the cost that most of humanity has paid since the beginning of the Agricultural Revolution to enable those achievements is immense. Many of us, most of us, lost our freedom and autonomy as soon as we settled (or were dragged) into this new existence of needing to work for others to survive, and our ability to take care of our fundamental human needs – those we developed over hundreds of thousands, even millions, of years – fell into a pit of darkness.

For our needs, these weren't revolutions, they were a devolution. *The Devolution.* And with each advancement we made in technology and society and GDP, the masses have been forced to devolve further and further away from what we need as humans.

Our close connections to family and community were whittled away, time for relaxing and leisure disappeared, the opportunity to have varied, adventurous days was forced into one or two days on the weekend (and

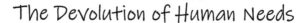

The Devolution of Human Needs

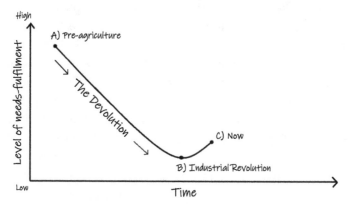

Figure 3.2. The Agricultural, Scientific, and Industrial Revolutions, collectively, pushed us further and further away from a state of having our needs fulfilled, creating various chronic poverties. (The graphic is not to scale and purely for illustrative purposes.)

A) Before the Agricultural Revolution: human needs were fulfilled as they had evolved, in balanced and sustainable ways, because this was the environment in which they were created.

B) The Industrial Revolution: the low point of The Devolution, where needs-fulfillment was arguably at its lowest in history.

C) Now: humans have managed to claw back some of our ability to fulfill our fundamental needs because workplaces are slightly less industrialized as we shift to knowledge and information work. But those rigid work traditions are proving difficult to shake off, and we're still, for the most part, unnecessarily living with poverties.

must compete with the laundry), and the ability to choose what we do on a daily basis became a long-forgotten, laughable myth.

Figure 3.2 is a conceptual graph of our level of needs-fulfillment over these different periods, from before the Agricultural Revolution to the present.

The Industrial Revolution was the very bottom (B). During this time, kids weren't just part of the labor force, they were *preferred* because of their relatively minuscule wages and high expendability; workdays of twelve to sixteen hours were common; there was a severe division of labor and housework for men and women; and only one day of rest was allowed (because God said).

It took some time, but luckily we started to see the impacts that this sort of work environment was having on the lives of workers: people were dying or getting sick because of long hours and poor conditions, kids included.

These impacts were revealed through the concerted efforts of unions, and some employers realized that it was good business to look after their employees. For example, Henry Ford doubled the minimum wage for his employees in 1914, and then reduced the workweek from six to five days twelve years later in 1926, both for *mostly* altruistic reasons.[35]* Governments started to set some rules for what business owners were allowed to make employees do, and for how long, and, thankfully, some societies said that it's not okay for kids to be working and dying in coal mines.

So over the last hundred or so years we've managed to claw back a fraction of our ability to fulfill our human needs (C in Figure 3.2). Many countries now legislate a maximum number of days or maximum number of hours that people can work, ensure that kids aren't being used for labor, and have certain standards for health and safety.

But even at the start of the twenty-first century, when we have abundant knowledge and wealth, and unbelievable technology, we're still much closer to the level of unbridled labor we had in the dirty factories in the nineteenth and twentieth centuries than we are to the autonomy and balance of June and her tribe twenty-thousand years ago.

Our needs are *still* in a pit.

The employee sitting in an open-plan office from Monday to Friday, eight thirty to five or six, for over 90 percent of the year, and spending an extra one or two hours a day just getting to and from work, is starving. They simply don't have the capability to take care of their own needs in a sustainable way.

They have food, shelter, water, and access to medical care, but because of the poverties of other needs they fantasize about the weekends or their upcoming holidays. They dream of being *anywhere else*, and they build life rafts out of a few branches and risk their financial security in the ocean of freelancing or entrepreneurship.

They might drown, but many don't feel like they have a life in their current situation anyway, so it's worth the risk. Or they just sit there and starve, too scared to challenge what's normal because they need the money.

---

* To combat high levels of worker absenteeism and turnover, and to increase productivity, Ford realized that people need to be able to fulfill their needs (such as feeling financially secure and being able to rest).

There are many examples of poverties caused by the rigid workplace:

Subsistence

Because of a deeply embedded culture of overwork in Japan, 71 percent of men in that country "routinely get less than seven hours of sleep each night."[36] And in the United States, also at least partly due to the stress and length of their workdays, one in three adults aren't getting at least seven hours of sleep on a regular basis. (Other major causes of not sleeping enough include obesity, physical inactivity, smoking, and excessive alcohol use,[37] all of which can be heavily influenced by rigid work practices, as discussed in the next chapter.)

Pathologically speaking, it has been found that "sleeping less than seven hours per day is associated with an increased risk of developing chronic conditions such as obesity, diabetes, high blood pressure, heart disease, stroke, and frequent mental distress."[38]

Protection

A study in the United Kingdom found that only half (53 percent) of people exercise more than once per week. The top reasons given were that they are either too busy or too tired.[39]

Another study, also in the United Kingdom, found that 37 percent of people *never* exercise or play sport. Never! Similarly, 40 percent of the respondents in this study claimed that lack of time was the main reason for not exercising more often.[40]

We can safely assume that at least one of the reasons people feel they don't have enough time to take care of their health, in this simplest and most powerful way, is due to the rigidity of their work (more on this, again, in the next chapter).

Leisure

A strong sign that people don't have enough time and energy to fulfill their leisure needs (and other needs, including creation, affection, nature, and freedom) during the normal workweek is that 81 percent of fully employed adults are found to suffer from "Sunday night blues" or the "Sunday scaries"[41] – that feeling of existential stress and anxiety about diving back into the too-muchness of the next long and rigid week.

The World Health Organization has recently included burnout in the 11th Revision of the International Classification of Diseases as an "occupational phenomenon" defined as "a syndrome conceptualized as resulting from chronic workplace stress that has not been successfully managed. It is characterized by three dimensions:

1. Feelings of energy depletion or exhaustion
2. Increased mental distance from one's job, or feelings of negativism or cynicism related to one's job
3. Reduced professional efficacy."[42]

In some of the most rigid workplaces in the world, burnout is running wild. A survey of fifteen-thousand U.S. doctors found that 44 percent "were experiencing symptoms of burnout." A large U.K. law firm found that 73 percent of its lawyers were feeling burnout.[43]

And a Gallup poll of U.S. full-time employees found that nearly a quarter (23 percent) feel burned out at work "very often or always," and 44 percent feel this way at least sometimes.[44] Drained of human needs, especially regarding rest and play, these people are just getting through the day.

Affection
Loneliness has become a crushing epidemic across much of the world (especially in Western societies), and is likely to be one of the main causes of a corresponding spread of depression, anxiety, and other health and well-being problems.[45] The United Kingdom has recently appointed a Minister for Loneliness to focus on this issue.[46]

It may seem unfair to say that work has any part to play in the loneliness epidemic, especially when you can argue that work, for many people, is one of the main avenues for social connection.

But *that* is the problem!

First, working long and rigid hours gets in the way of genuinely connecting with people outside of work, such as spending time with friends and family, or creating connections in the community. A YouGov study in the United Kingdom found that "almost half (49 percent) of respondents say that being busy in their day-to-day lives stops them from connecting with others as much as they would like to."[47]

Second, even though the workplace is a major source for human interaction, these interactions are often only skin-deep. Work isn't usually where we open up and share our troubles and dreams with others. This isn't surprising, since many of us maintain a professional distance at work, or we want to avoid professional fallout when relational issues arise, or we don't feel that we can trust those we compete with.

One Gallup study on U.S. workers found that only two out of ten people have a "best friend" at work[48] – that is, someone they can confide in, care about, spend quality time with both in and out of the office, trust, and, dare I say, love.[49]

Combining these two points, it could be said that many people with normal jobs spend most of their waking hours disconnected from true social interaction and affection, a complete reversal of the daily lives of June and her tribe.

Nature

A systematic review found that, because they don't get enough sunlight, 80 percent of shiftworkers, 77 percent of indoor workers, and 72 percent of healthcare residents were vitamin D deficient.[50] A deficiency of the sunshine vitamin has been linked to osteoporosis, certain cancers, cardiovascular and respiratory disorders, inflammatory bowel diseases, cognitive disorders, and a long list of other crappy stuff.[51,52] This is just one of the many ways (and one of the worst) that work environments and cultures, and the lack of daily freedom, get in the way of our proper connection with nature.

Understanding/Creation

Work doesn't always satisfy our cognitive needs. Often there's little variation, and when there is it's either at the mindlessly simple end of the spectrum, or it's highly specialized to the point of still being mindless, thus not providing the stimulation our brains require.

One survey of thirteen-hundred professionals around the world found that 65 percent of us are bored at work, with legal (81 percent), financial (68 percent), and accounting (67 percent) being the most boring. Research and development (45 percent) and executive management (49 percent) were the least boring.[53]

We often don't get to use our minds as they were designed to be used while we're at work; we can't use our minds in varied and complex ways with consistent discovery and novelty. Someone who spends the majority of their time the way most of us do is starving their brain.

Freedom

The mere feeling of freedom is one of our strongest needs, and it's one of the biggest needs we aren't meeting in the workplace.

A survey of nearly one thousand freelancers found that the top reasons they give for preferring the unpredictability of freelancing over a typical office job all related to freedom: work-life balance (70 percent), desire to choose *when* I work (62 percent), freedom (56 percent), desire to choose *where* I work (55 percent), and desire to be my own boss (49 percent).[54]

Without freedom it's much harder to fulfill our *other* needs in sustainable ways. From the same survey, 60 percent of respondents "said freelancing has helped them become healthier, and 66 percent said they are less stressed as a freelancer." Escaping their normal jobs allowed them to start relaxing and take care of themselves.

These are just a few examples, but they're enough to show that the rigid workplace is really fucking us over as a species.

What can be done about this situation?

One option is to wait thousands or millions of years for our fundamental needs to slowly evolve to disconnection from other humans, being surrounded by artificial light and bricks, constant busyness, doing the same things day after day, not requiring sleep or physical activity, and mindless servitude. Evolution never really reaches an end point, so this is not such a silly idea; it just requires patience.

Another option is to start moving away from unchecked capitalism, today, and toward a way of working that considers employees as humans, and to start valuing people's needs as much as shareholder profits and CEO salaries.

We also need to recognize that human sustainability and capitalism aren't mutually exclusive, but in fact synergize beautifully, as I'll discuss in Part Two of this book.

It's time to combine our astounding advancements in technology and understanding of the universe, *and* our knowledge of what we need as humans, to fight back against The Devolution. It's time to prioritize our needs, in all areas of society, especially the workplace. It's time for us to leap out of this pit.

Coping

Polite skeptics may, at this point, be tempted to say that everyone who works for them is fine and happy, and none of this applies to *their* workplace. *No one who works for me is in poverty!*

Although humans have evolved to require certain things to feel whole, alive, and healthy, we have also evolved to be highly adaptive and can cope with terrible environments, such as drought, war, ice ages, concentration camps, and open-plan offices. If nothing else, *Homo sapiens* is a survivor.

This means that we can subsist in this rigid, traditional work environment and work long hours, even when most of our needs are starving, and it can take years before we realize that something is wrong. Many of us think that it's normal to ignore our human requirements and prioritize work in order to provide for ourselves and our families. It's only when we're surrounded by beeping monitors that we realize, with deep regret, that we've sacrificed our happiness for the sake of work.[55]

If something isn't a direct and obvious threat to our survival, we're usually okay with it. Our traditional workplace doesn't have sharp claws and big teeth; it's not something we instinctively run away from when we see it. Sure, occasionally we gloriously quit from a particularly heinous work environment; but usually we put up with it and ignore the voices inside that say "this isn't good," because, as far as we know, it's normal. We slowly succumb to ill health and other problems, not realizing that we're being attacked by this way of living.

I'd felt the black cloud building for some time. At first it was little things: occasionally getting to work late because I couldn't get out of bed, turning down invitations to meet friends so I could stay home and watch movies by myself, my waistline expanding with a bit too much comfort food, having trouble focusing on my work.

Because of my long hours at work and commuting two to three hours a day, I could easily put a tick next to each of the demonstrations of poverty set out in the previous section.

Slowly and surely, I was consumed. I became numb. I couldn't make the simplest of decisions. I sat and stared at my monitor at work, trying my best to at least look busy when someone walked past.

I was going through the motions of life, pretending to be a person.

"I think I might have depression," I told the HR manager, my hands cold and shaking as I forced the words out into the open.

It wasn't the first time I'd gone through mental health problems during my career, but this time I decided to tell my employer in the hopes that they would be understanding, and perhaps try to work with me as I found help. And thankfully they were understanding, at first. They gave me time to see a therapist, and my boss helped to plan new deadlines for my projects.

The therapist confirmed that I was suffering from severe depression and anxiety. We talked mostly about work, and how I felt trapped by my current existence, and how I didn't feel alive because my life was nothing but work and sitting in traffic, and that I knew that there was something fundamentally wrong with the way we work, and how I was constantly working, even after hours, to try to escape from work and free myself.

She suggested that I should work a bit less, and that even though it's admirable that I'm trying to start my own side business, maybe I should focus on my day job and learn to be content with what I have. She took me through mindfulness exercises – breathe in, breathe out, focus on a tree outside, breathe in, breathe out – that would help me cope with life in its current form.

Henceforth, every day, when I started having trouble focusing, I'd breathe in, breathe out, look at leaves brushing against the office window, and close my eyes. And once a day I'd walk outside and sit on a park bench for fifteen minutes.

It did help to a certain extent, and I now do my best to do some simple meditation on a daily basis to escape from information overload and re-center myself. But the *real* solution came only a few weeks after I told my employer about my situation. They fired me.

The letter on the table had some fluffy statement about the "position being unnecessary, and it will be divided between different functions." Whatever. I was too numb to argue. On top of the dubious timing of my firing, this was my third time being made redundant in the space of five years. It was the final nail.

On my drive home, I swore off working for other people and being in a normal eight-thirty-to-five office job forever. I knew the damage it had done. "*Never. Fucking. Again.*" I would be free, at any cost. With this thought, a thin ray of sunlight pierced the black cloud for the first time in years.

After a final, sobbing breakdown, and after spending my last few dollars on food and exorbitant rent, I moved away from the city to stay with family in a small tourist/retirement town on the coast. I fell into a job as a lifeguard at the local pool, and after writing a few articles on LinkedIn, managed to become a contributing writer for a flexible job-search company.

The pay wasn't great for either of those jobs (especially compared to what I was receiving in a "normal" job) but for the first time in years I started to feel content. The healing process began.

The lifeguarding took up three or four days a week, sometimes half-days, sometimes longer days with a few-hours gap in the middle, and the writing I could do whenever and wherever I wanted; the only commuting was a five-minute drive to the pool.

With this newfound flexibility I had the freedom to attend to my human needs, all of them, every day.

I slept as much as I needed to sleep. I took my dog for a nature walk each morning and evening. I regularly worked on things I was passionate about (writing and editing). I exercised every day (obviously my free pool access helped!). I could do housework whenever it needed to be done, in the gaps of the other stuff I was doing, rather than using my precious weekends for it.

I met with friends to hang out *during weekdays* (it was tough to stop feeling guilty about that). I could make love at ten on a Tuesday morning (I hadn't been able to do that since skipping classes back at university).

I spent time doing nothing but appreciating the beauty of the world around me. I'd spot a type of bug with cool wings that I didn't know existed and then wonder how insects evolved, or I'd see a constellation of stars that I'd never seen before because I finally had time to look up.

Thanks to the dismissal from my last rigid job, the major *root cause* of my depression was solved: I no longer had any poverties. I no longer craved weekends because I was *living sustainably*, fulfilling my fundamental human needs, every single day. I no longer needed to cope.

This, for me, was revolutionary, and it was one of the reasons I decided (and was able) to write this book. I'd seen firsthand that it's possible to be enormously productive *and* free; these things weren't mutually exclusive. In fact, they both flourished at the same time, because of each other. It quickly became my mission to help that concept spread as fast and far as possible.

I don't recommend that everyone rush off to become a lifeguard (it will make you hate kids and their parents). But my point is this: even though I was still working thirty to forty-five hours a week, and even though I'm earning much (much!) less now than I was in the corporate world, the freedom to avoid long commutes, have control over my start and finish times, and have flexibility and freedom in general, has given me a life that people throw money at the lotteries in the hopes of one day winning. I'd won without buying a ticket.

It doesn't require the Wild West of freelancing to get those things. Employers need to realize that *they* have the power to make incredible differences to their employees' (and their own) lives. And then they need to ask how the current work structure produces poverties and work with everyone in the business to find out how they can make a difference that allows people's needs to be fed.

Even simple things, such as letting someone work remotely for one or two days a week, can vastly reduce stress and increase health and engagement. Or letting people leave when their work is finished, rather than them feeling that they have to stay until five ten just because the boss hasn't left yet, makes them feel that they're a trusted adult with control over their own existence.

How many of your people are coping?

Work Is Not the Devil

At this point you're probably wondering why I hate work so much, and if there's any point in reading a book by some dirty socialist who's completely against it.

Well, I'm not against it. Far from it.

We need work.

Or rather, *our needs need work.*

Going back to the lottery fantasy at the start of the chapter, what would really happen after you quit your job? Maybe you'd travel around the world, perhaps spend a month in Greece on a yacht. Then you'd come back and upgrade your house to a mansion with an infinity pool and a cinema. Maybe you'd finally take those singing classes you'd always thought about. There would be abundant computer game time. Probably some partying and champagne. And all of this interspersed with bountiful time with friends and loved ones.

But in this life of luxury and leisure, you'd start to get bored. Real bored. And you'd start to feel that some things are missing. Playing PlayStation all day isn't all you expected. Constantly going to the beach has started to lose its appeal. Even spending too much time with loved ones and your entourage of friends is wearing thin.

These things were fun for a few months but now they're leaving you with an empty, useless feeling. Some gaps are forming in your humanness.

You're getting up at ten every day; and your brunch of smashed avocado on sourdough toast isn't filling you up the way it used to.

Maybe part of the reason that many lottery winners blow all their winnings within the space of a few years is that they're trying to fill that empty feeling with more and more material things, or trips, or giving money away to family or charity, not realizing that by quitting their jobs they escaped from something they need.*

Work helps to fulfill an incredible number of our fundamental needs. Work is a direct satisfier, to various degrees, of at least seven of the ten needs in Max-Neef's modified list: subsistence, protection, understanding, participation, creation, identity, and affection. Even if we weren't paid for work – if money didn't exist – we would still do *something* other than relax on a beach, eat, or hang out with friends.

We have an inbuilt desire to create, to challenge ourselves with a project that has a beginning, middle, and end, and to do so with the joint effort of other people. It's something that fosters connection and cooperation, which have enabled humans to survive and dominate the planet. It's part of how we identify ourselves – we can feel proud to be an expert, and we can pass that knowledge to others. Our minds are powerful and active; if they're not being put to use they get unbearably restless. When we work we get blissfully lost in the flow of doing, in discovering, in testing, in asking Why? We're tinkerers and problem solvers, from before the time we figured out how to harness fire. And we need missions: something to fight for, or fight against, with passion; something that drives us.

What June and her tribe were doing was work: teaching youngsters, studying the movements of the animals they hunted, building spears and weaving nets, painting cave walls, tracking the stars and moon, caring for one another, singing songs, sharing their history, trading with other tribes. Yet no one was paying them to do these things. They did it because that's who they were. It's a part of being human.

An article in the *Sydney Morning Herald*[56] about a multi-millionaire surgeon who had declined retirement, even though he had more than

---

* Other reasons they lose all their winnings is that they have no idea how to manage that amount of money, having never had that much, and they perceive those winnings as bonus money and thus completely expendable.

enough money to do so, completely missed the point of why he wanted to keep working.

The author speculated that Daniel (the doctor), like other wealthy people, was so incredibly hard working and driven to succeed that he just couldn't imagine not working; that is, he was wealthy because of his inherent drive to succeed, so he could bear the pain of working.

Daniel must be incredibly driven and disciplined in order to have achieved his success, but I propose that he continues to work because in doing so he satisfies many of his fundamental human needs: it's the challenges, the opportunity to make a difference, using his mind and skills, and his connections with patients and colleagues that keep him working. *The work itself* adds value to his life, regardless of how much money he's earning.

These needs are within all of us, not just the super wealthy and successful. It just so happens that the wealthy are often in a better position to choose work that they're passionate about and have more freedom to pursue it in a way that they choose.

And the less well-off often dislike work because it may not be something they enjoy doing, and they don't have as much freedom to choose how and when the work is done – they lack flexibility. If these people suddenly became rich, they might retire for a while, but then they would realize that they want to do more than relax and have fun. They would find work, in some form, and do it in a way that suits them.

We're going to continue our little switcheroo on our lottery fantasy.

As it turns out, even though many, many people buy lotto tickets for their chance to attain freedom, the majority, when asked what they would do if they did win, said they would continue working in some fashion.

When Gallup asked people in the United States in 2013 what they would do if they won ten million dollars, over two-thirds (68 percent) of respondents said they would continue working, many even in the same job at the same company.[57]

Another survey by CareerBuilder found that just over half would continue working if they didn't need a job financially. The most common reasons to continue working were "I would be bored" (77 percent), "Work gives me a sense of purpose and accomplishment" (76 percent), and "Financial security aside from the winnings" (42 percent).[58]

Many people see value in working besides a paycheck. But they still demonize work and long for escape, or at least an avenue of escape for when they can no longer bear it, because society has created a bastard-ized version of what work *should be*.

We've allowed work to take up a disproportionate chunk of our lives, and to compete with the rest of life instead of being a part of it. Rather than being a positive, wonderful thing that allows us to be whole in so many ways, it drains many of our needs and creates poverties.

The thing we want to escape is not work itself, but *long and rigid work*, and we *should* escape from it. We can do that by moving back to a world where work is just one of the things we do, in reasonable proportion to everything else.

That people *want* to work kicks up all sorts of questions.

First, and I'll make this point a few more times: how terrible is our traditional, rigid workplace if it's managed to make many of us despise this fundamental life necessity? It has been forced down our throats to the point where we can't stomach it. If we were force-fed $100 steaks (or $100 parmesan polenta steaks for the vegetarians), they would taste horrendous. In the same way, we've managed to make work completely inedible when it should be satisfying and delicious.

Second, is retirement necessary? Are we retiring from work, or are we retiring from terrible workplaces and unsustainable lives? If work is something we want to do, and it provides substance to our lives, would we really want to suddenly end it?

Ask Warren Buffett. The dude is nearly ninety years old. He has more money than Scrooge McDuck. Has he stopped working so he can go fish-ing and look after his garden? What about Richard Branson? He owns a damned island! He could play computer games on his own beach while his personal assistant pours cocktails into his mouth through a gold fun-nel. Neither of them needs to work, but they do. Are they in the special minority of people who are driven to succeed, or does work feed their lives in ways that money and luxuries can't? (It's the second one.)

With our populations getting older across much of the developed world, this is an important point. (I'll expand on this in the next chap-ter.) Flexibility allows people to work longer, to their benefit, by making work more palatable, thereby reducing the strain on the welfare system and the younger working generation, to everyone's benefit.

The last question, and the most important for this book, is: if people like work, and have an ancient, internal drive to work, do they need to be monitored and micromanaged, kept in an open-plan office so everyone can see if they're working or not, and be forced to collaborate with their team? And do they need to be kept at work until five to make sure they've earned the right to go home? Or could they be trusted to work with autonomy and independence because of the inherent benefits that work provides? (I did warn you about my sarcasm.)

A New Description of Flexibility

Now that I've introduced important concepts about what it is to be human and how work fits into the picture, here's a new description of flexibility:

> Work flexibility is a practice that can maximize the positive effects of work on an individual while reducing or eliminating the negative effects. People want to work. They want to feel productive and to have feelings of achievement and belonging, and to have a secure income. They just want and need the freedom to fulfill the other important parts of their lives as well. Flexibility enables people to be free to be a whole human, as much and as often as possible.

For the rest of the book, and whenever you're thinking about work structures and managing others, I ask you to consider this description. It's a reminder that people aren't inherently lazy and indolent, and if they have freedom, they won't automatically abuse it. If you help them fulfill their human needs, they will *feel* like they've won the lottery, and they'll have the energy and appreciation to give you their very best.

CHAPTER 4

Busting Traffic and Other Worldwide Problems

Only a crisis – actual or perceived – produces real change. When that crisis occurs, the actions that are taken depend on the ideas that are lying around.

— Milton Friedman[1]

THE WORLD HAS QUITE A FEW CRISES kicking around at the moment. Many continue to worsen because the popular solutions thrown at them are just expensive band-aids – they fail to address the root causes of the problems.

In this chapter, I'll take the opportunity to dive into some crises that are impacting society and the world around us that have been caused, at least in part, by work rigidity and can be solved, to a large extent, by you, the business leader, providing flexibility for your people.

The crises we'll talk about here are:

- Aging populations and retirement
- Gender inequality, domestic violence, and identity challenges
- Preventable health problems
- Traffic congestion and pollution

Aging Populations and Retirement

Working your whole life in a rigid workplace is like swimming entire laps of a fifty-meter pool without taking any breaths.

It's tiring.

It's stressful.

It feels never-ending.

And when you get to the end of the swim (retirement age), you just want to stop and get out. That's what most people do. They work their whole lives, taking short, gasping breaths on the weekends and holidays, after each long, breathless lap, before putting their heads back under the water to desperately swim for another week, month, year.

As any swim instructor will tell you with a raised eyebrow, swimming this way, without breathing, is unsustainable, just as working this way, without taking enough time to look after human needs, is unsustainable. The result for one is that you don't enjoy swimming, hence you dread going to the pool and celebrate when swimming season has ended. The result for the other is that you don't enjoy work, hence you dread Monday mornings and celebrate when you can leave on Friday and never come back.

Retirement is a funny thing. When you consider all the human needs that work helps to fulfill (subsistence, protection, understanding, participation, creation, identity, and affection), it's odd that we would abruptly cut it out of our lives when we can. But when you think of how our traditional workplaces starve many of our needs in other ways, our joyful exit makes sense.

Leisure and freedom, for instance, are two of our most deprived needs during our working years, so they're two of the biggest things people look forward to when they retire: to finally *rest*, after being busy for forty-five years! And to have the freedom to decide what to do with their days. Affectionate time with family and loved ones is another starved need that retirees can finally feed; grandchildren beware!

The initial relief of escaping work (and the daily commute) through retirement is short-lived, however. Problems rear their heads, both for the individual and society.

The health impacts of retirement are a good place to start when determining if it's good or bad for people. Studies show that health results in the *short term* after retiring are either neutral or slightly positive. One reason for this could be the immediate relief employees feel after leaving rigid workplaces and finally being able to fulfill their needs for leisure, freedom, and affection. Also, retirees can spend more time taking care of their health. But a comprehensive study by the United Kingdom's

Institute of Economic Affairs discovered "large negative health effects of retirement among both women and men" in the *long term*.

The researchers found that retirement[*]

- decreases the likelihood of being in "very good" or "excellent" self-assessed health by about 40 percent;
- increases the probability of suffering from clinical depression by about 40 percent;
- increases the probability of having at least one diagnosed physical condition by about 60 percent; and
- increases the probability of taking a drug for such a condition by about 60 percent.

And to emphasize the long-term impacts of retirement, the researchers revealed that doubling the number of years in retirement

- decreases the likelihood of being in "very good" or "excellent" self-assessed health by 11 percent;
- increases the probability of suffering from clinical depression by 17 percent;
- increases the probability of having at least one diagnosed physical condition by 22 percent; and
- increases the probability of taking a drug for such a condition by 19 percent.[2]

They stated that the reasons why retirement affects health remain ambiguous, and possible causes include less social interaction (if work was the main source of human contact), lower incomes leading to lower investment in health-increasing activities (playing sports, exercising, traveling), and less physical activity in general (if, for example, someone's work was physical in nature). Based on the previous chapter, it could be said that the unfulfillment of other human needs also played a major part in these negative health effects by, for example, creating poverties in understanding, identity, and participation.

Another study, of blue-collar workers in Austria, found a significant relationship between early retirement and increased rates of death. Due to region-specific changes to unemployment insurance schemes, people in some parts of the country were able to retire up to three-and-a-half years

---

[*] Compared to people who are still working, controlling for age and all factors besides retirement.

before others. It was found that men who retired early (on average, nine months earlier than others) were 13 percent more likely to die before the age of sixty seven. The study attributed the early deaths to "changes in health-related behaviors (e.g., physical inactivity, drinking, smoking)."[3]

Interestingly, women's mortality rates in this study were unaffected by retirement age. The authors propose that the difference in mortality effects between men and women in this case is that "giving up the job is associated with loss of social status and identity for the main breadwinner [men], while work (and giving it up) is not central in life for the additional income earner [women]."

In other words, these poor blokes who retired were suddenly afflicted by poverties of identity, participation, affection, understanding, and creation (not so much protection and subsistence, because Austria has a strong social welfare system); and then they tried to feed those starving needs with food, alcohol, cigarettes, and lounging around too much.

Another problem with full retirement is that populations across the developed world are getting older. We're living longer, having fewer kids *and* waiting longer to have said kids. For the first time in history, there are now more people in the world over the age of sixty five than there are children under five; it's estimated that by 2050, one in six people (16 percent) will be sixty-five years of age or older.[4] (Most developed countries have already reached this figure; Japan has the highest proportion of sixty-five-year-olds, at 28 percent.)[5]

Economically, this *may* end up being a bad story.

As populations age, you end up with a greater number of people depending on government support compared to people who are employed and thus funding that support; there will always be some people who can't fund their own retirement.

There's also a greater strain on healthcare because it's used disproportionately by older people. "The hospitalization rates among Australians sixty five years and older are more than four times their younger counterparts," and they also visit GPs twice as often as younger people.[6] This pattern of increased demand on health services will be seen around the world. These services are already strained in many places, which affects quality of care in many ways.[7]

The Australian Productivity Commission, on the topic of the country's aging population,

> was particularly concerned about a lowering of the growth of labor force participation rates and overall a decline in labor supply, along with a reduction in labor productivity and national incomes. Due to these trends in economic outcomes, the Commission projected an increase in the fiscal burden related to expenses for health services, aged care and pensions in future years. The health care sector was singled out for special attention, as the Productivity Commission considered it to be Australia's greatest future fiscal challenge, with the share of public spending on health in GDP expected to rise sharply, from its current level of 6.5 percent to 10.8 percent in 2060.[8]

So it appears that full retirement is making us unhealthy, killing us early, and straining the economy. According to the evidence, it seems it would be a great thing for the health of the older population, and the health of the economy, if people worked longer into their lives.

One way we could get this to happen is for governments to incentivize people to continue working by increasing pension ages, based on the average healthy life expectancy of adults for that country. Another, more positive and less Big-Brother-y solution is in the hands of the capitalists: make life and work more sustainable by providing greater flexibility to your entire workforce.

Going back to our swimming analogy, what if work didn't feel like swimming without taking any breaths? What if we did what our swim instructor told us to do and slowed down our rate of strokes and took deep breaths at regular intervals? What if we were able to work *and* fulfill other human needs, by resting and having more time to live, even during an average Monday or Tuesday? Wouldn't both swimming and life be more enjoyable and less of a panic? Wouldn't they both be much more sustainable?

Increased flexibility, for both the older workforce *and* everyone else, will have two wonderful effects:

- First, and the effects will be immediate, is that many people at retirement age are fully aware of the benefits that work provides them and they would continue working if they were given more flexibility, such as working part time, or remotely, or with flextime, or some combination of these.

A survey of Australian workers found that *"73 percent of older workers said they would work more hours and stay in the workforce longer if flexible options were available."* Again, people *want to work*, seemingly regardless of age. From purely an economic productivity viewpoint, the authors of this study said this "could add an additional 2.1 million potential work years to the national productivity resource – equating to $134.8 billion, or 1.3 percent of Australian GDP."[9]

Additionally, individuals' health and well-being would improve, and the economic burden for healthcare and aged care systems would decline.

Studies show that people who work part time later in life enjoy the "best mental health and well-being outcomes" compared to those who are either unemployed or who work full time.[10]

- Second, and the effects will be long-term, is that if work is less painful and life-sucking, people will be in less of a hurry to get the hell out when they reach retirement age. They won't be starved for leisure, affection, freedom, and other needs, so they'll be more willing to continue reaping the positive effects of work. They're also likely to be healthier longer, and thus more capable of working longer. (I go deeper into the health benefits of increased flexibility later in this chapter.)

  On top of needs-fulfillment, people can spend more time and effort developing skills and knowledge, ensuring that even as they age they'll be up-to-date in knowledge and ability.

  The Austrian blue-collar study, which can be applied to much of the working world, and different colors or collars, showed that with greater flexibility and less need to be the breadwinner, men would be struck with smaller identity crises when they do eventually retire, because work wouldn't be the only way they enriched their lives. This would reduce their desire to eat, drink, and smoke away the associated pain. (More on gender equality and the identity of humans in the next section.)

And although this chapter isn't about the benefits of flexibility for business or productivity, there are great incentives for business owners to help people continue working later in life by allowing more flexibility.

Older people generally have more life and professional experience and have a lot to offer in terms of mentoring younger workers and maintaining a clear head through problems. They've been there and done that, they've learned through their own failures and successes, so they have powers of foresight that younger people in the workplace are still developing.

Older people, especially now, tend to be better communicators and have better overall soft skills than younger people, whose anxiety levels hit the roof when they need to use a phone to *talk* to someone. (I'm allowed to say this, because I'm a self-confessed talking-on-the-phone avoider).

 Bottom-line benefits have been found in firms that have greater age diversity and practices that support "age-inclusive HR practices." This comes from improved performance as well as reduced employee turnover.[11] A global survey also found that 86 percent of people prefer to be in multi-generational teams, and "85 percent say that an age-diverse team helps them come up with innovative ideas and solutions." (The biggest challenge in these multi-generational teams was the difference in communication preferences.)[12]

And contrary to stereotypes, older people are not by default afraid of new technology and less able to learn things. In fact, one study found that people over fifty five had less trouble working across multiple devices than eighteen-to-thirty-four-year-olds.[13] Old dogs *can* learn new tricks.

The ability to work part-time, remotely, or with reduced hours with full pay, or even just having flexibility with start and finish times, can help people happily remain longer in the workforce, for their benefit and for the benefit of the economy, society, and the businesses for whom they work.

Gender Inequality, Domestic Violence, and Identity Challenges

The rigid workplace has a lot to answer for when it comes to gender inequality and a range of issues at home and in the workplace for both women and men.* It has also created a fissure between fathers and their children, between women and their lives, and between men and their identity (and health, and happiness).

---

* When talking about men and women, I acknowledge that these issues apply to LGBTQ couples to differing degrees when they're split along traditional gender roles at work and home.

In modern times, people in most countries have grown up in societies where there's a great disparity between genders. Men have been the workers, spending most of their days working hard and then coming home to a few beers and dinner.

Women have been the caregivers, looking after kids, maybe squeezing in some low-quality, part-time work, and doing the majority of housework and management – also hard work, but never-ending and unpaid.

Because of the rigid nature of most workplaces, with long days and required presence at the workplace, the path of least resistance has been to have one person (usually the man) focusing purely on work and maintaining a secure, full-time job, and the other person (usually the woman) being unemployed or casually employed. Both are trapped.

Thus, we've had a stark division of labor at work and home, and deeply entrenched gender roles, resulting in the following issues for women, men, and children.

Issues for Women

1. Men end up with too much power over their partners because they earn most of the money, thus provide housing, food, and other things required for survival and security. Many men then feel entitled to control, and women have less power to negotiate, leave, or find quality work.

   Domestic violence is inextricably linked to inequality both in the workplace and at home. On this topic, the Australian government, in its *Fourth Action Plan to Reduce Violence against Women and their Children*, states:

   > There is no single cause of violence against women and their children; however, gender inequality sets the stage for such violence to occur.
   >
   > Evidence shows that the key beliefs and behaviors relating to gender that drive violence against women are:
   > - Condoning of violence against women
   > - Men's control of decision-making and limits to women's independence
   > - Stereotyped constructions of masculinity and femininity
   > - Disrespect towards women, and male peer relations that emphasise aggression[14]

2. Women have less opportunity for balance in life, which isn't surprising given that, whether they work or not, they undertake the vast majority of household chores and management. "Worldwide, women carry out twice as much unpaid domestic and care work ... as men."[15]

   A telling statistic from an Australian study is that women are 24 percent more likely than men to feel rushed "often" or "always" in their everyday lives. This feeling of consistently being rushed was found to be a barrier to physical activity as well as being associated with "poorer self-rated and mental health."[16]

   Rushing from task to task and fire to fire not only inhibits the ability of women to look after their health but it also gets in the way of fulfilling all of their human needs, such as the opportunity to fully use the mind in varied and concerted ways, feeling part of something bigger (having an identity beyond parenthood or work), rest and leisure, and so on.

3. The women who have "made it" in the rigid workplace have had to do so at great cost to themselves and their personal lives. They were essentially told that they had to embody "manliness" – being more ambitious, being stronger in negotiating, being bolder, asserting themselves (and other similar recommendations from Sheryl Sandberg in her book *Lean In*) – along with foregoing or delaying having a family.

   Women have had to drive gender equality in the workplace, single-handedly, using their individual power in the face of systemic bias and discrimination. They have had to be superwomen, and as Michelle Obama put it in a recent speech, "that shit doesn't work all the time."[17]

Issues for Men

1. With less exposure to women, children, and caregiving (and to men who show respect to women), men don't develop important aspects of their identity: empathy, love, and the ability to show emotions in healthy ways. They are then emotionally crippled, and they deal with this in problematic ways, such as aggression, drinking, drugs, talking in disrespectful ways about women, gambling and overeating, sexual immaturity, and notoriously high rates of suicide.

2. Being caught up in working so much, men have less time and energy to develop themselves in rounded ways by fulfilling their fundamental human needs, such as looking after their mental and physical health, learning, reading, relaxing, being with their children and/or partners, having quality male friendships, and using their minds outside of a work context. And they're left with various poverties, which subsequently produce stress and a lack of well-being.

Rigid work has almost crippled men, creating a one-dimensional creature that's incapable of realizing their full potential as both a man and a human. This identity is passed down to the next generations, as Tim Winton, author of *Breath*, describes vividly:

> So many boys are learning how to be men from people who are really bad at being men. . . . I think boys just put themselves together from spare parts; and what's closest to hand is often cheap and defective, and that makes it dangerous. They're learning how to be bad men because there aren't enough good men in their lives showing them how to be good men.[18]

Issues for Children

1. Fathers who have more work-family conflict – one of the results of working in rigid patterns – have poorer mental health, relationship quality, and *parenting capabilities*. All three of these influence a "child's socio-emotional development and well-being independently of the mothers' contributions."[19]

2. With fathers and mothers divided into strict gender roles, children see and feel the power differences in their parents' relationships. This affects how they perceive the relative values of men and women, which perpetuates gender stereotypes as the children grow up.

3. Kids are heavily affected by the domestic violence, caused partly by the power imbalance created by work rigidity, that they and their mothers face. With exposure to violence and abuse, these children are more likely to be perpetrators or victims of violence when they become adults, enforcing a cycle of abuse that lasts for generations.[20]

The First Step

Having had to toil twice as hard to get decent work while having to do most of the housework and household management, women have been the major drivers of work flexibility for the last couple of decades.

They knew that it wasn't enough to "lean in" and be superhuman to have it all. They knew there was a better way: *If only I could structure my own day and week, I'd be able to get all this work done and be a mother!*

And that was the answer: flexible work.

Being able to choose how, where, and when to get work done has been infinitely valuable to those who didn't want to have to choose between decent work and having a family.

Women knew that they could be the CEO, or a member of parliament, or simply have well-paying, non-brain-numbing work, without putting off having a family. Women are, after all, fully capable multitaskers – they just needed to prove that it could be done.

After years of fighting for this right, it's become somewhat normal for women to access flexibility in most organizations. This was the first step away from the problems above, at least for women, and the results speak.

An article by Remote.co, about how working remotely affects gender equality in the workplace, compared fifty-three fully remote companies (sixteen of which took part in interviews during the research) to large traditional companies and other startups. It was found that:

- Women make up 42 percent of the leadership at the sixteen remote companies that were interviewed (compared to 14.2 percent at S&P 500 companies).

- Of the fifty-three remote companies in the research, 28 percent have a female founder or co-founder (compared to 18 percent of all startups in 2014).

- Of those fifty-three remote companies, 19 percent have a female CEO (compared to 4 percent of S&P 500 companies).[21]

These incredible differences show that when women are free to get their work done without the rigidity of the old-fashioned boys club (where time at work is the most important measure of value), they're empowered to get shit done and lead and start businesses.

In another study, done in the United Kingdom, researchers found that women "who were able to use flexitime [alter their start and finish times] were only half as likely to reduce their hours after the birth of their child." And those who accessed remote work were also much less likely (by about 36 percent) to reduce their working hours after childbirth.[22]

Various other types of flexibility have enabled women to continue their careers without moving to lower-quality or less-senior roles. Job sharing, for instance, is being used with great success in high-level positions, and part-time work is being more commonly used in managerial roles.

But although increased flexibility *for women* has gone a long way to enable them to continue and succeed in their professional careers, many still end up facing the stigma of using that flexibility, resulting in discrimination called flexism.

When flexibility is still an exception in the workplace, when it's used only by people who ask for it the loudest, such as women with caregiving responsibilities, it's seen as a disruption to normal operation. It's tolerated rather than accepted and celebrated. This creates the perception that those who use flexibility (women) have less commitment to their careers and companies.

A study by Bain and Company found that more men than women perceived that women's careers are hindered by "competing priorities" (i.e., choosing to prioritize family over work), whereas the biggest reason given by women that they're less often in senior positions is that they don't fit the mold of the existing style of management.[23]

Men also miss out on the benefits of flexibility when it's not allowed, even though many want and need it.[24]

More needs to be done. The next step is being taken, albeit slowly.

The Next Step

The word being used in companies at the more progressive end of workplace flexibility is *normalization*. They've become aware of the issues presented above regarding discrimination toward those who use flexibility, such as part-time work, flextime, and parental leave.

Companies have realized that if only some of the working population are allowed to use flexibility, the practice remains abnormal, unusual, the exception. And many of those who use flexibility are minorities, which leads to numerous issues (detailed in Chapter 8, where I talk about the differences between policies and programs). Normalizing flexibility is crucial in order to address the difficulties currently faced by women, men, and children.

And how do we normalize flexibility? Men.

Men need to be *allowed* to work flexibly when they request it *and* be encouraged to use it. The latter is important because it hasn't been normal for men to use flexibility. They're twice as likely as women to be rejected when they request a change in their work structures.[25] And when they do so, they step out of what's normal. This comes with risk to their careers and subsequently to their sense of identity and self-worth.

When a company steps up and decides to make flexibility normal for everyone, it kicks off an elegant and beautiful cycle for men, women, and children:

- **Men:** When men have greater flexibility, they can fulfill other important parts of their lives, such as pursuing passions, connecting more with family and friends, and having time to rest, relax, seek adventure, and fulfill all their needs in a sustainable way. They can also do more of the housework and household management, which helps break down traditional gender roles and increase equality. Flexibility reduces the burden on men to be the breadwinners, so they can fulfill their needs in a balanced way and become multidimensional and whole in their identities.

- **Women:** When companies freely offer flexibility, they have systems and training for optimal use of the practice, and there's no stigma attached to using it. So women can fully realize their career goals, gain promotions, and increase their paychecks. And when men do more of the housework, women who have jobs will have more time to relax and fulfill other needs.

- **Children:** Kids get to spend more time with both mom and dad, neither of whom are stressed and run off their feet. Family time will be higher quality and intentional. Boys will learn how to be good, whole men from good, whole men – no missing or defective parts.

Breaking the trap of rigid work benefits us all!

One great example of the effects of allowing more men to access flexibility (and providing encouragement to take it up) is Iceland's equal parental leave.

In 2000, Iceland's government adopted a law that increased parental leave allowances from six to nine months. This leave is divided between mothers and fathers, with each given three months of *nontransferable* leave, with the remainder to be divided however the parents choose.[26] The objective of the change was "to ensure that children get to spend time with both parents, and to enable both men and women to balance work and family life."[27]

The results of this change were dramatic.

First, due to the nontransferable nature of the leave, the percentage of fathers who took parental leave increased from about 3 percent in 1997 to 90 percent in 2008, and it has hovered at about 80 percent in the years since – the Global Financial Crisis negatively influenced labor security and the desire and ability to take leave.[28]

Second, men have developed better relationships with, and under-standing of, their children in those important early months and years. One survey found that "72 percent of fathers say that taking parental leave has helped them to understand the needs of infants and 83 percent agree that taking paternal leave has increased their emotional connec-tion with the child."[29] Another study by the World Health Organization found that, compared to earlier generations, children in Iceland today are much more likely to "discuss problems with daddy."[30]

The third, and probably most important, result is that caregiving re-sponsibilities were divided evenly between parents (for cohabiting cou-ples) by the majority of parents, and this division lasted for the term of the study: *three years after the birth of the child*.[31] Just three months of paternity leave changed family dynamics drastically in favor of a more equal standing, with effects not just in the home but in the workplace.

Another study found a "direct correlation between involved father-hood and long-term relationship stability. . . . Fathers who took sole charge of babies before they turned one were as much as 40 percent less likely to subsequently break up with their partners."[32]

The researchers stressed that it was difficult to pinpoint the cause and effect of this correlation, but, as British MP Jo Swinson said, "For couples where care is shared, not only does that couple have more in common, which can enhance the relationship, but it becomes a shared endeavour, which helps reduce stress."[33]

Preventable Health Problems

People are living a lot longer now than ever before. But even though our life expectancy has increased dramatically, our quality of life, mentally and physically, hasn't increased proportionately, and in some ways it's getting worse. Our major killers and causes of disability and poor health are no longer infectious and parasitic diseases, as they were before the mid-twentieth century; they're chronic, noncommunicable diseases, usually due to lifestyle and age.

In Australia, more than 70 percent of diseases are chronic, including musculoskeletal disease (e.g., arthritis), depression and anxiety, cardiovascular disease, cancer, diabetes, and hypertension.[34] And these chronic diseases are associated with one or more of the following lifestyle-related risk factors: poor diet, physical inactivity, alcohol, smoking, and stress.[35]

Globally, heart disease is the leading cause of death for both males and females, accounting for over 12 percent of all deaths;[36] depression is the leading cause of disability;[37] and in OECD (Organization for Economic Cooperation and Development) countries, over half of all adults are overweight or obese,[38] a major contributor to many of the diseases above.

This section describes how our rigid workplaces play a large part in the development of these health issues, and how flexibility can be used to solve these problems and improve physical and mental health.

(I distinguish between mental and physical health in this section, as I have in other parts of this book, only to describe specific effects, but they're so closely related and interdependent that I mostly talk about health in general. Edward Bullmore, author of *The Inflamed Mind*, makes the case that the traditional dualist perspective of separating mental health and physical health should no longer hold weight, since the brain is part of the body, and it's been shown that stress, bodily inflammation, and depression are all connected.)

The Ten Riders of the Workapocalypse

Jeffrey Pfeffer, in his highly illuminating and deeply depressing book *Dying for a Paycheck*,[39] introduced the term *toxic workplaces* to describe what I have referred to as rigid or traditional workplaces.

These workplaces, Pfeffer argues, create social pollution in the form of increased physical and mental health issues and premature death on an immense scale (one-hundred-twenty-thousand excess deaths per year in the United States alone, and over one million in China). These deaths are due to poor management processes in which humans are treated like robots, with society and individuals picking up the tab.

Pfeffer calls for a greater focus on "human sustainability" and offers solutions such as measuring the social pollution of businesses. He recommends publicly calling out those who fall below acceptable limits, in the same way we would name, shame, and punish an oil company responsible for a spill, and by celebrating those that *do* prioritize the health and well-being of their employees.

But there are ways that individual businesses can put their foot down and make a difference, today, without waiting for major policy changes or social pollution measurements and shaming. They can do it by implementing greater flexibility for employees and managers.

I want to show how flexibility gets directly to the root of the ten workplace exposures introduced by Pfeffer, which are, "with almost no exceptions, as harmful to health, including mortality and having a physician-diagnosed illness, as exposure to secondhand smoke, a known and regulated carcinogen."

Of these "ten prominent workplace exposures related to employer decisions that affect human health and longevity," flexibility addresses nine. Presented here are Pfeffer's ten workplace exposures and how flexibility can go a long way to reduce the effects for almost all.

1. **Being unemployed (sometimes a consequence of being laid off):** Flexibility allows greater employment for, among others, women, people with disabilities, older people, and those who are geographically restricted. This directly reduces this exposure for many demographics.

   Flexibility also allows someone who already has a job more opportunities to upskill and decentralize their work, so that when that dreaded "restructuring" letter arrives from HR, there will be less of an impact. The employee will have the skills and connections to find new employment faster, and/or they'll already have supplemental income.

2. **Not having health insurance:** This one isn't relevant except for the fact that flexibility, by improving mental and physical health, reduces the need for health care and the level of insurance required by employees. (But, of course, being able to access medical services should be a fundamental right for all humans regardless of employment status!)

3. **Working shifts and working for longer than the customary eight hours:** One of the tenets of flexibility, especially in this book, is to

reduce the daily and weekly hours of work, including (and especially) for shift workers. Reducing hours can be done in a way that doesn't hurt the business, that's mutually beneficial, and that considers humans as humans rather than robots. The following chapters explore the link between flexibility and productivity.

4. **Working long hours in a week (i.e., more than forty hours):** As with the previous exposure, flexibility is about moving the focus away from hours worked and putting it onto value created, so we move away from cultures of working long hours for the sake of working long hours, which are prolific in modern society.

5. **Confronting job insecurity (e.g., because colleagues have been laid off or fired):** By giving people more time and energy, flexibility allows people to have other pursuits, and it allows them to upskill in other areas, thus expanding their work options, both of which create greater job and income security.

    People often report higher engagement levels with their work when they have access to flexibility. Higher engagement levels lead to greater productivity and creativity. This increases employees' value to their businesses, which increases their job security.

6. **Facing family-to-work and work-to-family conflicts:** Out of the ten, this exposure had, by far, the largest effect on physical and mental health. Flexibility is the best way to reduce this conflict, and it was originally used mainly by parents (usually mothers) who needed and/or wanted to work *and* have children. When the rigidity of work is decreased, either in location or hours, it's easier for people to handle their family needs, thus reducing the stress guilt of not being able to give their best to their jobs and their families.

7. **Having relatively low control over one's job and job environment, including having relatively little freedom and decision discretion at work:** Freedom is one of our fundamental needs. Starving this need is bad news for our health, hence it's no surprise to see it as one of the top harmful workplace exposures.

    Flexibility, which means focusing on results, and allowing autonomy with how, where, and when work is completed, helps people feel in control at work.

8. **Facing high job demands such as pressure to work fast:** Some might argue that flexibility, such as working fewer hours in a day, might increase the pressure to work fast, but it actually relieves that pressure.

   It reduces the pressures associated with normal workplace structures, such as long commutes, long meetings, distractions by coworkers, and sitting in an open-plan office with constant surveillance (called inferred pressure). And it creates a culture of job effectiveness and continuous improvement by reducing wasted resources and time. Instead of working fast and being busy, people think about whether a task is necessary and find better ways to do things, which reduces demands and their resulting pressure.

9. **Being in a work environment that offers low levels of social support (for instance, not having close relationships with coworkers, relationships that would provide social support to mitigate the effects of work stress):** Flexibility, especially remote work, might be seen as contributing to this problem, since it involves a risk of low social interaction and support at work. But flexibility enables greater social networks to be developed *outside* of work, which, since you can choose that social network rather than being forced into one at work, might be higher quality and provide greater support.

   Social isolation can be a problem with remote work, but the chapter on how to roll out flexibility provides solutions.

10. **Working in a setting in which job- and employment-related decisions seem unfair:** Decisions that people would feel are unjust are those that add to their feeling of being pressured, such as being given too much work, being given work that an employee isn't qualified to do, support being taken away, or changes in work hours or locations without the employee's input. These issues can be resolved with a more flexible approach to work.

Why do each of these exposures affect our health in the first place?
Stress.

Each one of these exposures, and other workplace exposures, including harassment and bullying, terrible bosses, and commuting to and from work, induces stress, usually over the long term because many of these exposures are consistently present in rigid workplaces. This long-term stress harms our health in two major ways: directly and by inducing poor health behaviors, such as increased use of drugs, alcohol, and McDonald's, and decreased use of gyms, nutritious food, walking trails, and cycling paths.

Direct Harm

In the same way that work itself isn't the devil, stress isn't inherently bad. It's a useful motivator. Without any sort of stress, we would likely lie down and slowly (or quickly) die. Stress stimulates us to act.

Being hungry gets us to look for food. Smelling smoke tells us that a fire is nearby, and we should investigate it or leave the area. A tiger jumping out from behind a bush causes us to run faster than normally possible. The stress of our own internal motivation, or the competition with someone at sport or at work, can drive us to greater levels of achievement. Stress is a bad thing when it's high and never-ending: chronic stress, which is useless and only leads to poor health and unhappiness.

When we're stressed, our bodies physically prepare us to take action: to either stand our ground and face the stressor (fight) or to get the hell out of there as quickly as possible (flight). It does this by elevating our heart rate, directing blood to move away from our internal organs and toward the muscles in our limbs – the tools most useful for running and fighting – priming us to defend our survival. It also releases chemicals that increase our alertness, such as adrenaline and cortisol.

Very few things in the natural world create unending stress. A tiger attack or flood are normally over pretty quickly. The rigid workplace, on the other hand, *does* create unending stress – for eight or more hours a day, forty eight to fifty two weeks a year, from our early twenties until we retire or die. That's depressing.

Just being *at work* for most of the day, travelling to and from work, and the associated poverties of human needs, cause relentless stress for many of us. We're chronically in this fight-or-flight state, with increased heart rates, blood directed away from our major organs, and increased levels of adrenaline and cortisol.

The damage this does is immense. Our blood pressure is permanently increased and arteries are hardened. Cortisol breaks down cells and causes inflammation. And our health in general suffers.[40]

This stress also changes our behavior.

The Choices We Make

Not only does the rigid workplace increase the direct effects of stress on our bodies, it also reduces our capacity to make good decisions about our health.

Richard H. Thaler won the Nobel Prize in Economic Sciences in 2017 for his work in behavioral economics, specifically on the psychology of individual decision-making, and even more specifically for his development of *nudge theory*. Nudge theory, in a nutshell, proposes that people's decisions can be influenced by subtle psychological tricks or cues or by reshaping the choices available to them. With nudges, a person's free will and choices aren't removed, but because human behavior is predictable, it's much more likely that the tricks or cues will encourage someone to choose one thing over another.

This is a powerful tool that can be used for good or for evil. In the right hands, it can help people save more money, stop speeding, eat healthier food, and stop smoking. In the wrong hands, well, just ask the advertising and marketing industries.

With a few strategically placed signs or television ads, or big yellow arches next to a main road, people can choose oil-drenched food with little nutritional value over cooking at home, impacting both their waistlines and their wallets.

Or they can fall into the world of gambling by downloading a sports betting app after being bombarded by an endless parade of gambling ads.

Or they may apply for yet another credit card to receive a temporary zero-percent interest on balance transfers because of a promotional email; banks know that this balance won't be paid in time and they'll make their money anyway.

Thaler and Cass R. Sunstein, co-author of *Nudge: Improving Decisions About Health, Wealth and Happiness*, believe that there's a dichotomous world of decision makers. First is the perfectly rational and perfectly fictitious *Homo economicus*, who makes decisions based on infinite information and resources, and who can unfailingly predict the outcomes of their decisions, and thus will always make the optimal choice for their subjective needs or goals.[41]

They will be fully aware and knowledgeable of the long-term health and financial costs of eating a burger and large fries for dinner, decide that the costs outweigh the short-term satisfaction of eating something glistening and salty, and go home and cook a cheaper and more nutritious meal.

And then there are humans. Real humans have limited time, energy, information, material resources, and understanding of the impacts of our choices; we have biologically programmed biases that cause us to quickly jump to conclusions with that limited information; we favor short-term pleasure or rewards over long-term goals; *and* we tend to be self-centered.

What this means is that humans tend to make pretty crappy decisions for our long-term health and finances, the environment, and other people, exemplified by our current obesity epidemic, plastic pollution, global warming, and other bad stuff humans have done and are doing to ourselves and the world.

I'm feeling pretty bold today, so I'm going to challenge one of the concepts put forth by this Nobel Prize winner and his colleague, the one that says that humans are generally useless at making their own decisions.

Humans are capable of so much more.

I don't believe that there's a dualist "perfect and fictional *Homo economicus*" and "perfectly flawed human," between which exists nothing. I believe, rather, that there's a spectrum of human capability, on which each of us moves up and down according to our internal resources (energy) and external resources (time and money).

On one day, Bob is fully capable of driving past the big yellow arches, going for a jog, and then cooking a nutritious meal; on another day, Bob, drained of time and energy after a long, stressful day, succumbs to the convenience and glistening sheen of fast food, and gets two burgers and a large serving of fries with a big glass of sugar water to wash it all down.

Thaler himself agrees that it's because of our lack of resources that we make imperfect decisions; he thinks the best solution is to increase the making of good decisions through nudges. But what about the other part of the equation? What about increasing our resources so that we're able to make better decisions ourselves?

I'm not refuting the effectiveness and usefulness of nudges. I'm saying that increasing the resources of humans to enable them to make better decisions can have fantastic results, especially in the realm of personal health.

Well-being programs at work are examples of using nudges to improve health outcomes, often without consideration of human resources and capability.

Many businesses around the world try to encourage better health decisions by their employees by providing helpful nudges: bowls of free fruit in meeting rooms, free fitness classes, educational pamphlets about sleep and vegetables, and tracking number of steps and rewarding top steppers.

In the United States, especially, where employers have the burden of paying for health insurance and thus have a strong financial reason to have healthier employees, well-being programs are almost ubiquitous in firms with two hundred or more employees.[42]

But while businesses are providing helpful nudges, many of those same businesses are sucking up people's resources through rigid work practices, making it harder for employees to make good decisions about their health in the first place.

Have you ever been stuck in traffic after a long, stressful day and still felt like going to the gym? Even if your employer is paying for it? Even if there's a poster on the wall at work listing the top ten benefits of exercise?

I find most corporate well-being programs to be at best creepy and patronizing and at worst a terrible invasion of privacy and an encroachment on personal freedoms. Over half (55 percent) of large firms that offer health benefits to employees in the United States offer biometric screening, such as blood pressure, blood sugar, cholesterol, and BMI, to measure workers' health risks, and, "increasingly, companies are also *imposing penalties for employees who do not improve on various biometric and lifestyle measures* [italics added, because holy shit!]."[43]

(This also opens up new doors for discrimination, such as not hiring or promoting people with increased health risks, such as being older, having a disability, or being overweight.)

A company in Japan called Crazy is using nudges to fight against its country's "sleep debt" by incentivizing sleep. Because of a culture of sacrifice and unwavering commitment to the companies they work for, people in Japan often work incredibly long hours compared to other countries, and as a result they end up sleeping far less than the recommended seven to eight hours. This deprivation causes ill health and mortality rates resulting in a reported $138 billion loss to Japan's economy yearly.[44]

Crazy is trying to help. Employees' sleep habits are tracked by an app on their smart phones, which draws data from sensors embedded in their mattresses. If they consistently manage to sleep more than six hours per night during the week, they can accumulate a financial reward of ¥64,000 (US$594) in a year. This wellness initiative has been mirrored by several other companies, including Teijin and Hitachi, who track and reward not just sleep but also physical activity.[45]

As wonderful as this may seem – helping employees improve their health and lives through data and incentives – it again disregards the fact that businesses are the *root cause* for their employees' lack of sleep.

When we nudge people to get enough sleep, aren't we forgetting that humans are naturally adept at sleeping? Most of us even enjoy it! It's something we've been doing since we were living in trees, long before corporations and well-being programs existed.

Many people, not just in Japan but around the world, stopped getting enough sleep because of long, rigid hours of work and management cultures that supported and allowed these practices to become normal. (Occasionally the problem is crying babies or barking dogs, but mostly it's the work thing).

I say fuck that! Before any business managers have the gall to say they're looking after workers with fitness programs or biometric testing or sleep tracking, they need to stand up, hold their hands on their hearts, and declare that there's nothing else they can do to ensure that they're not *hurting* those workers' abilities to be healthy. Before bringing in the fitness trainers and sleep devices, here's a completely free and highly successful well-being program summarized in three sentences:

1. Ensure that work isn't taking up all your employees' time and energy.

2. Ensure that employees have the freedom and flexibility to prioritize their health.

3. Employees will then have the capability to make good choices themselves.*

---

* I believe there *is* a place for a business to help employees with extra health and well-being initiatives, such as free fitness classes, greener workspaces, more natural light, and mental wellness support, but these must be used in conjunction with reducing the potential harm of psychosocial effects caused by workplace rigidity.

It's evident that various forms of flexibility would help improve people's health-related behaviors.

Reducing hours per day or days per week at work increases the time to do other things, including sleep and exercise. Working remotely reduces the time and stress of commuting and frees employees to plan and structure their days, both of which increase their chances of sleeping and exercising more and cooking good food.

But here's some evidence!

One study linked various (rigid) workplace factors to reduced ability to sleep. It found that:

- Lack of choice in daily work routine caused people to sleep, on average, 2.3 minutes less per day than those reporting more choice at work.

- Unrealistic time pressures and stress at the workplace caused people to sleep eight minutes less per day.

- People who work irregular hours (e.g., shift work) sleep 2.7 minutes less per day.

- People who commute between thirty and sixty minutes each way to work sleep 9.2 minutes less per day than those with a commute each way of zero to fifteen minutes. People who commute each way over sixty minutes sleep 16.5 minutes less per day than those with shorter commutes.[46]

The authors note that although these seem like small effects, they're cumulative; i.e., someone who's affected by all of these, which isn't uncommon for rigid workplaces, may be missing out on nearly half an hour of sleep every day, which is enough to have a dramatic effect on their health.

Another study, which, conversely, looked at the effects of flexible work on sleep behavior, found that people with a results-only work environment* slept almost *an hour* (52.3 minutes) more per day than those with a traditional work structure. Of the 52.3 minutes, twenty minutes were a *direct* consequence of ROWE – people had more time to sleep – and thirty-two minutes were an *indirect* consequence – people had greater schedule control and less negative work-home spillover.[47]

---

* ROWE (results-only work environment), as described in Chapter 2: people can choose when and where (and how) to complete their work. The only thing measured is what is produced or completed.

Almost an extra hour per day of sleep is life changing, and no bribery was required.

Many people are fully aware of how much their health and lives are affected by rigid workplaces, and conversely how much flexibility could help. In a survey of over three thousand workers,[48] most of whom were professionals, 77 percent of respondents said that "having a flexible job would allow them to be healthier (eat better, exercise more, etc.) and 86 percent said they'd be less stressed." Another study found that remote workers exercised more, by twenty-five minutes per week, than in-office employees.[49]

Spiral Up

Aside from helping us not get fat and die prematurely, flexibility can turn the whole health picture upside down, into something positive and multi-colored.

When we begin living sustainably, when work isn't the all-conquering force in our lives, we can start to develop better personal knowledge and habits.

The World Health Organization defines health as "a state of complete physical, mental, and social well-being and not merely the absence of disease or infirmity."[50] There is a continuum of health ranging from total ill health to total health[51] (or from "dead to Superman," as my chiropractor Dr. Adam East more colorfully puts it).

When we're sick or injured enough that we decide to do something about it, a doctor or pharmacist will treat that sickness or injury enough so that it's no longer a problem, or it's less of a problem than it was. But the health journey is so much more than not being sick or injured. It's the accumulation of everyday things that either improve or damage our health over time, and thus dictates our overall position on the health spectrum.

Greater work flexibility enables a reduction in things that damage our health (e.g., stress) and an increase in those things that improve our health (e.g., adequate sleep), allowing us to spiral up this continuum of health. This leads not only to higher quality of life, but also to less illness and disease in the future.

In addition to increasing our time and energy, flexible work provides greater freedom to structure the day the way we want and to do health-related activities without judgment. Some things that are great for health

The "Dead to Superman" Spectrum

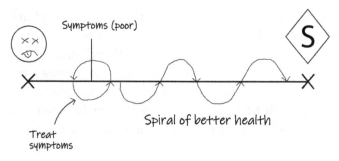

Figure 4.1. Doctors and pharmacists treat poor health, which is when people have symptoms such as pain and depression. But the journey to better health is more nuanced than simply alleviating obvious symptoms. Upward spiral!

are quite unacceptable, or illegal, to do in an office. Examples of those things go well beyond just exercising, sleeping more, and eating better:

- Mindfulness and meditation, practicing gratitude and forgiveness, yoga, tai-chi, breathing exercises, humming loudly or singing to stimulate the vagus nerve

- Dancing! – alone or with a partner

- More sex, and time for *proper* lovemaking and intimate connection, even just with yourself; healing of sexual trauma and learning about the body

- Relaxation: watching kids play, reading a book, listening to music, sitting on the grass in the sun, being idle and doing nothing, all undervalued in modern society

- Addressing chronic back and hip pain through visits to chiropractors or physiotherapists and finding and fixing the root causes for these pains instead of just living with them

- Ripping off your shirt and stretching or doing lunges in the sun for twenty minutes while you consider a tricky section of a quarterly report

- Learning how to reduce dependency on social media, focusing more on your own life and creating and fostering true connections with family, friends, community, and nature

- Addressing childhood or other trauma – the cause of many physical and mental ailments – through therapy and/or research

- Reducing other sources of stress, be it family conflict or financial issues, by focusing on setting life straight rather than rushing from fire to fire at the end of the day

- Going to the dentist (Poor dental health affects the heart and mental health, and many of us leave the dentist off the calendar until we have a serious problem. For many it's a cost issue, but for others it's low on the list of priorities of everyday activities.)

- Learning how to cook decent food, giving yourself options that will make you proudly scoff every time you pass the golden arches

- Figuring out which fundamental needs may be chronically unfulfilled, and then filling them regularly

- Building your knowledge about your own health

All of these activities, and many more, create resilience, all influence each other for the better, all increase our quality of life. And all move us up the spectrum toward being health superhumans.

I'll end this section with a quick story.

I haven't been sick for over three years.

OK, maybe I've had *one* small cold.

But since leaving the rigid workplace and working with full flexibility, I haven't had those debilitating illnesses I would consistently get at least two or three times a year, the ones that put me out of action for a few days or an entire week, or caused me to have a chest cough that lingered for months. I honestly can't remember what it even feels like to be that sick. (Fate, come at me!)

Part of the reason for my improved health could be that I spend less time in workplaces, so I might be exposed to fewer germs. But I spend time around the general population doing other things, so I don't think that's it.

I believe it's because my bodily systems aren't constantly stretched to the limit because I'm able to look after my health every day. I've reduced or removed stressors and many associated terrible health decisions, and the good things I do every day for my fundamental needs combine to push me toward health resilience.

Not only have I rarely been sick in the last two years, but my health has improved in other incredible ways (TMI warning!):

- My libido is higher now, in my mid-thirties, than it was for much of my twenties, which, for a man, is the opposite of what it should be.

- My lower back pain (from sitting too much while commuting and being stagnant at a desk) is mostly gone, and I can sprint and jump again – I thought those days were over.

- The flexibility in my limbs is better than it's been in over a decade.

- I hardly ever feel the need to self-medicate in the form of alcohol, pornography, or videogames.

- And I'm experiencing less depression, having attained a state of consistent contentment. (I don't strive for happiness, since I think this is a fleeting emotion, but rather for deep satisfaction.) The black cloud does still occasionally hit, but I have the time and knowledge now to take care of it, so its effects are much lessened. I have greater resilience.

Who knows what other changes are going on inside my body, and which future problems have been averted?

The moral of this story is that, because of flexibility, *I have the time and energy to prioritize my own health*, and that has changed my life.

Traffic Congestion and Pollution

In 2017, traffic congestion cost the U.S. economy $305 billion ($33.7 billion in New York City alone).[52] This cost comprises the lost productive hours of people stuck in traffic, increased cost of goods transportation, wasted fuel, the social cost of extra pollution, and various other factors.

In the United Kingdom, this figure was £37 billion (US$46 billion); in London it was £9.5 billion (US$11.8 billion).

In Germany it was €16.4 billion (US$9.2 billion).

In Australia it was A$16.5 billion (US$10.6 billion).[53]

But honestly, who cares? Do you? Do you know what $305 billion looks like? Have you ever held that much money in your hands? Does it affect your everyday life if your country collectively loses that money?

Sure, it adds to the prices of our groceries and products through increased transport costs, but it's not something we really notice. No one says, "Why the hell are my chips $3.50 now? They were $3.40 last year. Bloody traffic!"

What we do notice is the everyday pain.

We wake up earlier and earlier, having our precious sleep stolen by that damned alarm, just so we can get ready and make it onto the road before it starts clogging up.

We feel the frustration of having our travel time blown out by random and increasingly frequent traffic jams that add thirty minutes to an hour to our trip, making us late for work even after we leave home super early. And when we get to the front of the queue we find that it was caused by . . . nothing?! Often it's a phantom traffic jam, created by the butterfly effect of small variations in driving behavior – someone brakes slightly for the car in front, causing the next person to brake a little more, and so on, and that builds up to gridlock.

We feel impotent anger when we finish a long day of work, and we just want to get home to our loved ones, but another minor accident or breakdown has brought the motorway to a standstill. We sit in our cars, listening to traffic reports, wishing we were somewhere else, *anywhere else*, and wondering if this job is really worth it, and pondering if there's more to life.

It stings us when we put gas in our cars and for some unknown reason the price has mysteriously jumped up by forty cents from what it was yesterday. But what can we do? Not put gas in the car? Not go to work?

A survey of fifteen-thousand professionals from eighty countries found that 40 percent of respondents said that the daily commute was the worst part of their day, and one in five were regularly late for work due to travel disruptions.[54]

In summary, traffic sucks.

The same solutions to congestion come up over and over again in the news, and during political elections, and at town hall meetings: new roads, better public transport, congestion charges, and, increasingly, ride-hailing (such as Uber), and autonomous vehicles.

Expanding Roadways

This is a solution that appeals to our logical minds: more road equals more space for more cars equals congestion gone. It's wonderful in its simplicity, hence it remains one of the most popular promises to frustrated commuters.

Shall I list some of the problems with this solution?

- Roads are expensive to build or expand, often in the hundreds of millions or billions of dollars for even a section of highway.

- Roadworks *create* congestion by blocking lanes or reducing speed limits for as long as it takes to build.

- They take a long time to build, usually years.

- Expanding the capacity of a roadway tends to induce more people to drive or to live further away from work, which results in increased pollution and use of resources, and, soon after, the same (or worse) congestion than before the expansion.[55]

Public Transport

This has an important place in improving the movement of the masses. But it's only one part of the overall answer.

In a country like Australia, where people prefer the personal comfort and freedom that a car provides, and towns and cities are spread over large areas, public transport will account for only a small percentage of commuters. And the rideshare of one of the main public transport modes, buses, is heavily affected by congestion.

When congestion worsens, people prefer to be in their cars rather than sitting on a bus because service becomes delayed and erratic[56] (which again increases congestion, which causes more people to not use the buses, and so on, in a spiral of traffic-y doom). It's difficult to reverse the trend of congestion by getting more people onto a service that's affected by that very congestion, so getting rid of congestion requires other solutions.

Ride-Hailing Services

Contrary to Uber's claim that it helps reduce congestion, it's actually increasing congestion. Traffic congestion in San Francisco, for instance, increased by 60 percent between 2010 and 2016, with Uber and Lyft vehicles responsible for more than half of that increase.[57]

It's not hard to see why this happens. If the cost of an Uber ride is only marginally more expensive than, say, taking a bus or a train, yet has the advantage of being a privately chauffeured ride directly to a destination, a certain number of people will leave public transport (or their bike, or their walking shoes) to be the sole passenger in a vehicle that takes up space on the road, on the way to that destination, and on the way out.

In other words, Uber isn't just replacing people driving their own cars; it's increasing the number of car trips, thus increasing traffic. Recent studies show that "43 percent to 61 percent of [ride-hail] trips substitute for transit, walk, or bike travel or would not have been made at all."[58]

Autonomous Vehicles

The people waiting for a fleet of autonomous vehicles (where we have mobility as a service (MaaS), similar to electricity or water service) to save the day are likely to be disappointed.

The car company Audi, after conducting research on traffic flow in Ingolstadt, Germany, surmises that "a city with 100 percent self-driving cars will reduce commute times by a third, even with 10 percent more vehicles on the road";[59] which isn't a terrible result, but it shows that self-driving cars will only be one piece of the congestion puzzle. They're not a silver bullet, especially because it will take some time, probably decades, before we reach 100 percent and finally ban silly humans from clogging up the roads with their imperfect reaction speeds and temper tantrums.

We're going to look in more detail at two other traffic solutions, both of which are forms of demand management – reducing demand on existing roadways by changing travel times or reducing or eliminating travel:

- *Congestion pricing* is one of these solutions, heralded by many as the most feasible one for major cities, and it has already been utilized with considerable success.

- *Flexible work* is a magnificent beast that's quietly flying under the radar: specifically remote work and flextime.

We're going to look at these from the perspective of one person – Rahul. Rahul lives in Brisbane, Australia. He's a normal, everyday sort of dude who has a job and a partner and a kid. Rahul works on the opposite side of the city from where he lives, about a forty-minute drive from home. His partner's workplace is only about five minutes from home, and their child goes to a nearby school. It's also a great neighborhood, so this is where they've decided to stay for the foreseeable future.

But Rahul hates his morning and afternoon commutes. Every second or third day there's bound to be heavy, inexplicable congestion, blowing his trip out from forty minutes to over an hour and a half, so he leaves quite early to avoid being late. (The traffic-was-shit excuse can only be used a certain number of times before people start to raise their eyebrows.)

He never gets enough sleep; he never has breakfast with his family; he rarely feels like exercising or doing anything other than eating and watching Netflix by the time he gets home; he can't remember the last time he just relaxed at home; he feels stressed when he gets to the office, so he doesn't feel like he's doing his best work; and he's pretty close to just slamming his foot on the brakes the next time someone decides to tailgate his car.

If he wanted to get out of the traffic and take public transport, his only other really viable way of getting to work, he'd have to drive to the local train station, transfer to a bus, and then walk the final ten minutes to the office. He tried it once and it took him, door-to-door, over an hour and forty minutes. When he returned home that night, nearly twelve hours after leaving, he swore off it forever. "Screw global warming!"

So, he continues to drive.

Punishing the Driver

In comes congestion pricing.

The government has been toying with this idea for a while after realizing that *something different* needs to happen to turn the tide of worsening congestion. It's choking the cities and impacting their growth and liveability. Building new roads is expensive, takes a long time, and hasn't worked. In fact, people seem to materialize from nowhere and fill up each new road within a couple of years of its opening. Charging people to drive at peak hours seems to have reduced traffic in other countries. "Let's do it!" they said.

Fast forward through whatever long-winded processes are required to get to the point where Rahul is now being charged to drive on the main roads he needs to take to get to his office. He pays A\$20 per day,[60] or \$100 per week, or \$400 per month, or \$4,800 per year, in congestion charges. Rahul is paid reasonably well (one of the reasons he's determined to stay in his current job), but this charge, on top of his fuel, other road tolls, and maintenance of his car, is starting to impact his savings. There goes the house he was hoping to buy someday.

He wonders what he can do. He could go back to his long public transport trips, which would save money. Even though he'd have a lot less time with his family, he could be productive on the train – do some extra reading and whatnot. Maybe.

The congestion charges apply only during peak hours, so he considers asking his boss if he could start earlier and then finish earlier. No. He knows his company. He knows his boss. Not only would they say no before the question had left Rahul's mouth, it would make them question Rahul's commitment to the company's mission and values. It would hurt them to have employees come to the office at whatever damned time they want. Who would manage them? It'd be chaos!

Rahul does some digging for solutions and finds a communal ride-sharing website where he could pay a small fee and catch a ride with another driver, or he could earn some money by picking someone else up. Being adventurous, he decides to create an account. Unfortunately, he doesn't find anyone going from his location to his destination and gives up after a few weeks.

Just to recap, Rahul's commuting options are:

- Pay an extra $4,800 a year in congestion charges to continue driving to work.

- Spend an *extra* two or more hours per day commuting by public transport, resulting in a total commute of more than three hours per day, or more than fifteen hours per week, putting him in the super-commuter category,* *not* a good category to find oneself in.

- Potentially risk his job and career by asking for flexible start and finish times in a rigid workplace.

- Use ride-share when a convenient sharer finally becomes available, and then find that it's not convenient to depend on a stranger to consistently be on time, and to be consistently on time himself, because life and stuff happens.

- Find a new job closer to home that pays less and/or isn't in his chosen field.

---

* Over ten hours of commuting per week.

- Move the whole family closer to his work, requiring his kid to change schools and his partner to either find a new job or do the same commute in the opposite direction.

The technical term for this is being stuck between a rock and a hard place and a spiky thing and some other unpleasant object. Yet another term is choosing the least of several evils.

Don't get me wrong – marginal changes to a system can produce the desired effects for at least part of a population. There will be some people who are near convenient public transport, or within walking or biking distance, but have chosen to drive because they love their sweet wheels (Australia is renowned for its love of the motor vehicle), and a congestion charge will push them to seriously consider leaving their cars at home. Positive results have been found in cities where it has been implemented – Stockholm, London, Milan, and Singapore; each has had large drops in traffic volume in the city centers. But even though congestion charges have had some success, it has some problems.

For instance, there are many people, like Rahul, who don't have other viable and convenient travel options. With a congestion charge they're forced to make a large compromise one way or another, be it financial, domestic, or health-related, or, more likely, all of these in varying measures. It's a *dis*incentive, a punishment. Mixing metaphors, it's like using a big stick to herd cats.

It also does nothing to address the root cause of commuting in the first place – people need to get to work, regardless of whether they're paying more to do so. On top of that, a congestion charge takes several years to implement, at great cost, and people may just take different routes, thus still polluting and causing congestion on non-charged roads.

Flexible Work, Flexible Roads

Let's look at a different, and currently fictional, scenario. The Australian government, instead of going with the congestion pricing strategy, decided, after a compelling speech from a progressive back-bencher, that it would try something that's completely new on the world stage: incentivizing companies to provide flexibility, remote work in this case, for their employees.

The government has created a National Flex Fund, which provides businesses with tax breaks of $2,000 for each employee who can demonstrate that they regularly work remotely or travel outside of peak times.

The aim of the fund is to make more businesses mindful of their impact on the roads, and to spread the awareness of work flexibility in general it offers various other health, social, and productivity benefits that carry over to government spending.

The size of the fund for Brisbane alone is $100 million, a drop in the bucket compared to the billions spent on road upgrades and other traffic costs. (The widening of a section of the highway between Brisbane and the Gold Coast is estimated to cost over one billion dollars.)[61]

Rahul's firm, although quite traditional in its management style, was attracted by the tax breaks and decided to take part. Rahul, with his terrible commute, was one of the first to put up his hand when asked for remote work volunteers. He was accepted for a trial, and he's now working three days a week from home, or sometimes from a local coworking hub that's only five minutes from his home when he gets sick of his desk at home and needs to see other faces.

He saw the benefits immediately. On his first remote workday he slept an hour longer than usual, and then cooked breakfast for his family, and then sat and ate with them. He then walked his kid to school for the first time ever. Upon getting home, he opened his laptop and got to work, feeling refreshed, half an hour earlier than he normally would at the office. After a hugely productive and relatively uninterrupted day, he went down to the park for a run, at the same time he would normally be sitting in traffic. He finished off the day with a deeply present and engaged evening with his family.

After a while of this, Rahul's health is improving – he gets more sleep, exercise, and home-cooked meals, and less stress. His connections with his kid and partner are growing, and he's helping out a lot more at home, with duties such as cleaning and household management, like keeping track of appointments and his kid's events. He's saving $35 per day when telecommuting ($10 on fuel, $5 on tolls, $20 on coffees and lunch), which is a savings of $105 per week, or $5,040 per year for a forty-eight-week work year.

He has also lessened his carbon footprint by preventing over 1.5 tons of carbon dioxide from entering the atmosphere over the course of a year (based on driving sixty kilometers a day and the average car emitting 182 grams of CO_2 per kilometer).[62]

Rahul is also more energized at his job, even on the days he goes back into the office (with a renewed appreciation for time with his coworkers and the novelty of working in different locations). His manager has seen a marked uptick in his performance and enthusiasm for his next projects, and Rahul has been asking for more responsibility.

Besides the plethora of benefits for Rahul and his family, the least of which is escaping the stress of traffic a few days a week, removing people in large numbers from the road can make incredible differences to congestion, the main aim of the National Flex Fund.

Rahul is one of four-hundred employees from his firm who now work remotely more than half the week, and he's one of fifty thousand in his city who are experiencing the direct benefits of less commuting, more freedom, *and* not contributing to traffic (and saving thousands of tons of CO_2 from entering the atmosphere).

There are about six-hundred-fifty-thousand people in Brisbane who drive to work.[63] So the reduction of fifty-thousand drivers equates to 7.7 percent fewer people being on the roads in peak traffic times. This may not sound like it would have any effect on overall congestion, but it has been found that even small changes in traffic volume can have incredible effects.

For example, one study that analyzed the impact of public transport strikes on traffic found that the temporary *increase* in the number of cars on the roads by 7 percent (due to train strikes in Melbourne) resulted in a hugely disproportionate increase in congestion; namely, the number of severely congested roads in the city increased by 133 percent, 58 percent more vehicles experienced congestion, and the average travel speed across the network decreased by 20 percent (actual travel time increased by 73 percent).[64]

That's a bad day.

Conversely, some studies report that reducing traffic by just 4 to 5 percent can increase average travel speed and decrease congestion substantially, by up to 30 percent.[65]

Here's why this happens. Traffic flow is determined by driving speed and traffic density (number of cars per unit distance per lane). Roads have a maximum flow rate of cars above which the flow becomes unstable, and even a slight disturbance, such as someone slowing down to change lanes, can result in stop-and-go traffic or complete gridlock. Below this maximum flow rate, traffic moves smoothly.[66]

If a road often jams because there are too many cars trying to drive at once, reducing the number of cars even by a small percentage can put the flow rate below its maximum, and then traffic becomes stable and can flow easily.

Increasing the percentage of the workforce that works from home, or reducing their days of work, or changing their start and finish times, can help immensely with traffic flow during peak times by reducing the demand for the roads at these times. The less rigid our workplaces become, the less rigid our road demand becomes. Put another way, *flexible work creates flexible roads!*

There is an elasticity to traffic when people have more freedom to choose when or if they travel. Road use becomes an elastic market. If someone travels to work at a particular time and notices that traffic is becoming bad at that time, they could choose another time to travel or avoid traveling in general.

Not only does the worker benefit, but the road at that time will be less busy, and all the other drivers will benefit as well. This is what congestion pricing attempts to do through punishment (increased costs), but flexibility allows it to happen in a positive, non-punish-y sort of way, and at much less (or zero) cost to implement. And it can happen *right now*.

Why isn't flexibility already the top contender for reducing congestion? Why aren't we reading this headline: "Road crisis: government seeks companies to take up flexibility." Why aren't city planning documents filled with strategies to incentivize flexible work? Compared to all other solutions, it's cheap, fast, simple, and reduces pollution; no one loses and everyone wins.

The issue is that there's a vast disconnect between the people working to reduce congestion (traffic engineers, construction companies, politicians), who focus mainly on increasing the capacity of roads and other technical stuff like traffic light timing or congestion charges, and the people who have control over travel demand at peak times (business owners and managers).

It's not a traffic engineer's job to find out why people are using the road in the first place, much less help reduce that demand. It's their job to build bigger and better intersections and roads. Their underlying assumption is that lots of people need to use the roads, and their goal is to provide the best infrastructure.

On the other side, businesses don't see themselves as being responsible for traffic. Or if they're aware of their contribution to traffic, they don't think that their one business could make any difference. Furthermore, there's no obvious short-term incentive for businesses to pay attention to their role in congestion, even when they see the direct negative results in stressed and late employees and increased freight costs.

That's why flexibility doesn't come up as a solution. It's not easy to see the connection between work and traffic, and the incentives for any one stakeholder aren't clear.

"We're going to work with local businesses to create elastic demand for roads" is more abstract and less catchy than "We're going to spend a billion dollars on a new highway!"

I hope that this little story about Rahul has made the connection between flexibility and traffic problems clear to government and business leaders. And whenever you see congestion on the news, or politicians promise new roads in a political campaign, or you're crawling through traffic on your way to work, think of Rahul, and think of the magnificent beast of flexible work. We can bust this bastard one flexible business at a time.

Part Two

DEFINITELY NOT ROBOTS

CHAPTER 5

Energy Buckets,
and Why the Compressed
Workweek is Dumb

THIS IS MY FAVORITE CHAPTER, because it has graphs – Wait! Don't close the book yet! These graphs are fun and easy to decipher and make it easier to describe the difference between humans and robots.

But before getting into the excitement, why does it even matter?

Well, in the previous two chapters I've described why flexibility is important for the individual, for society, and for the planet, so there are good reasons for the humanist, the altruist, the feminist, and the environmentalist to take flexibility seriously.

But the capitalists, the people in charge of this flexibility – the managers, CEOs, heads of state – the ones with the power over the structures of work – might be tempted to say, "Why should *I* be the one to sacrifice profits/surpluses/shareholder returns just to help society? There are millions of other businesses around the world, we're just doing the same as them: trying to make some money and create jobs. We already *are* helping society by giving people bloody work!"

So, this part contains the most important message of the book:

Flexibility is good for business.

Flexibility helps to decrease waste and increase profits in many ways. Rather than being a cost and a sacrifice, it's an investment.

I want leaders to understand the value of flexibility so that it's rolled out to people en masse rather than to individuals who have to sacrifice their reputations by asking or pushing for flexibility for themselves. It's only when everyone has access to flexibility that we have a purposeful, strategic program, Levels 3 and 4 on the Flex Scale, rather than the bare minimum of Levels 1 or 2. Flex for all, as opposed to intermittent flexibility for just parents or caregivers, has a greater impact on individuals and society by increasing the number of people who benefit. And it requires systems in place that will ensure that the practice is optimized and allowed to succeed.

Faced with the evidence that flexibility benefits business, the polite skeptics will consider these cases as outliers; that, somehow, they got lucky, and the approach wouldn't apply to their own business or industry. "My employees are so busy that flexibility wouldn't work."

This part of the book is a deep dive into *how* flexibility, perhaps non-intuitively, boosts productivity, makes people feel like they're doing less when they're doing more, reduces stress, and increases collaboration and innovation.

My goal is to change people's perception about flexibility from "it's a cost we bear to help mothers and to avoid litigation" to "it's great for people *and* it's great for business." And the biggest perception that needs to change is that we consider humans to be robots.

What Is Productivity?

Another wee point to clarify before we get to the graphs (I know, the suspense is unbearable!) is that we need to agree on what productivity is.

When most people in the workplace talk about productivity, they're talking about input: how many things are being done, how hard someone is working, *busyness*. Or they're talking about output: how many things are being produced, how many sales are being made, how many coffees are being poured.

But we're going to be more rigorous and show that there's a vast distinction between productivity and input and output, and that there's a big difference between robot productivity and human productivity.

To start with, the economic definition of productivity is the ratio of outputs to inputs: how many things are produced (output) per unit of resources or time to produce those things (inputs). For example, one hundred widgets made per hour, or ten tons of steel produced per one hundred tons of iron ore. Here's what the equation looks like:

$$\text{Productivity} = \frac{\text{Outputs}}{\text{Inputs}} \left(\text{e.g.} \frac{\text{Apples Picked}}{\text{Worker Hours}} \right)$$

This is a reasonable definition for a machine, and we'll use it later when we talk about a robot, but it's only part of the story for humans. The human story is much more nuanced.

A human can sit in a chair, not making or producing anything material, yet still be highly productive. Or a human can be the busiest person in the building, rushing here and there, doing a thousand things, yet be completely unproductive.

Imagine that a telemarketer, Jack, is making twenty calls to potential customers per hour. He's efficiently running through the pitch provided by the company, quickly being rejected, and then moving with high speed onto the next call. In a game of pure numbers, Jack has a high input.

With his current way of doing things, one out of those twenty calls is resulting in a sale. He's content with this record because he's just doing as he was told and assumes that this is a reasonable rate of sales. But his productivity, sales per hour, as you can guess, is probably not as high as it should be.

Next to this person is another marketer, Jan, who's making only ten calls per hour. Her input is low compared to Jack's; she's not working anywhere near as fast as he is. She's also using the script provided, but she's putting more effort into being personable to the clients, and she's going off script when she sees an opportunity to ask more questions about the client's needs and how the product will suit. She's even making permanent changes to her processes based on what seems to be capturing the favor of clients. She's even doing research into finding the best clients in the first place.

With this method, Jan is making five sales per hour – four more (400 percent more) than Jack. She's adding 400 percent more value to the business than Jack. Even with her much lower input, she's being 400 percent more productive than Jack.

This is a simplistic example, but you can see that input – busyness and working hard – and productivity are quite different. A human, who can think and plan, can be much more productive than a robot that just performs a mechanical task.

The more nuanced part of human productivity is that the impact of Jan's work goes beyond her own high level of sales. Her methods, and her desire to continuously improve, will spread to other people in the organization, thus increasing sales and reducing waste. This is why it's so important to see productivity as more than just the number of tasks completed or widgets produced, or even the financial value of one person's work.

True productivity comes from working with intent and being aware of the value one is providing to the business's big picture. True productivity comes from the ability and desire to think, learn, and change.

Another term for human productivity is *work goodness.*

People aren't just *doing*, they're also *thinking*, and *caring*. Doing means getting stuff done, thinking means planning, strategizing, and improving, and caring is the desire to do a good job, otherwise known as engagement.

Work goodness is multifaceted. It includes the quality of the work (is it right the first time, or will it need to be redone?), seeking ways to improve work, questioning the relevance of tasks, searching for ways to reduce wasted effort, materials, and time (*eliminating* work can be the most productive activity we do!), innovating and creating for the business as a whole, and wanting to be there, which influences all of the above.

Robots and Humans
Robot Productivity

Now that we have a good working definition of productivity, let me introduce a robot. Robots come in a million types, shapes, and ability levels, and they're becoming more advanced every day. But here we're not going to talk about the T-1000 from *Terminator,* or Bender from *Futurama*, or WALL-E from *WALL-E*, or any other cool robot which (who?) can think, plan, and strategize.

I'm going to keep it simple and talk about a robot that lives in a manufacturing plant and performs one task. Our robot puts lids on row after row of glass bottles.

At 100 percent productivity, its design specification, it caps one thousand bottles per hour. To simplify the comparison between human and robot, we'll assume this robot operates only on weekdays and only from nine to five.

As you can see in Figures 5.1 and 5.2, and as you'd probably expect, the productivity of the robot doesn't change over the course of each day or from day to day during the week. It caps one thousand bottles per hour on Monday morning; it caps one thousand bottles per hour on Friday afternoon. This robot has linear productivity.*

---

* I'm aware that robots are often unpredictable. They're shut down for repairs, maintenance, and cleaning, and they're slowed down or sped up in the search for optimum production and quality, but this isn't a book about robot maintenance, so we're going to ignore these variables.

Productivity of a Robot – One Day

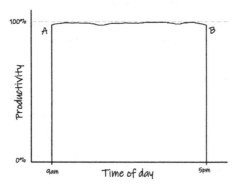

Figure 5.1. In this graph of productivity versus time of day for a robot, the robot is turned on at nine and is instantly at or near maximum productivity (A). It remains at or near 100 percent productivity for the entire day, with only slight variations when it's slowed down for quality purposes or for other reasons. It's turned off at five (B), at which point its productivity drops instantly to zero. (It's assumed that the robot doesn't need to be shut down for maintenance or cleaning during the day and that it runs over lunchtime.)

Productivity of a Robot – One Week

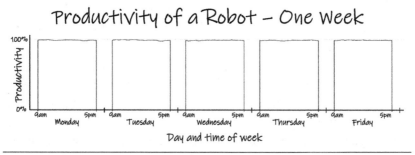

Figure 5.2. In this graph of productivity versus day and time of week for a robot, the robot is turned on at nine and turned off at five each day, and it remains at or near 100 percent productivity for the entire day and week. It's operational only from Monday to Friday. (The time between each day is scaled down to reduce blank space.)

Human Productivity (Assumed)

Now for humans. The way we manage humans in the traditional workplace assumes that a human's productivity over time looks something like Figures 5.3 and 5.4, which, as you can see, is pretty close to that of a robot.

The human in this instance, like the robot, only works from nine to five; but they also have a lunch break for an hour. During the times and the days the human is supposed to be working, we assume they have linear productivity and that their productivity remains at or near 100 percent for the entire workday and workweek.

It's important to remember that 100 percent productivity for a human isn't just *doing* – going through the motions of work – but also *thinking* and *caring*: they're giving their best.

Saying this out loud (and putting it in graph form) probably seems insane. Any reasonable person wouldn't assume an employee is still at their highest level of productivity at four on a Friday. Or that someone can work at this level for an entire day. Yet the way we structure our traditional workplace and manage others is proof of this assumption.

We insist that people work eight or more hours a day, five or six days a week, because we're worried that we'll miss out on the productive time of that person if they don't work the maximum legal amount of time. (Businesses and unions battle over how much time people have to work, with neither looking at the true issues.)

We make people ask permission and sign forms to take a day off or leave early to attend to a personal matter, worried that this downtime will affect productivity and hurt the business.

We pay people the same amount per hour regardless of whether that hour was supremely productive or completely unproductive. Often, we don't know the difference.

We use types of flexibility such as time-in-lieu, where extra time worked one day can be taken off on another day, assuming that each hour of work is worth the same as, and is directly interchangeable with, another, like currency.

Any strict adherence to time, or use of time worked as a measure of productivity, or attempts to increase the amount of time people work, shows that we equate time worked with productivity.

This way of thinking makes perfect sense for a robot. One minute of machine downtime is indeed a lost minute of productivity, which will either be made up or lost forever. Downtime is a critical measure in a manufacturing plant because you're not producing but you're still paying overhead and operating costs.

But thinking that humans have linear productivity, and a minute of work lost is a minute of productivity lost, is one of the strangest lies we tell ourselves. The entire foundation of the normal workplace, and many arguments against flexibility, is based on this lie. "If they work fewer

Assumed Human Productivity – One Day

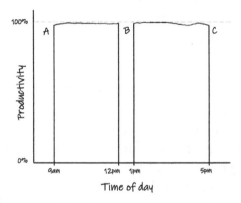

Figure 5.3. In this graph of assumed productivity of a human versus time of day over one day, the human starts work at nine (A), then works at or near 100 percent productivity until lunch (B), at which point productivity is 0 percent, but it jumps straight back to or near 100 percent as soon as lunch is over, remaining there until the end of the day (C). This person may still take short morning and/or afternoon breaks, but productivity will instantly ramp back up to 100 percent as soon as that break is finished. (Breaks are not shown.)

Assumed Human Productivity – One Week

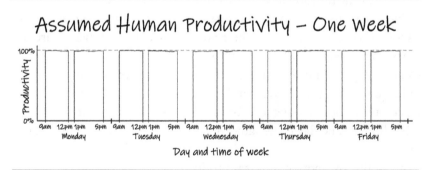

Figure 5.4. In this graph of assumed productivity versus day and time of week for a human, the human starts work at nine each day and finishes at five. They have a lunch break from twelve to one. They work from Monday to Friday. It's assumed that when the human is supposed to be working, their productivity is at or near 100 percent.

hours, they'll get less done." We take this as a fundamental, unbreakable, obvious law of productivity. Any idiot knows it.

For example, Ian Brinkley, a chief economist in the United Kingdom, when talking about a national reduction of the working week to four days, said, "A four-day week is a 20 percent reduction in working hours.

You're going to have to get a big improvement in productivity to cover that. It's unlikely that any productivity-enhancing effects from reducing hours would be big enough to cover the cost of reducing working hours."[1]

But this assumption that humans have linear productivity fails the second we look at what a day of work actually looks like, especially in our rigid workplaces.

For instance, when a coworker interrupts us while we're working, it takes, on average, twenty-three minutes and fifteen seconds to get back into the flow of what we were doing before the interruption.[2]

The assumption crashes when data says that only about two or three hours per day are truly productive in a normal workplace. A survey in the United Kingdom of 1,989 full-time office workers found that 79 percent didn't consider themselves to be productive throughout the entire day. In fact, the average amount of time they did consider themselves to be productive was two hours and fifty-three minutes per day.[3]

The assumption dies when we look around an office at three and realize that 30 percent of the people are scrolling through Facebook, 30 percent are texting their partner that their brain is so dead and asking them what they feel like eating for dinner, and the remaining 40 percent are pretending to work because their boss is walking past.

Then there are just some days we're on, some days we're off, and some days we shouldn't be at work. There are differences in biological chronotypes: some people work better in the morning, some in the afternoon, some at night.[4] And there are a million other factors in our lives that influence human productivity and guarantee that it's not linear, and that it's certainly not at 100 percent for the entire workday and week.

For humans, no day is the same; no hour is the same; no minute is the same.

When the assumption of linear productivity falls, so do all arguments about arriving and leaving at a particular time, making up for lost time, signing forms to take a day off, and monitoring employees' activities.

I don't mean to be patronizing, and I know that no manager actually thinks of their workers as machines with constant 100 percent productivity (or I would hope that's the case), but as a society, because of the traditions we all grew up with, this is the assumption we make. And it keeps us stuck in our traditions.

This assumption needs to be burned up and have its ashes thrown off a cliff.

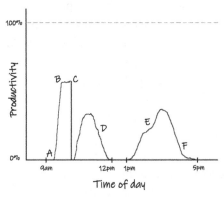

Realistic Human Productivity – Rigid Day

Figure 5.5. In this graph of realistic productivity versus time of day for a human in a rigid workplace, the human starts work at nine each day and finishes at five. They have a lunch break from twelve to one.

Human Productivity (Realistic)

What does productivity look like for a real person in a normal, rigid workplace?

Let's go back to the graphs.

Normally, most of us start the day with a long or stressful (or both) commute. We get to our workplace and work is the *last* thing on our minds. Our cortisol levels are high, and we need to de-stress by preparing for the day: chatting with coworkers, making coffee, turning on the computer, checking the news, maybe waiting for the morning team meeting. This is point A in Figure 5.5.

Having prepared for the day and settled in, our nerves calmed by the sweet, sweet caffeine, we open whatever it is we're working on and, well, start working (point B).

But it isn't our best work. We're not operating at or near maximum productivity. For one thing, we know we're in for a long day, and we're probably partway through a long week, so we're conserving our energy. Two, there's no incentive to be hugely productive, since we can't go home early, so we go through the motions and get work done as it needs to be done. And three, interruptions abound! Questions from coworkers and bosses, meetings, phones ringing and loud conversations in the next cubicle, etc. (There's a meeting at point C in the graph; notice what it does to productivity.) These elements all make it extremely challenging to get into a productive workflow.

By the time we get to eleven and beyond (point D), the relentless efforts to work without getting into a satisfying flow cause mental exhaustion, and we're just waiting for lunch and probably checking our favorite social media or news sites.

Getting back from lunch, we're not feeling well rested (especially if it's a short lunch where we have to eat as fast as we can). We might be drowsy after having just eaten, and we're getting set for another long period of work, so there's no need to push too hard (the long upward slope toward some sort of decent work, point E).

And then F is the slowdown to the end of the day. That feeling of ennui usually hits at three or four in the afternoon; I can't recall anyone I've worked with (or myself) being at the top of their game between four and five in the afternoon.

This is just one day. Figure 5.6 is an example of a realistic workweek, showing even wilder variations. Monday we're a little slow to get started. Tuesday we're a little more productive. But we didn't sleep well Tuesday night, resulting in pretending not to be a zombie on Wednesday, exhibiting maximum presenteeism, taking up space but adding zero value.

Thursday might be a more productive day – maybe fewer meetings, or a little more sleep Wednesday night. And Friday – ah, Friday – the day we wish we were somewhere else. We finish some tasks and plan for next week (or, more likely, for the weekend). We're tired, we're done. When is five o'clock coming?

Remember, we're not talking about the ability to merely go through the motions of work. This can be done for many hours and many days if we're talking about simply *doing* (laying bricks, typing words, greeting customers). While this still counts as working, it's not true productivity, which we earlier referred to as *work goodness*.

Work goodness means being fully functional and immersed in a flow state, where we can question and improve our work to create new solutions and paradigms and give our best.

It might *feel* like we're being productive at four when we're expending energy and effort to read that same sentence for the fifth time in a row. But is your productivity anywhere near what it was in the morning when your mind was fresh? Are you anywhere near as capable of

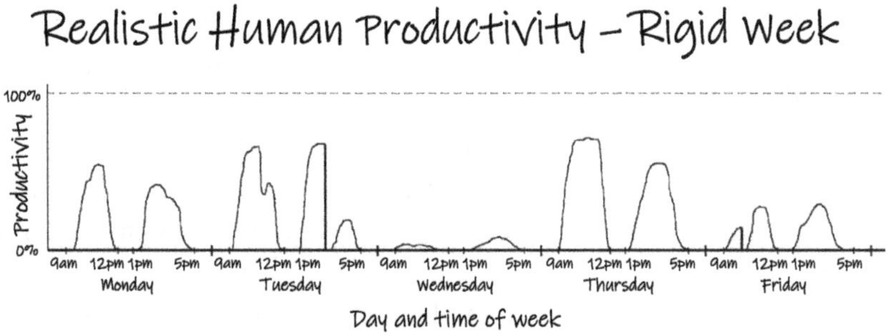

Realistic Human Productivity – Rigid Week

Figure 5.6. In this graph of realistic productivity versus day and time of week for a human (rigid workplace), the human starts work at nine each day and finish at five. They have a lunch break from twelve to one. They work from Monday to Friday.

thinking through a problem and producing a solution? When you're serving a customer, are you giving them your best or just your adequate?

An interesting and frightening illustration of how our abilities vary while working long, rigid hours was found in a study on the consistency (quality) of judges' parole decisions at different times of the day.

The judges were significantly more likely to be lenient and release prisoners at the start of the day and just after lunch than at any other times. Said the researchers: "You are anywhere between two and six times as likely to be released if you're one of the first three prisoners considered versus the last three prisoners considered."[5]

These highly trained and experienced professionals, who hold people's lives in their hands, made decisions willy-nilly based on how long they'd been working for the day. That's like having a machine that's designed to make circles slowly revert to making squares as the day wears on.

I'll say this one more time: human productivity is far from linear.

My analysis above should raise some questions, such as why on earth would I pay someone by the hour if not every hour is the same? And aren't we wasting the company's and the individual's time by operating for all those hours at sub-optimal productivity?

And if we combine these ideas with the last couple of chapters, we should be angry. Not only are we not being productive with this rigid adherence to time and place, we're causing incredible problems for individuals and society. We're sucking energy out of employees for little productivity. It's like driving a car in first gear – you use a hell of a lot of fuel and get nowhere.

When an employee is sitting there at four waiting for five to arrive, it costs the business, the employee, the employee's family, and the world. The business is using their precious time and energy and benefiting not one bit.

That makes me sad and mad, and I hope you feel the same.

The Energy Bucket

Why *can't* humans just be 100 percent productive all day, every day, like a robot?

It comes down to one thing: different energy sources.

Energy is a clear concept when you talk about a machine: you plug it into a power outlet, flick the switch, electricity flows through its circuits, and through the wonders of physics it does whatever it's programmed to do. The same goes for a machine that's powered by combustion, or hydraulics, or wind, or whatever. They all receive their energy directly from some power source, and as long as they're connected to that power source, they'll keep doing whatever it is they do, to their maximum capacity. Disconnect them or turn them off and they stop. Simple.

Humans are more complicated. Yes, in a practical sense we do have a direct energy source. After we eat food, our body converts it to energy for our cells, which allows us to move, think, and breathe.

But if a human has enough food to eat, will they automatically be energized and working to their full capacity at their job?

What about someone who's eaten enough, but only slept an average of four hours for the last few nights? Will they be productive? Or will they be functioning as if they were drunk?

Let's say someone has had enough food *and* regularly gets seven or eight hours of sleep, but they've received an eviction notice and need to find somewhere to live by the end of the week. Would this person be highly productive and focused on getting their job done, using their brain to its full creative capacity? Or would the fear of not having a secure residence be taking up most of their mental space?

What about the person who's well-fed, and well-slept, and has secure housing, but is currently in a rough patch with their partner, and hasn't had sex, or even been hugged or kissed, for a few weeks? Will they be giving their best at work? Or will they feel empty and deprived, and uninspired in the office?

What about the person who hasn't had a holiday for twelve months? Will they be skipping through the door ready to change the world? Or what about the person who comes in on a Friday morning after a full week of long days, who hasn't had any chance to relax?

What about the person who hasn't learned anything new and has been doing the exact same thing day after day after day for months? Will they be putting their all into their work, finding ways to improve processes, reduce waste, or please customers?

What about the person who has no control over their job? Where they do it, when they do it, how they do it. It's set in stone. They don't have any freedom to make decisions or be creative. Will they be tapping into their energetic and productive potential?

What about the person who sees no meaning in their work and is just there to make some money? And they have no idea how their work fits into the bigger picture of what the company is trying to achieve? Will they be putting in more than the bare minimum?

What if someone hasn't seen a tree, or been under the sun, for a few weeks? What if they don't have any natural light or views of the outside world from their workspace?

Are these things starting to look familiar?

Are you getting sick of rhetorical questions?

As you might have guessed, we're revisiting the fundamental human needs. They were introduced in Chapter 3 as requirements to be fully human. Any unfulfilled need causes damage to our bodies and minds, and for optimal health and well-being we should have a balanced fulfillment of *all* our needs.

I'm now going to extend this concept to work productivity, and say that if we want an employee or manager to be functioning to the best of their ability, they, again, need a balanced fulfillment of all of their fundamental human needs. A dearth of any single need will take away from that person's ability to be fully productive. To help conceptualize this as our energy source, I've created the *energy bucket*.

Imagine a bucket.

This bucket is floating above your head. In this bucket is a luminescent gold substance that looks and behaves like a liquid, but it's completely weightless.

This shiny liquid is your energy – your *capacity* to be productive, your capacity to *do*, to *think*, and to *care*.

The bucket and the energetic substance float around with you day and night. The fuller the bucket is, the more capable you are of *doing* and *thinking* and *caring*. The emptier it is, the less capable you are of *doing* and *thinking* and *caring*. This is the energy bucket (Figure 5.7), and it has the following characteristics.

1. It's divided into ten compartments, one for each of the fundamental human needs discussed in Chapter 3. The only way to fill the bucket is to fill each individual compartment, and the only way to fill each compartment is to satisfy the particular human need represented by that compartment.

    You can't fill the creation compartment by eating. You can't fill the participation compartment by reading a book. You can't fill the freedom compartment by hugging your partner. You can fill each compartment only with whatever satisfies that need. (Remembering that some things can satisfy multiple needs at the same time,* such as dancing, which helps to fulfill participation, affection, creation, identity, understanding, subsistence, and protection needs all at the same time to various degrees.)

2. The compartments aren't comparable in volume or in the number or amount of satisfiers necessary to fill them. For instance, to fill the subsistence part of the bucket, you would need food and water every day, whereas to fill the affection compartment, perhaps a good lunch or dinner with friends once a week is enough.

    These requirements are different for different people, different stages of life, different cultures, even different days. But a safe rule of thumb is that each compartment needs regular fulfillment. The optimal amount is personal, and you *feel* when it's filled or it's not.

3. The gold liquid, our energy, is constantly draining from each of the compartments: it fuels our capacity to *do* and *think* and *care*, and

---

* Max-Neef refers to these as *synergistic satisfiers*; I call them *bucket boosters*.

The Energy Bucket

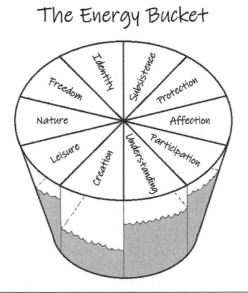

Figure 5.7. Each compartment of the energy bucket corresponds to one of the ten fundamental human needs from Max-Neef's modified list. It's displayed here as transparent to make clear that the compartments are separate from each other and that their levels of fullness are independent of each other.

it also evaporates over time. If you're sitting around doing nothing, every compartment will still empty out (except perhaps leisure, which is refilled by doing just that, or nature, if your nothing involves grass and sunlight).

As soon as any of the compartments is filled and the source of satisfaction is removed, it begins to empty. For example, if you finish eating a meal, your subsistence compartment will likely be full, but as that food is used for energy, and your stomach empties, that compartment also empties until the next meal.

Meeting with friends will help fill the affection and participation compartments, but as soon as you leave them these compartments will slowly empty until you do something else with other people that satisfies these needs, such as coming home to your family or meeting colleagues for lunch.

4. Some things drain the entire bucket much faster than others. Things such as stress, commuting, being in an open-plan office, too much pressure from work or too much work, social rejection, abuse, and

bullying. These things are the opposite of the things that add to the bucket, and they drain it, fast.

5. The goal with the energy bucket is not to have every compartment 100 percent full at all times. Not only would this be impossible, especially when filling one compartment often drains other compartments (work can fill participation and understanding but drain leisure and freedom), it's also unnecessary. As long as each compartment is filled often enough that a person doesn't feel chronically deprived of any particular need, they will have enough energy to *do* and *think* and *care*.

    In fact, emptying and filling the compartments provides healthy and motivating hunger followed by satisfaction, much as a meal is truly satisfying only when you're hungry. Some deprivation is a good thing.

    What we want to avoid is chronic unfulfillment – compartments *never* getting a chance to completely fill, or remaining empty for long periods of time. That's when we move away from hunger (good) and toward poverty (bad).

6. If one compartment is chronically unfilled, even if all the others are completely full, it drastically impacts a person's ability to *do* and *think* and *care*. This is a poverty of a human need, and, as described in Chapter 3, a poverty of *any* individual need creates pathologies, and it certainly takes away from someone's ability to be fully productive at work or in any other arena of their lives.

    Someone who has worked fourteen days without a break would have a completely empty leisure compartment. Even if this person somehow managed to keep every other compartment filled, they wouldn't be able to give their best to their work. They'll have a poverty of this one need, and their brain (and body, if their job is physical) will be starving for a chance to switch off and relax.

    At this point, even if all other compartments are full, it wouldn't be right to say, "Well, their Energy Compartment is 90 percent full, so they should still be productive." No. If one compartment is empty, the whole bucket may as well be empty. It's only when *every* compartment is consistently filled that we can consider the energy bucket to be filled.

This concept occurred to me long before I'd read about humans having various fundamental needs, when I was working in a rigid workplace, doing eight-to-ten-hour days in an office and commuting over an hour each way.

I would get home and feel completely drained of all energy and enthusiasm; I had no capacity to do anything but sit in front of the TV, eat dinner, and then go to sleep.

I even noticed that same empty feeling the morning after an especially stressful commute. I was devoid of energy even before I turned on the computer. I felt the same way when I hadn't taken a day off in months.

On the other hand, things unrelated to sleep or rest or stress increased my energy and productivity immensely: hanging out with friends, doing something creative, going for a walk in the woods.

I pictured a magical bucket that held and supplied me with all of my energy, and I said things like, "Man, my bucket is empty" or "Oh yeah, my bucket is so full now." (To which my partner would say, "What the hell are you talking about?")

Hence the *energy bucket* was born. In the years since, especially after learning about our fundamental needs, I can usually identify which compartments of my bucket are empty or full at any particular time. And I'm keenly aware that if *any* of my compartments are empty, my entire quality of life and ability to do my best work will be compromised.

The concept may sound like pseudoscience, but it's a giant step up from thinking that the only things people need in order to be constantly productive at work are enough food, money, and motivational speeches.

The concept of the *energy bucket* provides powerful and practical knowledge: how to boost productivity from its source. It enables us to determine if our power source is depleted or full, and *how* to fill it.

We fill it by being completely human, as often as possible! And we do that by ensuring that all of our fundamental needs are fulfilled on a regular basis. That's our power switch.

Empty Buckets Are Expensive

As people's energy buckets empty, their ability to do their best work – including being able to think properly and caring about what they're doing – is compromised.

That last point, caring about their work and the company they work for, is called *engagement*, and it's a critical metric in business.

Companies have realized that their employees being engaged is much more important than them merely being present, that someone who's there but would rather not be there *might as well not be there at all*. They're not worth the money you're spending to keep them there. Compared to someone who's engaged, they make more mistakes (which take time and money to fix), they're more likely to be injured or to injure someone else, they're less likely to go above and beyond their job description, they take more sick days, and they're probably going to leave soon and need to be replaced anyway.

Gallup quantified these effects by comparing "business units" that are in the top quartile in employee engagement to those in the bottom quartile and found that the latter had seen:

- Higher absenteeism (sick days) – by 37 percent

- Higher turnover in "high-turnover organizations" (e.g., retail) – by 25 percent

- Higher turnover in "low-turnover organizations" (e.g., government) – by 65 percent

- Higher shrinkage (theft) – by 28 percent

- More safety incidents – by 48 percent

- More patient safety incidents (for those in healthcare) – by 41 percent

- More quality defects – by 41 percent[6]

All of these differences are expensive: overall, highly engaged business units achieve 21 percent greater profitability than less engaged units.[7] Just one of these elements, turnover, can cost tens of thousands of dollars for an entry-level position, and one-and-a-half to two times an employee's salary for more technical or senior-level roles. (Costs include "hiring, onboarding, training, ramp time to peak productivity, the loss of engagement from others due to high turnover, higher business error rates, and general culture impacts.")[8]

It costs to have empty buckets!

Fill the Bucket

If we're aware of what fills the bucket and what empties the bucket, can't we, shouldn't we, use that information to avoid or reduce things that empty it, and increase or add things that fill it?

Given that this is a book about flexibility, I will of course be saying that flexibility helps to fill the bucket, and thus it increases engagement and productivity. But before I do, I'll step back from the "if I have a hammer, everything is a nail" position and emphasise that flexibility is only one tool on the belt, one important aspect of taking a human-centered approach to boosting employee engagement. All of these tools, coincidentally, correspond to filling various compartments in the employee's bucket. They include:

- Growth and development in a job and career
- Alignment between the job and their skills and interests
- Appropriate resources to do the job
- Feeling valued and cared for
- Clear goals and timely feedback
- Feeling like they belong to the team
- Their work demonstrating a noticeable impact on the business; the business demonstrating a noticeable impact on the world
- Autonomy and decision-making ability
- Good communication between them and their managers (and good relationships in general)
- Satisfactory pay
- Good relationships with other employees (e.g., no harassment and bullying, friendships, and connections)
- Good physical environment (e.g., air and light)
- Job security

That said, increased flexibility on its own is a *powerful* tool on this belt!

What might a productivity graph look like for a non-rigid day, when someone has the flexibility to take care of their needs in a sustainable way?

We'll consider the example of someone who is using two different types of flexibility: working remotely, from a home office, and being able to choose when they work during the day (flexitime). They're still working roughly seven to eight hours a day in this example.

To start the day, this person doesn't need to travel to their office, which removes the stress and time wasted in the morning commute. They're a morning person and decide that they get their best work done early so soon as they wake up, have a shower, and make a coffee, they turn on the computer and get straight to it (point A on Figure 5.8).

Their productivity at this point is at maximum because: 1) they're not drained from the commute, 2) they're harnessing their own productive rhythm of the day, 3) there are no interruptions from colleagues just dropping by, and 4) they're already energized and engaged from being able to live sustainably on previous days and weeks.

This person's productivity slowly drops over the morning (B) because they *are* still human, but for five to six hours they're working near their full productivity, doing amazing things that our previous example of someone stuck in a rigid workplace would struggle to achieve on *any* day.

Then they stop. Unlike the people in the rigid workplace, this person is not going to try to push through low productivity and is not going to drain their bucket for a low return while they wait for lunch or the end of the day. They've already accomplished so much for the day, they deserve a damned break (point C)!

They're going to use a few hours to *refill their bucket!* Or, to mix metaphors and borrow from the story of the lumberjack, they're going to go away and sharpen their axe, ready to chop down another tree later.

They have a lazy lunch while watching a couple of episodes of whatever is on Netflix, fully resting their mind with a leisurely activity. And since they know they'll be crappy at doing their work in the early afternoon after eating, they're going to the gym after lunch instead, improving their overall health and taking their mind even further off work, which will give a boost of energy for the late afternoon.

This is where we get to point D. Even though this person has already had a supremely productive morning, a morning that they could only dream about in their old open-plan office, they've realized that they can

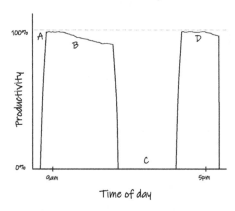

Figure 5.8: Example of the productivity of a human who works flexibly; in this case, they're working remotely *and* can choose when to do their work. This person is still expected to work seven to eight hours a day, but this isn't tracked or policed by management.

catch a second wind of high productivity with the way they've structured their day, where work and life coexist in an integrated way.

This highly productive *and* balanced day can be repeated multiple times in a week. Employees aren't holding their breath, and they're not putting up with poverties until the weekend. They're living sustainably, every day, and for multiple successive days they'll be able to hit high levels of productivity. This is unheard of in rigid workplaces.

Not every day will be exactly like Figure 5.8. There are ups and downs and unknowns in life, regardless of someone's level of flexibility. Some days might be terrible and the employee will get nothing done. But then they'll make up for it on another, immensely productive, day.

Or perhaps one day they decide to go to a judo class in the early morning, or they need some extra sleep and start work at ten. But then they work a solid, productive four hours until two, doing more than they would in a full day in a rigid workplace while also taking care of their health.

Different types of flexibility work for different people, but all of them will increase people's capacity to *do* and to *think* and to *care*, and that's good for business.

Ten-Hour Days?

I'm going to end this chapter by bad-mouthing a popular type of flexibility.

I mentioned in Chapter 2 that I don't like compressed workweeks, and now I'll explain why. The compressed workweek has some drawbacks that give flexibility a bad name, and in doing so it gives fuel to the polite skeptics. It also perpetuates a complete lack of understanding of human productivity.

Remember those pretty graphs from earlier in the chapter? The one for the *assumed productivity* in a compressed workweek would look very similar to Figures 5.3 and 5.4, where our human just keeps on being 100 percent productive for every minute of the day and week but now it's for ten hours a day, four days a week. There's no lull in productivity on any of those days except when they stop for lunch or finish for the day.

As we've already discussed, in real life people aren't even productive for an eight-hour workday, not even close (see Figures 5.5 and 5.6). So sticking *another* two hours of work onto those unproductive eight hours should hopefully sound completely, well, dumb.

In a ten-hour day, the negative effects of a rigid day are heightened:

- People will try to conserve even more energy in a longer day, so they'll spend even more time just going through the motions. Simply being *at work* for this long is hard work.

- People have even less time for the daily fulfillment of their human needs. With ten hours of work, plus one or two hours of commuting, only a few hours are left to do anything else, which will be mostly recovery time – eating something and sitting in front of the TV. This will hardly serve to refill their bucket.

- There's less incentive to be productive and a greater focus on time. In fact, there's a greater *dis*incentive to be productive: because this person is sacrificing so many hours *at work*, they feel that they don't need to achieve much more than being present in order to earn their money.

- People will spend more time each day in a state of stress, which will affect their productivity and their health. Long days of work, and the associated work-family conflict, are two of the worst workplace exposures for health. The human cost of this practice is expensive.

I can already hear the argument: the four days of toil are worth it for a three-day weekend. And, yes, that extra day of complete freedom has been a big reason for the popularity of the compressed week. *But*, by the time the long weekend arrives, the employee's needs are screaming. They've been swimming their laps without a breath.

They haven't had much exercise. They're sacrificing sleep to try to get other stuff done in the short amount of the day they have left. They haven't had much quality time with their family. They're not social with friends or the community on those workdays. And the list goes on.

Employees can't live sustainably during this workweek, so the long weekend becomes a binge of rest and recovery before they leap into the next exhausting set of four days. And much of that extra day off will be used for the errands and housework that couldn't be completed during the four highly rigid days of work.

The compressed workweek perfectly encapsulates the assumption that humans are robots, with infinite capacity to be productive. It truly is dumb. If you're looking to reduce the number of workdays as a form of flexibility (to provide more freedom to employees, reduce traffic, and reduce energy costs for buildings, for instance), simply chopping off that fifth day *without* adding those hours onto the rest of the week, and without reducing employees' overall pay, is a much better option. This is called *reduced hours with full pay*, and it will be explained in agonizing detail in the next chapter.

CHAPTER 6

Flexible Humans Are Productivity Monsters

I believe that drudgery and clock-watching are a terrible betrayal of that universal, inborn entrepreneurial spirit.

— Richard Branson[1]

IN THE LAST CHAPTER we started our journey decoupling time from human productivity, critical in our move toward greater flexibility in the workplace. We saw that people have productivity spikes and troughs, and the more we fulfill our human needs during the troughs, the more we refill our energy buckets, and the more impressive those spikes become.

This chapter builds on that theory of energy. In it we discuss further how the rigid workplace stifles true productivity, and how flexibility encourages it. We also cover two cool and effective concepts that I use to multiply results in my own work, and in the improvement projects I've led in various workplaces: Parkinson's Law and the Pareto Principle.

With greater flexibility, and hence a greater ability to be human, we're more able to see which activities are worthwhile, and we're more able to do those worthwhile activities with focus and greatness. I'll demonstrate this improvement with case studies of a seemingly radical type of flexibility: reduced hours with full pay – the five-hour day and the four-day week.

Parkinson's Law

In his 1957 book *Parkinson's Law*,[2] British naval historian C. Northcote Parkinson discusses the ways in which the number of civil servants employed in government tends to increase regardless of how much work needs to be done.

The underlying message of this book is as true now as it was over sixty years ago, maybe even truer in our age of limitless information: most work is unnecessary, bureaucratic rubbish, created to control and track people, and something with which to fill time and keep people busy. But the most important takeaway from the book is the famous opening line, which has since been called Parkinson's Law:

Work expands so as to fill the time available for its completion.

You'll know this law to be true if you've ever had an assignment at school. If you had two weeks to do the assignment, it would generally have taken two weeks to complete, even if it was something small or simple like a thousand-word essay. If that same assignment had a one-week deadline, that's how long it would have taken to complete. If you had to do it in two days, you would have been able to get it done in two days. And so on and so forth, until you reach the amount of time it would actually take to write the essay if you were focused and committed.

Most deadlines are arbitrary and are based on how long a previous, similar task took. As soon as a deadline is given, it creates an expectation for how long the work *needs to take, and then it takes that long.*

In the traditional workplace, if someone has eight hours in which to get their daily work done, it will generally take eight hours to get said work done, even if it could have been done in one hour.

Is this true? Does a day off reduce workers' results by 20 percent for the week? Usually no. They'll get everything done in four days that would normally take five.

So either something miraculous is happening and workers are able to conjure up superpowers during the days when they're working, or their work could actually be completed in a smaller window of time.

It's the second one.

Why Rigidity Stifles

Most work can be completed in a fraction of the time it normally takes. But the traditional workplace stifles true productivity, and it does so for the following reasons:

The Parkinson Effect

Something mysterious happens to our minds when we're given a time-frame in which to complete a task. The task will expand, like some alien blob from a 1940s horror movie, to completely fill the timeframe, like a gas expanding to fill a container.

If your teacher gave you a whole month to write the aforementioned thousand-word essay, a combination of things would happen.

First, you'd spend a lot of time thinking about doing it yet not actually doing it. "Thinking about," thy name is procrastination.

Second, the process of structuring, writing, and editing the essay would be slow and relaxed (or neglected and then rushed the night before, if your school days were anything like mine). It wouldn't be attacked with gusto and purpose from the moment you received the essay.

Last, the essay would end up being far more complex and intricate than it would need to be. At some point the law of diminishing returns would take over, and you would spend three out of the four weeks bumping your grade up from 95 percent to 96 percent (producing *no* difference in the result, as suggested by empirical tests regarding Parkinson's Law.)[3,4]

In a rigid workplace, the standard time spent at work – eight or more hours per day, five days per week – is the arbitrary timeframe in which to get our work done. *And we fill it up.*

Energy Constraints

In our normal workplaces, we put in forty, fifty, or sixty hours a week, plus the hours spent commuting, *regardless of our productivity level.* We feel this drain of humanity and energy to our core.

We have a finite amount of mental and physical energy, and during our long workdays and workweeks we conserve it by plodding. Just as you can't sprint a marathon, you can't focus 100 percent on your tasks and get them done quickly and effectively for an entire eight hours a day, forty or more hours a week.

Our minds and bodies know, on a Monday morning, that we're going to be at work for a long time, and that time won't change according to our level of productivity, so we settle into the minimum effort required to get things done in that time. We pad the day by adding filler, *welcoming and seeking distractions* from coworkers, Facebook, and various "emergencies" that pop up.

We slog through the hours after lunch until we can finally leave, lying to ourselves about how hard we're working, even though our energy buckets are empty and our productivity is close to zero by that point. As much as we can, we preserve our energy to survive another week.

No *Real* Incentive

In a traditional workplace there's not a lot of incentive to do more than needs to be done, in the time given.

If we knock out our weekly tasks in the first few hours of a Monday morning, what then? What would we do for the remaining several hours before we're allowed to go home?

We can't just pack up and go to the cinema – that's unspeakable. We can't go home and hang out with friends – that's unmentionable! We could find or create more work, I suppose, and knock that out of the park, but then what? And why? We may end up with a promotion, which is an incentive, but working at maximum intensity, day-in and day-out, even if it were possible, will more likely lead to a psychotic episode than a promotion.

The point is that in most workplaces there aren't any truly valuable incentives to do more than the minimum. Cinema tickets or shout-outs at weekly meetings are throw-away incentives, and very few individuals at a company truly care about the yearly targets and profits for shareholders – that's not why people work. People work to buy food, pay rent, and send their kids to school. People work to test themselves, to grow, to have a feeling of participation, to help others, to feel a sense of accomplishment, and to be respected.

They don't care about their managers' bonus checks. They care about what *they* get, the things that make an impact to *their* quality of life – more time with family, or less stress, or financial security. Those are *real* incentives, and rarely do workers get them.

Leaving at Four?

You've probably guessed what I'm going to suggest as a solution to this low productivity in rigid workplaces. Yes, flexibility combats this stifled productivity with the fervor and skill of a young Chuck Norris beating up a roomful of bad guys who kidnapped his girlfriend.

Let's look at how a specific type of flexibility – reducing hours in a day while keeping pay the same – does this, and we'll start small to warm up.

Lasandra, an accountant, usually works from eight thirty to five. She gets in at about eight twenty and leaves at about the same time as everyone else at her company, ten or fifteen minutes after five, in order to not seem too clock-watchy and desperate to leave (even though, ironically, it takes a lot of clock watching to time this exit correctly).

She works these hours regardless of her productivity. If she has a good, productive day, she leaves at five ten; if she has a God-awful day where she didn't manage to answer a single email or finish one calculation, and spent the entire day texting friends and trying to appear busy, she leaves at five-ten.

One day her boss announces that the company will soon be implementing an Early Minute Program: anyone who feels like they've finished their work for the day can go home as early as four.

They're doing this because the CEO has been considering experimenting with flexibility to try to reverse the company's low staff engagement levels and above-industry turnover rates, and he's recently read about other businesses having success with reduced hours with full pay.

This will be their flexibility taste test.

At first, Lasandra is skeptical and wonders how anyone would be able to go home a whole hour early. *There must be a reason we work eight hours a day,* she thinks. *Surely we'll get behind on our work, and then they'll just scrap the idea? I mean, I know I'm usually busy all day.*

A few weeks later it begins. It's a Monday morning. People joke with each other about the potential to leave early, and poor Mark, who consistently left at five on the dot in the old system, receives the predictable, "Oh, you'll definitely be using it" from coworkers.

But the morning banter is a little shorter than usual. People move off to their desks with a touch more purpose than on previous Mondays.

Lasandra sets her coffee down on her desk and makes a list to organize her day. She doesn't want to seem overeager to leave early, but she's determined to get out by about four thirty to hopefully avoid the worst of the traffic.

Nothing major is due today. She needs to process some data for the monthly report that will be compiled at the end of the week, and several invoices from suppliers need to be checked and filed. And, as usual, she'll receive random requests for work from various departments during the day.

With this knowledge, she sets to work. She blows through the supplier invoices before the first urgent (they're all urgent) request for data from someone in manufacturing, which she finds and sends quickly. She starts on the numbers for the monthly report at eleven. Normally at this time of day she'd be checking the news and waiting for lunch. Normally she might chat with Richard. Not today. She's imagining a smooth, fast drive home.

She processes the data with purpose. She enjoys going through the numbers and doing her own analyses (hence her choice of accountancy for a profession) and can often get lost in somewhat irrelevant, albeit interesting, Wikipedia pages (with some slight detours to Facebook to check the top posts). But she stays on task and finishes and sends the data for the presentation shortly after her lunch break.

Having finished everything on her list, she starts on some other work she wasn't meaning to do until later in the week. She also gives short turnaround times for the various other urgent requests that pop up.

To Lasandra's pleasant surprise, she has had an extremely productive day and could have left much earlier than four. Then four arrives, and no one leaves. Not straight away. No one wants to seem too eager.

At four ten, her boss, under orders from the CEO to lead by example, stands up and packs his things away. "Alright, I'm outta here, dudes and dudettes!" Everyone breathes a silent sigh of relief, and a few others prepare to leave as well, and get some ribbing from the biggest doubters of the program, the dedicated seat warmers.

Lasandra leaves at four fifteen. On her drive home, which, without the stop-and-start, bumper-to-bumper traffic, is twenty minutes quicker than usual, she wonders why they ever had to work till five in the first place. She wonders what she's going to do with this extra time when she gets home. And she wonders if they could shorten the day even further.

What happened? Was it magic? Did everyone end up working an extra hour the following day to catch up on that missed hour? Highly doubtful. If we go back to the reasons the traditional workplace stifles productivity, we can see how flexibility reversed the situation:

1. **The Parkinson Effect was reduced**
   Reducing the day by one hour reduced the arbitrary amount of time to get stuff done, so the opposite of the Parkinson Effect (known as Horstman's corollary) took place: instead of work expanding to fill the time available, it shrank to fit the shorter time.

This doesn't mean that the productive output diminished, it just means that it all fit into a smaller timeframe – the gas easily compressed into a smaller container. There was a little less distraction, a little more focus, et voilà!

2. **Energy was increased**

   In the example, since this was only the first day of the program, there wouldn't be much increase in energy. But in the following days and weeks, the extra hour a day would be used for more sleep, exercise, time with family, hobbies, etc., and this would help fill energy buckets and enable people to get stuff done during those shorter work hours, *and* to do it better.

   But on that first day, the knowledge that they could leave early led people to waste less time with the news, Facebook, and other distractions. They felt less of a need to preserve energy, so they were able to work faster and with more purpose.

3. **The incentive was real!**

   Being able to leave an hour early was a big and *real* incentive for people to get their work done. Lasandra's opportunity to avoid rush-hour traffic was a huge benefit (do I need to say any more about traffic?). She ended up with more than an hour of extra free time because, along with leaving early, her journey was also quicker than usual (she normally gets home after six, today she got home at four forty).

A small increase in flexibility – reducing the workday by a single hour – reduced waste, increased human energy, gave the employees an extra hour per day to put toward other human needs, and increased productivity by over 12 percent.[*]

What if we follow Lasandra's line of thought? What if we take it further?

"The Five-Hour Workday Is Here"

Like a gift from the heavens, this headline arrived on my news feed one morning while I was still in bed, while I was drafting this chapter. I clicked on it without high expectations. It would probably just be another

---

[*] This would result, at minimum, if everyone has produced the same in a thirty-five-hour week that they would in a forty-hour week; but this doesn't take into account extra productivity enhancements from increased engagement, improved health, fulfilment of buckets, etc.

political theorist trying to convince people that we don't need to work as much as we do, which is accurate, but usually empty and hopeful rather than practical and evidence-based.

It was so much more.

A financial services firm in Tasmania, Australia, called Collins SBA had trialled a five-hour workday in its offices for *eighteen months straight*. I sat bolt upright in bed and read on:

> After undergoing a lot of research – including examining similar models in countries like Sweden – the firm took a big risk and decided to undertake a three-month trial of a five-hour workday for all staff.
>
> According to the firm's operations director Claudia Parsons, the benefits were felt almost immediately. "Our staff produced the same workload, received the same pay, and had the same responsibilities. The idea was that if you could get all this done within a five-hour period, you were free to leave at 2:00.[5]

And it worked so well that they made the change permanent.

I LinkedIn-stalked the managing director of the firm and originator of the concept, Jonathan Elliot, straight away and messaged him for an interview before I'd had my morning coffee.

His wife had cancer. That's how it began.

While Louise was receiving treatment, Jonathan needed to drop down to part-time hours and leave work by about one or two in the afternoon each day so that he could support her and help look after their baby daughter.

He noticed that his family life improved with more time together, and he had much greater interaction with his daughter; when he worked full time, he could only put her to bed.

But he also noticed something completely unexpected: even though he was working far fewer hours, he was doing the same amount of actual work. He was still able to run the business, meet clients, complete reports, and everything else he used to do in a full day. Somehow all his work fit into a much smaller timeframe. This triggered a big question: Could this apply to everyone else in the business?

After he announced that they were going to trial shorter days with full pay, staff members were either excited by the prospect or worried that they wouldn't have enough time to get everything done. He even faced polite skeptics within his own ranks: *"Well, I struggle to get my work done at the moment in eight hours. Great idea, Jonno, but it's not going to work for me."*

But in the six weeks they had to prepare before the official three-month trial, employees experimented with their work and looked for ways to improve their efficiency. And they started to realize that it *would* be possible.

I asked Jonathan if he needed to bring in process-improvement consultants, or buy new equipment to streamline tasks, or make any other major changes to enable everyone to shrink their workday. The answer was no.

Everyone just worked with greater intensity. They frowned on anyone who interrupted their work for frivolous things. They reduced email waste, only sending messages when absolutely necessary. They took fewer breaks. And meetings were cut or reduced dramatically; staff became antsy when outsiders held meetings in the old-fashioned, meandering, and chit-chatty style.

Employees shared improvements they found with the rest of the team. Collaboration and teamwork grew organically out of everyone striving to achieve the same thing: to do their best work as quickly as possible so they could have more life! Process improvement was exciting – words never before uttered.

The business did eventually implement improvements based on what the workers found through searching for greater efficiencies, such as email management systems and faster ways to log into programs. But these weren't rocket science.

The effect of shorter hours for the business? Well, they certainly didn't lose three-eighths of their business by reducing their hours by that amount. They didn't lose any business at all. When told about the change, clients were enthusiastic about working with a progressive business that cared for its people (and the free publicity gained by the trial brought more prospects). Staff were flexible (there's that word) and available for urgent matters that came up when people were finished for the day.

The only thing the business lost, I kid you not, were employees who enjoyed working for eight hours and didn't want to change their processes or improve their work. But it gained high-caliber employees who were attracted by the idea of working for a company that valued and rewarded results over time worked, the sort of people who, when let loose to do their best, can achieve amazing things.

And sick leave fell by an average of 12 percent across the business, a considerable savings given that the average cost of sick days in Australia per employee per year is $3,608 (and potentially higher for more senior or critical positions).[6]

Then there were the benefits to the people and their surrounding communities, seen in the personal stories from employees and managers:

- Staff not only avoided heavy afternoon rush-hour traffic by leaving early, but many went to work earlier in the morning (arriving by about eight) and hence missed out on the morning jams as well. This reduced the commute times and stress of employees (and made the roads in Hobart just a bit less crowded).

- One employee saved enormous amounts of leave for a holiday for her anniversary because she hadn't had to use any during the year. She was living sustainably each day, so regular time off wasn't even necessary.

- Jonathan had much more time with his daughter. The time at home with her decreased his wife's burden and allowed greater connection with his family (see the benefits of *gender equality* described in Chapter 4).

- Other parents in the company said they were able to spend much more quality time with their kids, doing stuff they would normally only do on weekends.

- Staff reported partaking in more leisure activities and hobbies during the week, such as reading, playing sports, doing things outdoors, and cooking.

- No more TGIF! There was no longer a feeling of crossing the line on Friday afternoons at the company. The employees were living and working sustainably, so reaching the weekend wasn't worthy of celebration; they no longer even have celebratory drinks on Fridays.

After fifty minutes on the phone with Jonathan, I could hear the courteous impatience in his answers. This was already much longer than the short meetings to which he was now accustomed.

I thanked him kindly for his time and let him go.

Perpetual Goodness

Another company, this time in New Zealand, blew up the internet in 2018 with its trial of a four-day workweek. The director of this company, a man by the name of Andrew Barnes, was sitting on a flight from New Zealand to the United Kingdom when he happened to read an article about worker productivity that said that office workers, on average, were only truly productive for two to three hours a day.

"This can't be right," he thought. "Why am I paying people to be unproductive for close to twenty-five hours a week?"

Similar to what happened to Jonathan, this sparked an idea to try something different, to step out of what's normal and see what's possible. And similar to Jonathan, he also happened to have a business that he could use as a guinea pig. The company is Perpetual Guardian, an "estate planning, philanthropy and investment advisory" business in New Zealand with a staff of 240. Andrew would reduce everyone's week by one day while leaving pay unaffected, because he was "paying for productivity, not for time."

Instead of just giving this four-day week a go and seeing what happened, Andrew took his trial a step further and enlisted researchers from the University of Auckland and Auckland University of Technology to rigorously study and report on the eight-week trial, to hold it up to scientific scrutiny, and thus make it useful for other companies around the world (and to convince any skeptics, polite or otherwise, of its merit).

I visited Auckland to hear Andrew speak about the trial, and to ask way too many questions about process improvement and the fulfillment of human needs.

The first thing I liked about the trial was that staff members were treated like adults. Andrew told everyone what he wanted to achieve, and why, and then left it to each team to figure out how they were going to fit five days of work into four.

They were "empowered" and "trusted" to make their own decisions about their work and productivity, and the leaders and managers took a "coaching and supportive role as opposed to being directive."[7]

Before the trial, staff were encouraged to think about what productivity means, how they could ensure that their productivity wouldn't fall, and how they could serve their customers as well or better.

It turned out (unsurprisingly) that productivity was highly individual and based on roles and responsibilities. The improvements that people came up with were similar to those at Collins SBA with the five-hour day: less time on Facebook, more purpose and intent (e.g., less tolerance for interruptions), and various other small things that accumulate to make a big difference.

Because it was a team-based trial – the entire team either had the fifth day off or not, based on the team's productivity for the week, *not* the individual's performance – people were inspired to do their best to make sure they didn't let everyone else down. They collaborated heavily to find the best ways to work, together. As with Collins SBA, this wonderfully human trait of working together flourished with the new way of working and the lure of having more life outside of work.

The business itself still operated with the normal Monday-to-Friday structure. Each person took their day off in the way that best suited the team, to ensure that the employee benefited *and* the business could serve its customers fully.

If there were urgent requirements, staff were required to work the full five days, but they were happy to do so given the extra days off during other weeks. Also, no one would take their extra day off in a week that had a public holiday.

Researchers found the following:

Benefits to the business

- Profits increased: total revenue went up by 6 percent and profitability went up by 12.5 percent.[8] The billable hours completed by employees in four days were more than they had completed in five.[*] (They received quite a bit of free publicity because of media excitement.)

- Team engagement levels increased significantly, shown by comparing staff survey results from the year before the trial (2017) and post-trial (2018), in the following areas:[9]

  - Empowerment: 68 percent to 86 percent

  - Leadership: 64 percent to 82 percent

  - Work stimulation: 66 percent to 84 percent

---

[*] As with Collins SBA, this company, like a law firm or business consultancy, has objective measures for how much truly valuable work is done and billed for clients; and these billable hours by Perpetual fit easily into less overall time, thus spoiling arguments that reduced hours with full pay wouldn't work for lawyers or other professionals who charge by time increments.

- Organizational commitment: 68 percent to 88 percent
- Retention intention: 62 percent to 84 percent
- Absences (i.e., sick leave) decreased by 8 percent
- Service performance increased by 8.2 percent
- Creativity behaviors increased by 9.8 percent

Benefits to people (and broader society)

- Satisfaction levels changed in positive directions in the following areas (from pre-trial to post-trial scores):
  - *Work–life balance: 54 percent to 78 percent*
  - Stress: 45 percent to 38 percent
  - Life (overall view of life satisfaction): 74 percent to 79 percent
  - Health: 67 percent to 74 percent
  - Leisure: 63 percent to 74 percent
  - Community (how involved the employee feels with their local community): 66 percent to 73 percent
- A whole day less per week of commuting (20 percent reduction in driving for those who commute by car), with corresponding reductions in fuel use, emissions, stress, wasted time, etc.
- Anecdotally, employees spent more time with family during the week; they were also cooking, gardening, doing more housework (comment made by male employees), studying, completing projects around the home, swimming, running, and relaxing.

As with Collins SBA, the trial quickly became permanent practice after the results were determined. The employees and the managers have become more focused, not only on the personal and profit benefits, but on how this extra time and energy can be used to give back to the community (local and worldwide).

The thing that stood out to me during Andrew's presentation was that the total workload during the shorter week *felt smaller* to employees, even though they were completing *more actual work* in those four days.

This, to me, is fascinating. The only way I can explain this is to relate it to the second reason that rigidity stifles productivity: the conservation of energy. Just being *at work*, regardless of whether it's productive time or you're simply trying to pass the time, burns energy and *feels like work*.

It takes effort to get through the day, even during those times of mindlessly browsing the internet or texting friends. These unproductive things were easily cut in the new structure at Perpetual Guardian; time spent on the four most popular non-work-related websites was reduced 35 percent.

With less time *at work*, employees burned less energy (or put less effort into conserving their energy), and then used that energy to great effect!

Doing an academic study of the four-day week has turned the concept into a global movement, with businesses and national governments interested in its implications.

So many people contacted two of the leaders of the campaign, Andrew and Charlotte Lockhart of Perpetual Guardian, to ask about the practicalities of implementing a four-day week that they formed a nonprofit community called 4 Day Week Global. Check it out at 4dayweek.com, where there's a wealth of information and the original white paper.

Based on Perpetual's success, Microsoft ran a trial of a four-day week in its Japan offices. Called Work Life Choice Challenge 2019 Summer, the project entailed Microsoft Japan closing its offices on all five Fridays in August 2019, with employee pay remaining unaffected.[10]

The goal of the project was to improve the work-life balance of staff in three areas: 1) Self-growth and learning, 2) Private life and family care, and 3) Social participation and community contribution. The company paid for any expenses associated with these activities.

Microsoft supported the reduction in working time in a couple of simple ways: promoting thirty-minute meetings and getting employees to use online communication and collaboration more, with the company's own platform, Microsoft Teams, of course.

Again, incredible improvements were seen: staff productivity improved 40 percent compared to August of the previous year.

On top of the productivity gains, staff took 25 percent less time off during the trial, and electricity use was down 23 percent in the office. Employees also used 59 percent less paper, probably because of increased use of remote communication instead of paper. Unsurprisingly, 92 percent of the twenty-three hundred employees were satisfied with the shorter week.

Based on the success of this project, Microsoft again implemented a four-day week at the end of 2019, called the Work Life Challenge 2019 Winter, which focussed on rest, continued improvement of practices, and enjoyment of the challenge.

Flukes!

I know what some of you are thinking: these cases of reduced hours with full pay were flukes. The staff didn't have enough work to do in the first place. They were lazy and this just made them finally get some stuff done. *It sounds interesting, but, seriously, not for my business – we've got way too much to do.*

Hold on, my politely skeptical friends. Several times a year we *all* see proof of our ability to do more in less time. Whenever you've had a day off, how often have you had to spend an extra eight hours at work the following week to catch up on everything you missed?

Never. (Or hardly ever.)

The entire workforce doesn't automatically work eight hours more in the week following a public holiday. We don't all go home at eight every day for a week after a public holiday. This is all the hard proof we need that Parkinson's Law is indeed active in our work lives. This entire lost day is mysteriously absorbed by the surrounding days.

Think about what happens in those four days leading up to the public holiday. We get everything done in four days that we would normally do in five. We do that by working with a little more gusto. We do it by spending a little less time being distracted or distracting others. And the changes don't increase stress; they're barely perceptible.

It makes me laugh (with frustration) whenever the four-day workweek is discussed in the news. The concept is usually dismissed as insanity by opponents, who say that our economy will come crashing down or will drop by the corresponding loss in productive time, or by people who say that it wouldn't work in their business because their business is different.

But does the economy drop by some significant amount every time we have a day off? It might if we were robots and our productivity was linear. But, alas, we're not, and it's not.

After seeing the results of these case studies, and thinking about why these results occurred, I hope you agree that our productivity would actually increase with an extra day off each week, or fewer hours at work during the day, because we'll have extra time and energy to be humans, and humans are great for business.

If you're in doubt, just go back over the three reasons why rigidity stifles productivity, and consider how having less time at work reverses these effects:

- Reduction of the Parkinson Effect: when you have less time to work, you get your work done in a smaller window.

- You need to conserve less energy in your bucket, so you spend less time with Facebook and texting and work with more intent.

- You have a *real* incentive to get everything done so that you can truly enjoy that extra day off.

The Pareto Principle

I could probably end the chapter there, but there's another critical point about these cases that we need to delve into. When we talked about Lasandra, we made a massive assumption: *all of her work is important.* In our hypothetical example, Lasandra kept doing the same work she would normally do without examining the value or necessity of each task, and she found efficiencies just by working with more purpose and removing wasted time.

But what happens when she starts using that extra time and energy to question the *importance*, *relevance*, and *methods* of her work? She can improve it, or she can completely remove it!

And that's the most exciting aspect of the real-life case studies of Collins SBA, Perpetual Guardian, and Microsoft: people questioned the hell out of their own work practices and tasks.

They hunted down value like hungry productivity monsters.

Unlike robots, humans can pick and choose what will provide the biggest value for our efforts. Rather than just finding incremental efficiencies, we can multiply our results if we scrap the pointless work, do more truly valuable things, and find better ways to do those valuable things.

The Pareto Principle, also known as the 80/20 Rule, is a strangely universal phenomenon that states that not all things are equal. Or that things, for the most part, are *very unequal.*

In 1896, Italian economist Vilfredo Pareto found that 80 percent of the land in Italy was owned by 20 percent of the population. He carried out surveys in other countries and in other time periods and found similar 80/20 distributions. Since then, the 80/20 Rule has been used to great effect in a variety of other fields.[11]

Quality control in manufacturing makes use of the fact that 80 percent of defects usually stem from 20 percent of causes. So rather than putting resources into fixing *all* of the problems in a random manner, you can decrease defects by 80 percent by finding and targeting those few main problems.

Similarly, Microsoft found that by fixing 20 percent of the most-reported bugs, they could eliminate 80 percent of errors and crashes in their systems.

In healthcare, 20 percent of patients use 80 percent of the resources.

Twenty percent of criminals commit 80 percent of all crimes.

Twenty percent of motorists cause 80 percent of vehicle accidents.

When I was looking at my personal finances the other day, only a few of my items of spending (rent, fuel, and grocery shopping) accounted for nearly 80 percent of my total costs.

This unequal distribution isn't always 80 percent and 20 percent – it can be 85/15, 90/10, 99/1, and so on. Nor does it need to add up to 100 percent; e.g., 1 percent of the U.S. population controls 40 percent of the wealth in the country.[12] This principle of inequality holds true in almost any situation you could imagine: a few things will always be more important or significant than most of the others. A great definition comes from the author of *The 80/20 Principle,* by Richard Koch:

> The 80/20 Principle states that there is an inbuilt imbalance between causes and results, inputs and outputs, and effort and reward. Typically, causes, inputs, or effort divide into two categories:
> - The majority, that have little impact
> - A small minority, that have a major, dominant impact

Is the workplace immune to this principle? Of course not. *Much of* what we do, in any industry, is at best unimportant, and at worst unnecessary noise that gets in the way of the few truly valuable things.

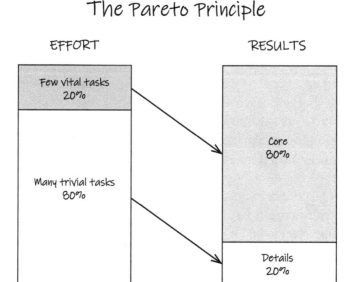

Figure 6.1. Illustration of the imbalance of the relative importance of causes/inputs/effort – i.e., 20 percent of the tasks (inputs) produce 80 percent of the overall results (outputs).

In my years as a process improvement specialist I've seen the same pattern, regardless of the industry or the type of work: there were critical processes, and there were the rest that needed to be thrown out or automated because it was sad and silly for humans to be spending any effort or time on them.

People waste time writing reports that no one reads (I've seen this countless times), fixing mistakes caused by others, moving things from one place to another and then back again, waiting around for other people to sign or complete something before they can start their own work, reading emails they don't need to read, sitting in long meetings, and a million other things that add no value to a business.

A heartbreaking story of this waste of human life on pointless tasks came up in an improvement project I managed at an insurance company. Jennifer (not her real name) spent two full days, every month, preparing two boxes of documents (some sort of invoices or reminders for corporate clients), and then she would wheel these boxes on a trolley to the opposite side of a labyrinthian building to another department to be sent out.

During the course of the project we found out what happens to those documents when they reached the other department. The paper in one of the boxes was immediately discarded, literally dumped into the recycle bin. The rest of the forms were sent to clients, who rarely used them; they went straight into the bin after going on a scenic journey through the postal system.

All of the time and energy (and paper) used for this task was waste. It added no value to anyone in the universe except the company's paper supplier. During the project, as we investigated these boxes of paper, Jennifer laughed in disbelief with the rest of us, but you could tell she was crying on the inside.

How much of her life had been spent needlessly sorting and stapling and folding and carting these redundant pieces of paper to the other side of the building? What else could she have been doing, either for her own life or to add value to the company?

That's one of the more ridiculous cases I witnessed, but these pointless or low-value tasks are everywhere! You just have to dig a little to discover them. You just have to ask a few different questions to figure out if something is worthwhile. Why do we do that? Why do we do it *that way*? Does the customer *really* need this?

What's worse is that this sort of no-value work is often *created* in rigid workplaces so that people have enough to do in the time that they're there! It may not be on purpose; it may be a legacy task from a previous era; but it's not right.

People often don't see the pointlessness of tasks because they're used to going through the motions, and they don't have the incentive or energy to question what they're doing.

Jonathan and Andrew, in the examples above, are doing the opposite. They're finding and creating value and eliminating waste. This is what I used to be paid to find; these employees found it themselves.

The Magical Supercomputer

We revere successful businesspeople and entrepreneurs, such as Steve Jobs, Richard Branson, and Elon Musk. They're often called geniuses for coming up with successful products and services and making billions of dollars.

But, apart from being smart and driven, and probably having a bit of luck, these people are just normal humans. There's nothing abnormally brilliant about them. To consider innovation and problem solving to be the domain of these and similar successful "geniuses" is to assume that only a few people can improve their work and the world around them.

But *everyone* is capable of innovation. It's natural for us to question the status quo and to use our curiosity to find better ways of doing things.

The most average human being on the planet has, contained in their cranium, the most sophisticated piece of computing hardware (yet) in existence. With this average human brain, which should be thought of as a *magical supercomputer*, they're capable of understanding language, the subtleties of behavior, economics, science and technology, and emotions. They can analyze and learn from the past and see into the distant future, and they can piece together patterns from disparate sources to come up with entirely new ideas.

The reason that we assume that most people can't do amazingly innovative things with their own work is that their supercomputers are usually exhausted: their energy buckets are empty, and they have no incentive to look for improvements. Sadly, many of our brilliant minds are stifled by "drudgery and clock-watching," as Richard Branson so keenly put it in the quote at the beginning of this chapter.

But the best ideas I saw in my projects didn't come from managers or from me, the specialists who are expected to have all the answers. They came from the people who did the work every day, when they finally had the time and space to think, and finally they were heard. In fact, many of those ideas had been there for years, sitting in the filing cabinets in their brains labelled "I tried to bring this up ages ago, but no one listened, and then I was too tired to care."

We can reverse this scenario. Well-rested and well-rounded people, who have the energy and incentive to use their magical supercomputers (and to *care* about using their magical supercomputers), are capable of astonishing things.

A Tiny Proviso

The four-day workweek, or five-hour workday, or any other fancy new length of week or day, are not the ultimate panaceas for work. These are just examples meant to challenge tradition, call our attention to the problems inherent in working too much, and show what's possible with seemingly crazy ideas regarding the ways in which we work.

But, if you recall the Flex Scale in Chapter 2, these initiatives only make it up to Level 3: Good Program. They're aspirational, but there's still some rigidity in their application.

Coming to work four days a week for eight hours a day, while better than five days of the same, is still somewhat rigid; it still doesn't take into account the natural and unpredictable fluctuations of human needs and productivity. And it still requires commuting to the office, and being in the office, every workday.

While people are hailing the four-day workweek as the next work revolution, we shouldn't assume that this is the best that we can do, or that it's the only way to get to higher levels of work-life balance and productivity. Let's not forget that there are many forms of flexibility, and that something like remote work, for example, also has amazing benefits, as I'll discuss in the next chapter.

Congratulations to Andrew and Jonathan and others who are helping to shift the needle in big ways. But it's important to remember that, a hundred years ago, the five-day workweek was heralded as a new utopia. There is always a touch of randomness in declaring how long a day or week of work should be.

CHAPTER 7

The Space to Choose

THE LAST COUPLE OF CHAPTERS WERE ABOUT TIME – how having freedom of time can produce enormous productivity benefits. Those benefits can then be used to promote (and accept) types of flexibility such as flexitime, part-time work, reduced hours with full pay, results-only work environments (ROWE), and so on.

This chapter is about location: remote work, or telecommuting, or working anywhere, or whatever other name you give this famous form of flexibility. It's about having the freedom to choose where to work, and how this can eliminate a vast amount of waste and distraction, allow for deeper flow states of productivity, save money on travelling and eating out, and various other good stuff. Remote work is its own special and amazing beast, but it also has its own challenges that need to be taken seriously, hence its own chapter.

But where do you even start when you talk about remote work? What hasn't been covered in the thousands of articles and books and podcasts on the topic? I'm going to take a human-centered perspective on the practice to show why it's in such high demand and why working away from the office boosts productivity and creativity.

I'll also talk about how to implement the practice and the environmental impacts (which are good). And at risk of attaining a new level of narcissism of which I didn't know I was capable, I'm going to talk about myself . . . again.

But first, some science.

Professor Nicholas
and His Surprising Experiment

Currently there is only one randomized, controlled trial that sought to determine what happens to productivity when people work remotely. This experiment took place at Ctrip.com International (now Trip.com Group), one of the largest travel agencies in China, with offices in Shanghai, Hong Kong, and Taiwan and a workforce of sixteen-thousand people.

The CEO and cofounder of the company, James Liang, as fortune would have it, was in a Stanford economics class taught by Nicholas Bloom. He told Bloom that his company was considering allowing its Shanghai employees to work from home, for two reasons: to reduce office space in Shanghai, where rental costs were skyrocketing, and to reduce attrition rates of workers who were getting priced out of living near the office and had long commutes.[1]

But "executives were worried that allowing employees to work at home, away from the supervision of their team leaders, would lead to a large increase in shirking."[2] They were uncertain about the effects that home working would have on productivity, wondering if it would offset the savings they might find in real-estate costs. That is, it was assumed that productivity would drop; the question was by how much.

Bloom, who I assume licked his lips at the opportunity to have access to such a large sample of remote workers and "exceptional access not only to data but also to Ctrip.com management's thinking about the experiment and its results,"[3] was more than happy to help. He and a team of researchers, including Liang, designed and ran the experiment.

Volunteers from two divisions put their names forward to work from home during the trial. Out of the 996 employees in these divisions, about half (503) volunteered. (In later interviews, it was found that those who *hadn't* volunteered anticipated high levels of isolation and loneliness, and that their chances of being promoted might decrease.)

Of the 503 volunteers, 249 met eligibility requirements (tenure of six months or more, broadband internet at home, appropriate workspace), and these people were randomly divided into the treatment (work at home) and control (remain in office) groups.

For nine months the treatment group worked from home four days per week and came into the office to work one day per week, while the control group worked all five days from the office.

The results were surprising, and good.

Since researchers measured productivity because the managers were worried about how much it would drop for the home workers, clearly no one was expecting the opposite to occur.

But over the course of the initial trial, the people who worked from home had a "13% performance increase, of which 9% was from working more minutes per shift (fewer breaks and sick days) and 4% from more calls per minute (attributed to a quieter and more convenient working environment)."[4]

This result doesn't include any of the elements of true productivity described in Chapter 5, such as the level of creativity and innovation of employees, the amount of rework (e.g., calling back to fix an error), efforts to improve work (e.g., by reducing time spent on administration), or the level of influence each worker had in improving other people's work. But even using the standard "how many calls were made per day" as the measure of productivity, this is impressive.

Even more impressive is the fact that it was obtained without any formal training on best-practice methods of working from home, without training for managers on how to manage a remote team, without any forethought about how to manage potential issues (such as feelings of isolation), without a gradual ramp-up to allow people to get used to working from home this many days per week, and without formal selection based on "ideal" traits of home workers. The only preparation for the trial was to set up the necessary equipment in employees' homes.

The study busted the myth about "bad" employees not being able to work remotely. Both the top fifty percent and bottom fifty percent of workers (based on pre-trial performance) who worked from home performed better, to a similar degree, during the trial.[5]

Another surprisingly good result was the difference in attrition rates between the control and treatment groups. During the trial, the group that remained in the office lost 35 percent of its employees (about standard for the business), and the work-from-home group lost 17 percent of theirs, 51 percent lower than the control group.[6]

Financially, the average savings for Ctrip.com for each remote worker was $1,900 per year. These savings comprised a $1,400 reduction in office and IT costs (the initial reason for the trial), $230 in productivity improvement, and $260 in reduced turnover costs.[7] This may not sound like a lot, but for context, the average yearly wage (including bonuses) for Ctrip.com employees at that time was about $3,840 per year.[8]

Due to these savings, Ctrip.com made the easy decision to roll out working from home for the entire company. The people who wanted to work from home but didn't get a chance during the trial could do so. And the people in the treatment group who wanted to come back to the office because they didn't like working from home could do just that.

The researchers continued to measure the productivity of workers after the company-wide implementation, and what they found was even more surprising. This time, the productivity of the home workers was *22 percent better* than that of workers in the office.[9] They were producing *an entire extra day's work per week* compared to the office workers.

Bloom attributed this improvement to a "learning and selection effect": people figured out for themselves whether they worked best in the office or home environment, and then chose that location. Working from home had the potential to provide higher levels of productivity than those found in the initial trial, but the people who didn't do well in that environment held back the overall gains in performance.

When people were allowed to choose, the full might of working remotely was unleashed. That's why this chapter is called "The Space to Choose": having the freedom to decide whether to use flexibility, and how to use it, is just as important as having access to flexibility in the first place.

For those wondering about the employees themselves: yes, they did benefit personally from working remotely!

Researchers found that workers in the treatment group were more satisfied with their jobs and the business (as demonstrated by the reduced attrition rate and surveys), they were healthier, they had more time with their families, and they saved a hell of a lot of money.

A survey of these home workers showed that:[10]

- Sixty-five percent got more sleep nightly.

- Fifty-five percent spent more time with family.

- Forty-four percent had more leisure time.

- The top reason why working from home was attractive to them was that they were able to change their lifestyle – eating, sleeping, shopping, etc. (29 percent gave this answer).

- Cutting their commute helped them save about 17 percent of their salaries (on direct commuting costs and saved time). Some employees also saved money on housing by moving further away from the office to cheaper locations.*

These numbers show that employee energy buckets were being filled in multiple ways. No wonder turnover and sick leave dropped so substantially for the treatment group! With more time, energy, and money to look after themselves, the sustainability of their daily lives increased dramatically.

There wasn't much preparation for this trial, which caused problems, the biggest of which was social isolation.

People who had been working five days a week in an office and commuting an average of eighty minutes per day obtained most of their social contact from the workplace. Their affection and participation needs mostly relied on coming into work. Then, suddenly, for the treatment group, this satisfier of social needs dropped to one day a week.

This was a huge shift, so of course "feeling lonely" was the most common negative comment from both the home workers (23 percent said this made home working less attractive) and those who chose not to participate in the trial and further rollouts. They anticipated and felt poverties of fundamental needs.

So, half the employees who initially worked from home changed their minds at the end of the trial and came back to the office. Two-thirds of the control group realized that they too would become lonely without the human contact provided by their workplace and decided to remain where they were.

In Part Three: How to Flex, I recommend ways that managers can structure and roll out a trial that uncovers and resolves issues such as this. For example, if managers and staff had collaborated in the development of the trial, the managers at Ctrip.com would have realized that four days working from home, without preparation or training, would result in isolation and loneliness; they might have decided that two or

---

* The average commuting time of employees was eighty minutes per day, with 21.3 percent having a commute time of over 120 minutes per day. On top of the health and financial benefits to employees, this also helped reduce Shanghai's traffic and pollution.

three days per week, or a gradual scale-up, would be better. This would have delayed the company's savings on office space, but in the long term they would have found more employees who were happy to work from home, and the employees would have handled the change better.

The lesson of this Ctrip.com experiment is more than "productivity improves with remote working." There are practical lessons, ones that I've experienced when I work remotely: balance is key, *and* it takes time to adapt. There are huge benefits to working remotely, but the potential drawbacks need to be taken seriously. I'll provide recommendations later in this chapter on how to reduce or avoid the negatives and boost the positives.

A Day in the Life

The Ctrip.com experiment showed us that improvements in productivity and job satisfaction are possible with remote work, even with the straightforward job of picking up a phone and talking to travel customers. But, as discussed in previous chapters, we can assume that the standard eight-hour shifts of the company's call-center operators weren't optimal for their productivity levels. The operators were assumed to be just as productive at nine as at four (linear productivity).

But because we know that productivity isn't linear, we know that the quality of their calls and the care-factor dropped off as the day progressed – they were still answering the phone and doing their job, but they were just going through the motions and not using their full productive and creative potential. What innovations and improvements could Ctrip.com be missing out on from its employees in this scenario?

Which brings us to this question: what happens when someone can combine freedom of location *and* freedom of time? When they can work from home or anywhere else, *and* structure their own workday? What if they have the space to choose exactly how they want to work?

I've been working with full flexibility for a few years now, and in that time, I've experimented with what works and what doesn't work (for me). I want to show what's possible when people are afforded this level of freedom, as well as some of the spectacular pitfalls that I've experienced.

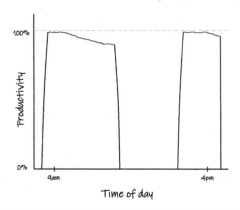

Human Productivity – Full Bucket

Figure 7.1. Example of the productivity of a human who works flexibly; in this case, they're working remotely *and* can choose when to do their work. This person is still expected to work seven to eight hours a day, but this isn't tracked or policed by management.

I'll start with the good stuff.

In Chapter 5, I talked about a person's productivity when they're afforded the flexibility of time and location – they could choose what times to work, and they could work mostly from home, so they could pretty much structure their day however they wanted to. That person (surprise, surprise) was me. The figure above shows, again, the average day.

I wake up at about six in the morning, do fifteen minutes of journaling, get some sunlight and exercise, come back home, shower, make coffee, then jump straight into my work by about eight.

I stay pretty much on task all morning, with a few short breaks to walk around, do some stretches, annoy my dog, or message a friend, until about one or two in the afternoon. I have a high level of productivity, which slowly drops off, or even slowly increases, over the morning.

I have a long, relaxing lunch. I make my own food, put on the TV, chill out, and eat. Then I have a short nap, or talk to a friend, or read, or play guitar, or meditate, or whatever else I feel like doing.

Then, if I need to, I'll do a couple more hours of work from about three or four in the afternoon. This is fully recharged work, which can sometimes be more productive and creative than my morning efforts.

Perhaps the smaller time block reduces the Parkinson's Law effect (work expands to fill the time available for completion) even further.

Perhaps the morning work followed by good recovery time allows my brain to fully awaken. Perhaps it's the melodic death metal music I put on at this time of day that erases any mental inhibitions.

This structure (which changes if it needs to, e.g., if I have to take my dog to the vet) works well *for me*. And even though the activities described above sound like a nightmare come true for managers who might be considering allowing employees to work remotely, I've produced superior work with this degree of flexibility, in both quality and quantity. And many other people who have this freedom of location attest to how much more productive and creative they are when they work remotely.

Not every day is like this, though. Some days I won't have that productive second wind in the afternoon. Some days it takes all morning to get into the right flow, and I might not be productive until a sudden burst between eleven and two. This can sometimes happen when depression pops up from nowhere, and I can't get out of bed till nine or ten. But then I'll have a long shower, make some coffee, and *still* end up having at least a few productive hours – the entire day is rarely lost.

That's life.

Life is different every day. Our energy levels are different every day.

Full flexibility, being able to structure and control our own workday, fits beautifully into the realities of life. It's a much more honest way of working and living than trying to push through eight or more hours and pretending to be busy when we can no longer push and our buckets are empty.

This way of working also puts the emphasis on real results. My publisher didn't care how many hours a day I worked on this book, only that another chapter was completed. My clients don't care if I'm editing their work at a café or in a coworking space or in my home office, only that their work is error-free and looking pretty by the time they need it. The actual product, the value I provide, is the only thing that matters.

This way of working also allows me to live sustainably.

But none of this happened straight away.

It Takes Time

It took a while for me to acclimate to working with full flexibility. In fact, I didn't really learn how to optimize its use, for my sustainable well-being and for maximum productivity, until one or two years after I started, and I'm still improving.

That was longer than it needed to take, but I had no idea what I was doing, having been thrust into that lifestyle to survive; everything I learned was through trial and error (and there were some big errors). But it was also a huge opportunity to experiment with what works and what doesn't – for me, but also for others.

One of my top recommendations, for anyone looking to implement remote work, or any type of flexibility, at their business: give it time to work properly. There are multiple reasons for this.

The first is *practicality*. It takes time to get used to new software or other technology (e.g., Zoom for videocalls to the rest of the team). It takes time to set up a home office and to ensure that distractions are minimized. It takes time to find a good coworking place or café for those days when you need to get out of the home office. It takes time to learn how to communicate, work together, and have effective meetings. And there are many other practicalities that take time to discover and address.

Another reason that getting used to flexible work takes time is that you need to *experiment* to find what works for optimum productivity and sustainable living. What sort of music helps you to concentrate? How long should time blocks be? How long should breaks be, and what should you do during a break? What's the best lighting? These are practicalities, but they're important on a personal level, too, because they determine how well flexibility works for each individual.

The last reason that the transition takes time, and why it took so long for me, is the personal work required to *become whole again*.

I'm about to reach beyond my grasp and get abstract, but something incredible happens with remote work and with flexibility in general. That extra freedom gives us the time, energy, and space to do those things that make us feel more whole as humans. But to use that time, energy, and space effectively, we need to become better at doing those things that make us whole humans. And we need to fix and develop ourselves in the process.

Don't reread that paragraph – let me give you a story instead.

Becoming Human

I've talked about how flexibility enabled me to get on top of my depression. But it took time. It was a multifaceted journey of healing, during which I fell over – a lot.

I used to cope (and still do on occasion) with depression and bad feelings by partaking in harmful addictions, the main ones being videogames, porn, fast food, and bingeing on Netflix.

No, these are not the worst addictions one can have, they're not alcohol, heroin, or gambling, but they have inflicted damage on my health and life in so many ways. They have been my escape from poverties and from pain.

When I left my old career and suddenly had full flexibility – all the freedom in the world – I went crazy. My addictions were unleashed. I'd spend a whole day playing videogames without blinking. I'd get through a whole series of whatever Netflix recommended in less than a week. And then I'd eat away the shame of wasting entire days on videogames and porn and TV by visiting the McDonald's or Subway situated about one hundred yards from home.

Like the Ctrip.com people, I was also extremely lonely after leaving the normal workplace, so I had an extra couple of poverties (affection and participation) that I was trying to cover up and escape from.

These addictions, and their underlying causes, were there before I had flexibility. But the burden of extra time and freedom allowed me to indulge in my problems in full, unadulterated, high-resolution glory.

Yet it was the extra time and freedom that made it possible for me to improve my life and outgrow my addictions. I could finally confront them and do something about the causes. And I started to fill my energy bucket in small ways:

- Walking my dog or exercising in the mornings
- Spending time in the sun and out in nature
- Seeing a therapist
- Cooking better food to make it harder to justify crappy takeaway
- Taking Latin dance classes
- Developing broader social circles and connecting more deeply with others
- Refocusing on passions, goals, and learning new things
- Meditating in the afternoons to re-center my mind
- Structuring my days to optimize these things and get my work done

My health, my well-being, my goals, my life all slowly started to look very different. Leaving behind addictions was only a side effect of my overall ascension to better levels of physical, mental, emotional, and spiritual health, levels that I'm sure I never would have attained while stuck in the normal workplace. I would have continued to go through the motions of life as a robot: unconscious, on autopilot, suffering without realizing what I was missing, without realizing that things could be different, never reaching my potential.

After exiting the rigid grind, I could finally heal and grow.

Full flexibility *required* me to become more human, but it also *enabled* me to become more human. It took time to shake off my old, robot self, but eventually I healed and became whole and alive.

Perhaps the employees at Ctrip.com *could* have comfortably worked from home four days a week, or even five, without encountering the effects of abject loneliness. But the trial should have started smaller and gradually scaled up.

The employees needed to learn how to work away from the office. They needed time to increase social connections outside of work (e.g., co-working spaces, volunteering, dance classes). They needed time to build greater connections with themselves by *being alone,* which doesn't necessarily equate to *loneliness.* Working from home takes practice, a focus on personal growth and fulfilling other needs, and the other good stuff I mentioned.

They needed time to become more whole and human.

In the traffic example in Chapter 4, I purposely gave Rahul only three days of working from home. If he had had more days to begin with, the benefits would have come at the cost of being socially isolated; he could have ended up in poverties of participation and affection, resulting in poor mental health and low engagement with his work.

But, with time, as Rahul got used to the practice and filled out his life in other ways, he could increase to four or five days of working remotely.

The same concept goes for non-imaginary people.

Recommendations for Remote Workers

I'll talk more about the manager's role in creating flexible work programs and trials in the next part of this book. But here are the most important recommendations for anyone who has the opportunity to work remotely.

There are entire books dedicated to working from home or working remotely,* but these are my rules for success (and avoidance of pain), based on my experience and research. Leaders can use this information to help develop ground rules and methods with their teams and as guidance for their own remote working practices.

1. **Create boundaries.** Without boundaries – temporal, physical, and mental – the lines between home and work can be blurred or erased completely. You may find yourself forever in work mode, never able to switch off and relax; conversely, you may always feel like you're in home mode, never able to fully switch on; or, more likely, you'll be in some purgatorial in-between, where you're not able to give your full self to anything. It's essential to create boundaries.

   I recommend the following:

   Temporal

   • Create and stick to routine start and finish times (but, of course, keep these flexible as required). This takes the effort out of deciding each day when to start and finish, and it makes it far easier to step in and out of work mode. There will be less need for daily efforts at discipline and motivation, because work is just what you do at that particular time.

   • Time block a certain number of hours for deep, concentrated work. Switch off notifications for social media and even for work-related emails and instant messages.

   • Have set times (before and after work, and during breaks) when you're not working or doing any work-related stuff. Ensure that your team and manager are aware of these times – after all, you've created ground rules and expectations with each other.

---

* A great book on this topic is *The Tracksuit Economy* by Emma Heuston.

Physical

- Have a dedicated office for work that's separate from living areas and bedrooms. Don't allow your business notes and folders and laptop to spill out into the dining room or living room – they don't belong there.

- Leave your office after work times, and don't use it too much during nonwork times, except for study or something similar. Otherwise, you'll quickly get sick of being in that space and sitting in that chair.

- Ensure that family members know that they're not supposed to be in your office during work hours (as much as you can, anyway, but with the coronavirus pandemic, I think we've became more used to seeing kids in the background of our workspace, which can be refreshing).

Mental

- Do something that helps define when your workday has ended. For example, I put on some heavy metal music, or take my dog for a walk, or go to my dance class, or start cooking, or some combination of these. (Most importantly, I leave my office!)

- If you're working regularly from home, make sure that you go and work somewhere that's *not* your home office at least one or two days a week. Find a café, shopping center (with a café), library, botanical garden, or coworking space, and work there for at least half the day. Many remote workers swear by the "coffee shop effect," where the buzz of activity around them and the difference in location give them creative and productive highs.[11] I've found this highly rejuvenating and energizing, and it helps me avoid cabin fever.

- Create and stick to times of the day and days of the week when you will and won't respond to messages. This can challenge people you work with who are used to being responded to all the time, but with clear boundaries and expectations, they'll get used to it quickly.

2. **Use your extra time and energy with purpose.** It's not hard to create a perfect Parkinson's Law trap for yourself when working from home. If you don't have a good reason to get your work done with gusto, you can end up using your entire day building up to writing that first sentence and doing so by going through every new YouTube video.

    What you need to do is incorporate *other* activities into your days. The best ones have set times and external accountability, such as activities that you do with someone else, or activities that you pay for, such as taking a class. Take a salsa class on Mondays at six, or see Michelle for morning coffee on Wednesday at ten, or read to the kids at the local school on Fridays at two.

    These activities give you things to look forward to outside of work, add structure to your week, and push you to work with purpose so that you have the freedom to do these things. They also help fill the energy bucket and shift you to a highly sustainable way of living!

3. **Experiment, and remember that it takes time.** Experiment with background sound – what works best for you (e.g., silence, classical music, ocean sounds), at what time, and for what type of work. Try out self-accountability and motivation methods, such as lists, diaries, project tracking software, and reminders. Find out how often you need to socialize, in what ways, and with whom. Determine the best times for meditation, exercise, hobbies, and/or napping. Try different types of lighting.

    I want to re-emphasise that *it takes time* to get this right. Be kind to yourself. Don't feel shame or guilt because you're not great at working remotely right away. And give yourself time to recover and heal from all that commuting and rigidity.

4. **Stick to the expectations and rules that you've agreed to.** It's still an unfortunate foible of remote work that trust from managers and colleagues needs to be earned. Employees need to demonstrate that they can get work done and communicate effectively so that no one needs to wonder whether they're going to reach deadlines or maintain productivity levels.

    Be like a cheerleader and hit your moves: execute everything that you said you would, such as meeting work deadlines, contacting people when necessary, and dialling in on time for meetings. Coworkers will see that you're reliable and fully capable of working remotely.

5. **Communicate, communicate, communicate.** This is also a reminder to myself, because I still suck at it. However much you think you should communicate with your manager and colleagues, it's probably not enough, especially if you haven't built up their trust in your dependability.

   Set reminders for yourself to call your boss at regular intervals, which can lengthen as trust builds. You can also have daily catch-ups with the team over Zoom or Skype. You can use Slack to ask quick questions or provide quick answers. And there's always email.

   Work out, as a team, rules about communication, and stick with them. And then communicate a little bit more. (I swear I'll try too.)

6. **Focus on health and well-being.** I've already harped on about health and well-being, but here we go again! Use this situation to your advantage, in as many ways as possible. Learn about your own health. Learn about your needs and the best ways to fill your bucket.

   Look into physical, mental, emotional, psychological, sexual, social, and spiritual aspects of health – truly holistic healing. This is a case of not knowing what you don't know until you know it, but when you start knowing, and start seeing unbelievable results, then you'll begin to understand what's possible.

Cutting the Commute

I sometimes like to jump in my car and drive to the city during peak hour. It's a sharp and tactile reminder of why I'm writing this book. Not many things in our daily lives take so much from us and give so little, and I like to be reminded of this needless pain that I've been fortunate enough to escape, at least for a while. If I can help even one person see the joy of removing traffic jams from their daily routine, then writing this book was worthwhile.

But something I forget to remember is that by driving much less, I've cut my personal carbon emissions significantly. This is something that many of us forget when we talk about remote work. But cutting one, or two, or any number of trips out of our weekly travel makes a significant difference to total emissions, and it's not a difficult or fancy way to fight climate change.

A report from the U.N. Environmental Programme (UNEP) found that motorized transport produces 23 percent of global carbon dioxide (CO_2) emissions, and it's the fastest-growing sector of greenhouse gas emissions. The report also said this sector "will be responsible for a third of CO_2 emissions by 2050 at current rates."[12]

Passenger vehicles account for more miles than any other vehicle types. Travel for work – getting to and from work and trips "for business purposes" – makes up a large percentage of these miles.[13]

Working remotely can make a significant impact on the distance we travel by car and consequently the emissions we produce. A 2012 congestion reduction program in Minnesota, called eWorkPlace, resulted in a significant reduction in the number of daily trips and distance travelled by employees when they worked remotely.

The program, which involved over four-thousand employees, assisted forty-eight businesses to set up and formalize their remote and flexible work initiatives. The results were measured by the University of Minnesota over a period of nine months.[14]

On average, participants worked from home 1.31 days per week.* On those days, employees took two fewer peak-hour trips, as you might expect when you eliminate the round trip to and from the office, and they saved 27.96 miles of travel compared to their in-office days. (Sixty-three percent of the respondents didn't leave home at all while telecommuting.)

In total, over the nine months, participants in the program saved 7.46 million vehicle miles of travel, and 8.14 million pounds of CO_2 emissions. The report adds that, of "tolls, transit, technology and telecommuting, [telecommuting] requires the least amount of infrastructure input" (i.e., it doesn't require any infrastructure).

The reason, I think, that we don't think much about the environmental benefits of working remotely is that they're not visible. In fact, they're

---

* Of interest to the Ctrip.com study earlier concerning what is the "ideal" number of days working from home, these employees felt that "to do their job the best" they would prefer to work remotely 2.29 days (on average) per week.

completely invisible. Not travelling is the absence of something. There's nothing to look at. It's not a sexy solution to reduce emissions. It's not a shiny new electric car from Tesla, or a row of wind turbines that you can point at and say, "Wow, that's definitely reducing emissions!"

When travel has been eliminated, the only thing to see are numbers and graphs of how many miles and how many tons of CO_2 have been avoided.

It's not exciting.

But the complete elimination of something is always more impressive than improvements in efficiency – it's a 100-percent improvement in efficiency, no matter how efficient your vehicle is! Leaving your car in the garage for an entire day while you work from home is a 100-percent reduction in distance travelled and CO_2 emissions emitted.

I don't know about you, but I find that pretty sexy.

Walking the Dog vs. Commuting

One thing that I'm eternally grateful for when I don't need to commute is that once a day, either in the morning or the afternoon, I get to take my dog, a beautiful black Labrador called Bear, for a walk in the bush near my home.

Not a rushed squeezing-in-a-quick-nighttime-walk-after-getting-home, but a relaxed one or two hours in the sun. This, above all my other weekly activities, keeps me centered and whole. It does so by filling every single compartment in my Bucket: affection (seeing Bear happily pursue a scent, eat grass, and do other doggy things), protection (exercise), understanding (observing trees, animals, and the world outside), participation (coming across other people walking their dogs or playing with their families – being part of the community), leisure (I leave my phone at home), creation (experiencing the beauty and chaos of sunsets, storms, green grass, a spider building its web), identity (letting go of ego and realizing, in the words of Tolkien, that I'm "only quite a little fellow in a wide world after all"),[15] freedom (I'm free to go wherever I choose, and so is Bear), and nature!

The times that we walk are usually when I'd be sitting in a car going to or from work in my previous rigid jobs, and that makes me feel even luckier. Table 7.2 on the next page offers a side-by-side comparison of my feelings about commuting vs. walking a dog.

I think the winner is clear.

Commuting	Walking the Dog
One of the top four stressful things we do every day	Reduces stress (except when picking up sloppy poop)
Lowers the chance of exercising for that day	Exercise!
Adds over a ton of CO_2 to the atmosphere per year	Prevents up to a ton or more of CO_2 from entering the atmosphere per year
Tailgating douchebags	Tail-wagging fur-kids
Chance of dying increases (e.g., by car accident)	Chance of being mindful and emotionally centered increases
Listening to honking, revving, and shouting	Listening to twittering, buzzing, and rustling

Table 7.2. Commuting vs. walking the dog – a side-by-side comparison.

Is that Flight Necessary?

We currently take over *four billion* individual passenger flights globally.[16]

It's become normal to fly.

It's so easy to just hop on a flight to the other side of the country, or even to other countries or continents, that we hardly even think about it. And we certainly don't think much about the damage it's doing to the planet. (Or, because we're only one of hundreds of passengers on a flight, we don't think that our individual contribution matters.)

From a macro view, the "global aviation industry produces 2% of all human-induced CO_2 emissions," and the industry is "responsible for 12% of CO_2 emissions from all transport sources (compared to 74% from road transport)."[17]

From the perspective of one traveller, you can blow all your CO_2 savings realized by not driving to work with just one flight. For example, on a standard domestic flight, 254 grams of CO_2-equivalent emissions* are produced per kilometer per passenger.[18] So on a round trip from Brisbane to Melbourne – 2,750 kilometers – 700 kilograms of CO_2 are produced *per passenger*.

For a North American frame of reference, "Take one round-trip flight between New York and California and you've generated about 20 percent of the greenhouse gases that your car emits over an entire year."[19]

---

* Includes both CO_2 emissions and "secondary effects" on global warming called "radiative forcing."

What does working remotely have to do with all this?

In the United States, for example, 29 percent of all flights are for business purposes.[20] The point to ponder here, which we've been forced to examine thoroughly during the coronavirus pandemic of 2020, is how many of those millions of flights for business purposes are truly required?

Is it possible that at least a portion of these trips are frivolous and unnecessary, like having a meeting that could have easily been done over our new friend Zoom (or put in an email), but we're simply too lazy to consider alternative means of conducting business?

And is it possible that a large portion of these business trips are in fact a way for people to boost their egos by being treated to all the trappings of interstate or international travel just because they can? One survey of millennials and their travel behavior found that most of them "found business travel to be a perk of the job, and 65% of them see it as a status symbol."[21]

I am speaking from experience. I remember feeling like a king during my first few business trips in my "normal" career. Free travel! Fancy hire car! Room service! Hotel room with two queen-size beds! Bragging rights: "Oh yeah, I've made it!"

But I also remember wondering, *how necessary was it for me to be there in person?* Did I *really* need to fly across one of the largest countries on the planet just to show my face, be shown a new machine, motivate people to work on a project, and chit chat with a plant manager over a coffee?

No. The answer is no.

Again, the coronavirus pandemic is helping us to realize with blistering speed that flying is often unnecessary. We can build connections, socialize with coworkers, close deals, work together on complex stuff, show our faces, and many other business-y things without producing 700 kilograms of CO_2 on a needless return flight. We can work remotely now with people anywhere on the planet.

With my current work, I have major clients I've not met in person once. But we've talked on the phone and had enough video calls and sent enough emails that we've developed deep and rich relationships – professionally and personally – and we've collaborated on huge projects. We've also made substantial business deals with each other without needing to meet face to face.

I'm not saying that we shouldn't fly at all. Travelling is in our blood, and the wonder of being able to see the other side of the world in less than a day can't be overstated. And yes, *some* business trips might be necessary. But when the airlines are running again, perhaps we can remember to use some moderation.

Someone might argue that their flight was going to happen whether they were on it or not, thus they're not responsible for the flight happening or the CO_2 emissions generated by that flight. But the more people fly, the more flights are needed. Each person takes up just one seat on a flight, but so does the person next to them, and the person next to them. Each of them has created the demand for that flight. And the more popular a flight becomes, the higher the chances that a new flight will be added to accommodate the demand.

Business travellers especially are more responsible than the average traveller for increases in demand because they tend to travel during peak times (mornings and evenings). At these times, planes are fuller, and one extra flyer has a greater chance of causing airlines to add a new flight to their schedule.

Choosing to work remotely – including, in this case, working from your local office – instead of flying for business reduces the demand for flights during these busy times. It does make a difference.

In Conclusion

Feeling in control over your own existence is one of the most valuable benefits of flexibility, and that fulfills one of our fundamental human needs: freedom. If you can give that to your people, they'll look after the rest of their needs, and your business, by themselves.

Whether people work from home, or from Jupiter, or long hours or short hours or part time, most of the benefits – all of the important ones – come from having the space – the freedom – to choose. That freedom includes being able to choose which types of flexibility to use and how they're used.

This is an important idea for the next part of the book, where we look at the practicalities of implementing flexible work programs. It's critically important to work closely with employees and managers to ensure that everyone feels ownership of the program, giving it the best chance of succeeding.

Part Three
HOW TO FLEX

CHAPTER 8

How *Not* To Flex

B Y THIS POINT YOU MIGHT FEEL INSPIRED because you know that flexibility can make employees feel like they've won the lottery, help reduce traffic jams and domestic violence, add years to people's lives, and increase profits for your business. You want to jump right in and get everyone at your organization flexing like Arnie at a Mr. Olympia contest.

STOP!

First, we have to talk about what *not* to do.

Because humans are humans and we're complicated beasts, and because many of us are scared of change and have biases and assumptions about other people, there are right ways and wrong ways to implement flexibility.

Issues often arise if managers or employees haven't worked out how to set ground rules and communicate them, if they don't have appropriate mindsets and attitudes about work, if there aren't technology solutions to enable easy communication and collaboration, and if there isn't an organizational focus on improvement and solving problems as they arise.

So, let's talk about why I have such a big issue with flexible work policies that don't have an overall strategy. Then I'll present a fun example of the wrong way to implement a flexibility program, which will illustrate why it's important to use rigor and, ironically, structure when putting it together.

Flexibility Policies Are Not Enough

In Chapter 2, I introduced the Flex Scale to show you how to measure the level of flexibility in your organization. If you remember, Policy (Level 1) was one level up from Rigid (Level 0). It was the first, nervous step toward flexibility, and it falls well below what businesses should be aspiring to.

Having a policy is helpful for outlining rules and processes for what flexibility looks like in the business, and who sorts out issues, and other things that are handy to have in an official document. But with nothing but a flexible work policy, flexibility usually remains the exception while rigidity maintains its place as normal.

And woe betide anyone brave enough to put their hand up for flexibility in a rigid world. Regardless of what's written in the official document, these people encounter judgment, jealousy, stigma, guilt, and pressure to over-perform and overwork, they're passed over for promotions, and they're often asked to find work elsewhere, either through convenient redundancies or overt pressure from management or colleagues. They're the annoying accommodation. The uncommitted slacker. The potential lawsuit. They're tolerated, like the drunk uncle at Christmas, until you can finally put them in a taxi to go home.

When a company grants a flexible work "arrangement" (honestly, I hate this word – it screams "temporary accommodation," like looking after your neighbor's cat while they go on a holiday to Fiji), it's often only for working moms. They were the people who fought the hardest for flexible work, and eventually they got it. But when they're the only people with access to flexibility, when a company merely has a policy, it comes with all the burdens outlined above.

Maja Paleka, a flexible-work strategist and consultant, calls this use of policy *tick-the-box branding*, which often accompanies proud statements from senior executives – "We have lots of moms, and even some dads, working flexibly so they can look after their kids." Maja summarized this effect on those working moms:

> [They] are working flexibly – either part time or leaving early – and are extremely grateful for the opportunity, but oh my goodness do they feel guilty. They know they have no choice – they have to use the opportunity, but they can feel the looks as they leave early to do pick up, and so they have learned how to

silently slink out the office so no one notices, or their leaving loudly is: "I have to go do pick up, but I will be online from 7 again!" They feel like they are working full time and then some to try to manage the perception that they are not pulling their weight, and they feel like no one notices this. But they still go back to feeling lucky.[1]

The other people who suffer with this sort of flexibility work policy are . . . everyone else.

An increasing number of dads are demanding to be actively involved with their children. Three-quarters of fathers in Australia wish they had additional leave for this reason,[2] and a survey in the United Kingdom found that almost 60 percent of fathers wanted their employers to provide more flexibility.[3]

Yet almost half of workers who request a change to their work structure are denied, and 27 percent of men in the Australian study who did access flexibility experienced discrimination, enough to scare other people away from asking.

Then there are the many other reasons for requiring flexibility, the biggest being the opportunity to be fully human. (This, however, is a far more philosophical discussion to have in a manager's office than talking about coming in late so you can drop kids at school. . . .)

Policies, by themselves, are really only beneficial to the guilt-ridden moms.

There are several reasons why policies that don't have an accompanying structured program or strategy for everyone can often cause more problems than they solve.

1. **Nothing changes.** Systems, technology, mindsets about work, and understanding of productivity and flexibility are all left relatively untouched. The few workers who try to work flexibly in a rigid workplace (and their managers, who are still managing a rigid workplace) are going to find the process challenging and annoying.

2. **Humans feel inequality.** If someone gets what others want, such as flexibility, those others feel envious, and that comes out in

unpleasant ways – comments about slacking off and missing out on promotions being just a couple of them.

The people who are working flexibly while others aren't also feel that inequality. They feel guilty for getting something that others have been denied, they feel undeserving and embarrassed, and then they overwork to make up for that feeling.

3. **There's no guarantee that anyone will be allowed to work flexibly.** It's still in the hands of each individual manager to approve or reject flexible work requests, and how they use that power depends on their ability, creativity, perception, and even their mood on the day.

   Recent legislation changes, however, in Australia and the United Kingdom, make it more difficult for employers to reject flexible work requests without good business cause. This challenges the subjectivity of the decision, but flexibility shouldn't be a fight between managers and workers (us versus them); it should be everyone working as a team, on the same side, trying to get work to work for everyone.

4. **The responsibility to ask for flexibility still lies with the employee, which can be terrifying.** When few others are working flexibly, the practice feels like the exception and not the rule.

   Anyone who walks gingerly into the boss's office to have the conversation about changing their work hours, days, or location will fear how they're perceived by their boss and their coworkers, and they'll worry that they're jeopardizing their career by just mentioning flexible work.

5. **The business and individuals without access to flexibility miss out on most of its benefits.** If only a few people are gaining these benefits, flexibility won't significantly benefit the business, and it certainly won't benefit the other workers.

6. **Flexibility needs to be earned.** With a policy rather than a strategy in place, people must work for the company for a while before they're allowed to request a flexible work arrangement.

   Rigid workplaces have the mindset that flexibility is a privilege, and that privilege can be accessed only after an employee puts in hard work and rigid hours as a rite of passage, after which they can be trusted to work flexibly. (Because new employees aren't given keys and passwords to the office and access to company systems and the carpark and the names of the best cafés in the area from their first day, right? *Right?*)

What this does, practically speaking, is lock people out of employment who *need* flexibility from day one, such as a single father who needs a job but can't afford full-time childcare, or someone with a cognitive disability who can work only a few hours a day before they need to rest, or someone with a physical disability who may struggle to get to the office every day, or someone who lives far away from the office and can't afford to move closer. Having to earn the privilege of flexibility is a form of discrimination that denies them and society of the advantages of their employment.

And businesses miss out on people who are skilled, educated, and motivated but need flexibility *before* they can take a job, not after a probation period. Huge, untapped talent pools are waiting!

Accommodating a lucky few isn't good flexibility. It will always be a special case and work-around that you have to deal with, and it won't be good for anyone.

But launching a proper flexibility program will make it normal. Solutions will be developed that will create productivity improvements you didn't know were possible. Developing a flexibility program *for all*, with purpose and strategy, is the way to go!

Implementing Flexibility Piecemeal Is Also Not Enough

At the risk of having you shout, "what the hell do you want from me?" I have to say that having a flexibility program for all is also not good enough if it's not done properly.

One of my favorite examples of a failed flexibility program was implemented (and subsequently trashed) by Richard Laermer at his New York firm RLM Public Relations. This program so perfectly embodies the wrong mindset about work flexibility that I'm envious that I couldn't create a fictional example as good if I tried.

In an article describing the project, Laermer writes:

> I began offering telecommuting as a perk a little over a year ago when I told everyone they could "phone it in" every Friday. I had

hoped home commuting would increase productivity and accommodate a more diverse work force – arguments often used
to justify the policy. But instead, my company's experiment ended up convincing me that telecommuting hurt my employees
(and my business) more than it helped.[4]

Every Friday, staff (not managers, or Laermer) were allowed to work
from home. That's it. This far into the book, I'd be disappointed if you
haven't already guessed how this turned out for everyone.

Yes, employees treated their Phone-it-in-Friday as a day off.

Some were hard to contact, and they rolled their eyes if they were
asked to come in on Fridays. One even said she couldn't meet with a client because she'd arranged a day at the Hamptons.

Laermer felt demotivated when there were fewer people in the office
(on that *one day* of the week), so he assumed motivation, hence productivity, was low for everyone. He didn't provide data to support this claim.

And then came the killer blow: the CFO felt sad that their "beautiful
office" was being wasted when it was nearly empty on Fridays. Thus, the
program was ended, leaving a bad taste in everyone's mouths and an angry article publicly denouncing flexibility, specifically remote work.

Let's list some of the ways this was doomed before it began.

1. From a needs-perspective, is it so unbelievable that people treated
   the day (FRI-DAY!) like a day off? After four days of rigidity – of
   commuting, being in an open-plan (albeit "beautiful") office with
   Laermer breathing down their necks, distractions, noise and bus-
   tle – one can imagine what the energy buckets of these employees
   looked like by the time Friday rolled around: Sahara-dry.

   With the sudden liberty afforded by not being under direct
   supervision for a day, of course the employees took the opportunity
   to fill their leisure, affection, freedom, and whichever other
   compartments in their buckets that were drained. Anyone would!

   I've been seeing this practice of one day of working from home
   being used more and more by businesses that claim to offer flexibility
   for their employees. It's not a good trend. It's another example of
   ticking the box – *look how flexible we are!*

   But, from a practical point of view, this practice doesn't give people
   the opportunity to learn how to optimize working from home or
   other locations. It remains an infrequent perk, or gift, which I'll

expand on in the next two points. Having one day of flexibility per week keeps the practice non-normal, the annoying exception to the rigid norm.

2. This perk was provided only to staff, not to managers or executives, which created an us-versus-them situation. Managers couldn't lead by example, and they didn't know what it was like for the employees to have Fridays away from the office. And they were likely jealous that they were left out.

   The managers were the police of the program rather than active collaborators. They weren't working with employees to find the best ways to make flexibility successful at the company, so any problems that arose remained problems. Those problems became excuses to end the practice as soon as possible.

3. There was clearly no strategy to this madness. Laermer himself called the remote day a perk, a reward, a gift. He didn't consider it to be a serious business strategy.

   If he had taken the idea seriously, staff would have been consulted on what sort of flexibility they needed (rather than just taking what they were given), and executives would have been on board instead of complaining about something as trivial as the lack of bodies in a building. There would have been supporting systems, ground rules, technology, data, and training (and other things detailed in the next couple of chapters) to ensure that people could be effective at their work regardless of where and when they did it.

Flexibility can't be an accommodation for the few who need it, nor can it be a perk or a reward, nor should it need to be earned.

Flexibility needs to be available to everyone, including managers (who, after all, are human too), and it needs to be a serious business strategy, fully supported throughout the organization.

You can't do it half-heartedly. You can't be sort of in. You have to be all in. Only then can you realize the beautiful benefits of flexibility, for people, for the world around us, *and* for business productivity. If you're not all in, you're going to miss out.

CHAPTER 9

The 3Ts of Flexibility

THIS CHAPTER SETS OUT THREE ELEMENTS that any flexibility program, big or small, *must have* to avoid situations like those discussed in the previous chapter.

These elements have a catchy name too: the 3Ts of Flexibility (which was a bit catchier when it started out as the 3Ts of Telecommuting, but that's *so 2017*).

The 3Ts are: The Talk, Training, and Trial. And, seriously, it doesn't matter if you have twenty-thousand staff and an entire department dedicated to rolling out this sort of thing, or it's just you and a partner working from a garage. In order to have a successful flexible work program, the 3Ts are non-negotiable.

The Talk

The biggest blunder made by the firm we discussed in the last chapter, with their phone-it-in-Fridays, was that they didn't have The Talk. The CEO just assumed that he knew what everyone wanted (one day of working from home, on a *Friday*), and that he knew the best way to give it to them, and then he just did it.

But, as in a romantic relationship, if you assume what the other person needs, and how they need it, and then you just do it, you're leaving yourself open to all sorts of problems. Proposing to someone who doesn't believe in marriage? Problem. Asking them if they're ready to have kids when they thought they were having a casual Tinder fling? Problem.

Like the talk you should have early in a relationship before you launch into a flexibility program at work, you need to have The Talk.

This talk doesn't have to be a symposium with PowerPoint presentations and Tim Cook or Elon Musk as guest speakers. It can be as simple as sitting down in a meeting room or at a café and having a chat about what flexibility means to everyone, including you.

This is a great opportunity to get to know people and what drives them personally. To find out what they love, where they feel that they have gaps in their lives, the ways work is either helping or hindering them in reaching their potential as humans, and where any non-fulfillment of needs might be getting in the way of their best work.

Make the meeting as non-judgmental as possible by showing your own vulnerability: talk about your kids, a novel you're writing, your badminton team, mental health problems, stress from driving every day, trouble with distractions at work, or whatever it might be. Talk about your fears about a potential flexibility program as well – what you're skeptical about, or what you worry may happen if people have more freedom and less oversight.

The meeting is a chance to find out what everyone knows about flexibility, and what they understand about productivity and how it's measured. It's a chance to find problems before they happen, which will be a big help when you start to implement the program.

Clearly this is a conversation that requires a balance of challenge and compassion. It requires a safe space in which people feel free to truly open up. It might be a good idea to have an expert, from inside or outside the company, to facilitate the meeting.

In contrast to the phone-it-in-Fridays debacle, Andrew Barnes successfully implemented a four-day workweek at Perpetual Guardian, and he did so by using The Talk.

He went into the meeting with an open mind and a blank whiteboard, and he didn't assume a thing, except that there might be room for improvement. He didn't assume what was best for his employees and managers. He didn't assume what they wanted or needed. He didn't assume he had all the answers. He *talked* to his employees. And he *listened*.

When it came to implementing the flexibility plan, Barnes gave every-one the opportunity to learn how to make it work. With this freedom, each team made the four-day week happen in their own, unique ways.

Another example of The Talk can be found in the most unlikely of places: A construction company called Mirvac implemented flexibility for all of its employees, including the construction workers.

We'll look further into this case study in Chapter 11 (The Forgotten), but I'll mention here that one important element of the program was that the business leaders let the employees tell them what they, as individuals, needed. The changes the business made were simple, but the program was hugely effective, and it was because the leaders kept their ears and minds open.

The Talk doesn't stop: it's a continuing conversation. It starts before the program is implemented, continues through the trial period, and is maintained well after flexibility is an embedded and normalized practice. Consistent communication is critical for the continued success of flex-ibility programs.

Training

The Talk can be incorporated into a training course or session, but it's important to ensure that the training travels both ways, that it's a con-structive conversation rather than a roomful of people being told what they should think.

People at a company will have different expectations and perceptions about work and flexibility, different values, different motivators, different pet peeves, and different biases.

Because humans are not robots, we have extremely subjective lenses through which we view the world. More often than not, we tend to stick to our perceptions and understandings until we're exposed to new ways of thinking.

After The Talk, during which people begin to understand each other's views and needs, formal training on flexibility helps them to understand the theories and implications of flexibility and its connections to health and well-being, equality, and the environment.

I recommend that the following topics be covered:

- What is flexibility? The different types, the benefits, and the poten-tial issues (this book is a good start!).

- Diversity and inclusion, unconscious biases, and discrimination, such as, for example, managers perceiving part-time work as lower in value than full-time work.

- Energy buckets and human needs, to create awareness that flexibility is needed for *so much more* than just caring obligations; it's about being more human.

- What is productivity? How does flexibility improve it? How is it measured? (Make sure that management doesn't consider "hours in front of the computer" as an appropriate measure for productivity – that useless measure can't live in the same world as flexibility.

- Continuous improvement, using tools such as Pareto Analysis, the Five Whys, and value-adding and non-value-adding processes. Analyzing root causes and avoiding quick fixes.

- Using technology appropriately, such as ensuring that communication programs aren't overused and can be turned off during particular times of the day.

- Setting ground rules as a team.

- Developing and running a flexibility trial.

The Talk and any related training should happen before you plan and run the flexibility trial.

Please, *please*, don't run multiple full-day training sessions. Humans can function at a high level for a limited amount of time per day or per week, so having a training session that goes for seven or eight hours, and/or a whole week, will ensure that people don't learn as well as they could. Those glazed-over eyes will deflect information like bullets off Captain America's shield. Keep it to a few hours, max, if you want information to be retained.

Trial

I've had a long, continuing debate with myself – screaming at myself in the mirror until we're both in tears – about whether the third T should be Trial or Trust, because trust is one of the most, if not *the* most, important aspects of implementing flexibility. Eventually I chose to call it Trial, because that's the best way to build trust. It's practical, it's the means to the ends, and it works.

I feel for frontline managers. They've got it rough. Pressures from above, pressures from below. Budgets to meet, drama to dispel, customers to please, quotas to fill, fires to extinguish, all while being coaches, mentors, and motivators. Articles telling them that managing is no longer enough: they have to lead, inspirationally, like Denzel Washington in the last ten minutes of *Remember the Titans*.

Then they have to deal with employees asking for more freedom and flexibility. Or their boss having new KPIs for diversity, well-being, engagement, and happiness. And then they're told that *they* need to work flexibly and leave the office early to make it easier for the employees to use flexibility and work fewer hours.

No wonder managers are resistant to flexibility!

But, in an inconvenient twist of fate, a crucial element of implementing a flexibility program is frontline managers encouraging *and* role-modelling its use. *Managers have to be the biggest advocates!*

So how do you turn the biggest skeptics into the biggest advocates?

Trial!

They have to see for themselves that this stuff works.

No amount of training and convincing will change someone's belief system. After years of doing something one way, people believe that it's the only way. It's not until they see the light for themselves that they'll believe in something new. And this is what happens time and time again to managers who resisted flexible work and then saw, in a trial, that it changed lives and turned employees into productivity monsters.

The three main case studies in Chapters 6 and 7 – Perpetual Guardian's four-day week, Collins SBA's five-hour day, and Ctrip.com's telecommuting program – all started as temporary trials. After seeing the results for themselves, managers were more than happy to permanently adopt the practices.

At Perpetual Guardian, for instance, Andrew Barnes said that "during the trial, managers changed their perception from not trusting their employees to do this [work a day less while maintaining productivity] to trusting them."

At Perpetual, and many other companies that have run flexible work trials, managers saw for themselves that productivity didn't drop when people had more freedom, so their fear was assuaged. In fact, the opposite occurred: people became more engaged with their work, more creative, more productive, more likely to collaborate with their team, and all those other wonderful things that managers work so hard to engender.

There may be extra work and hurdles to overcome when a company introduces flexibility, but it pays off and makes a manager's life easier overall. That's how you turn skeptics into advocates.

There are other benefits to running a trial before making flexibility a permanent practice. These include:

- A trial allows everyone – staff and managers, and even customers and clients if they're affected – time to adapt to this new way of working.

- Results of a trial can be measured: changes in productivity levels, absenteeism, turnover, engagement, health and well-being, customer satisfaction, errors or quality issues, and profitability. Measurement provides hard evidence for whether flexibility is successful or not from a business point of view.

- A trial gives people a risk-free period to try something they may have been concerned about asking for previously. Having a set time period for the trial, and having everyone involved, greatly increases the chance that people will try it and see the benefits themselves. (It's not always the managers who need convincing.)

- A trial allows problems with the program to be discovered and solved. Issues aren't an excuse to cut a trial short; they're opportunities to improve, learn, and optimize.

- A trial uncovers poor management and work practices that may have been hidden in a non-flexible work environment. For example, business success may have been measured by whether people arrived at eight thirty and left at five. With flexibility this measurement is meaningless, and success will need to be measured in more meaningful ways.

- A trial provides a blueprint for scaling up and rolling out flexibility to the rest of the organization if only certain departments or teams were part of the initial trial.

A trial should last a few months to allow employees to acclimate to the changes and allow potential problems and their solutions to become apparent. It may take a year or longer to see changes in people's health, but changes in health indicators (such as adequate sleep, subjective well-being, and exercise) will be seen sooner. Other results, such as changes in the number of sick leave days, productivity, employee engagement, and customer satisfaction, may be seen very quickly.

All staff must be involved in the development and implementation of the trial. You don't know what people want and need if you don't listen to them, so the trial won't fulfill their wants and needs, leading to issues and most likely failure.

I'll talk more about the specifics of structuring a trial in the context of the overall program in the next chapter.

A Warning About Technology

Technology was going to be one of the Ts, because technology and flexibility go hand in hand: improvements in technology enable working remotely, and as technology improves, more and more jobs will be able to leave the constraints of a single location.

But technology is a tricky friend, so instead of espousing its use with flexibility, or providing links to programs that will be quickly outdated, I decided it's best to provide a strong warning:

> On one hand, technology can be tool for working and collaborating from a distance, or for improving work processes in a team. On the other hand, it can be a tool for surveillance and micromanagement, and an even bigger disruptor of productive work than your loud colleague at the next desk.

As an example of the type of surveillance and micromanagement I'm talking about, a company called Time Doctor provides a service that

> tracks the websites and applications used while people are working. Managers can receive a report with this information. Managers can also receive a report listing potentially "poor-time-use" websites such as Facebook, and how long they were used.
>
> Time Doctor can also take screenshots of your employees' computers while they're working (this is an optional feature). The process of reviewing these screenshots is extremely quick for a management or HR person. The software also tracks keyboard

and mouse activity so you'll know if people are using their computers when they say they are.[1]

Services like this demonstrate a terrible distrust of employees. Part of the earlier description of work flexibility is that "people *want* to work"; it's up to you to foster that desire and not stomp it to death by starving employees of their freedom and privacy.

Some communication tools originally served to enhance productivity by allowing conversations and sharing of information and ideas with multiple people at once. But those tools can become time and energy traps of the highest degree.

Slack, for example, is an instant messaging service that's now used in many businesses. I've used it myself, and I've found that it does allow efficient communication from a distance, but damn! have I wasted some time on it. It becomes a drug. As with other social media *pings* or *bings* or *twangs*, Slack notifications provide a shot of dopamine straight to the brain, and it feels gooood. Each message not only distracts you from the task at hand, but it sets up a social reward feedback loop, further encouraging you to continue to send and receive messages from a colleague or friend.[2]

According to a study of large companies (five-hundred workers or more) by Time Is Ltd., the average employee sends more than two-hundred Slack messages per week, and power users belt out more than one thousand.[3] It was also found that at these large companies "there are more Slack channels than there are employees," meaning that each person has to keep track of multiple threads.

Instant messaging can also be a cheeky way of keeping tabs on employees when they're working remotely: *Why hasn't Naomi replied to the message I sent ten minutes ago? She hasn't even read it!* Don't fall into the trap of using surveillance methods – build a healthy relationship instead.

For the sake of people's health and well-being, businesses should encourage *less* time on phones and social media, even the professional platforms like LinkedIn and Slack.

If something *needs* to be said, pick up the phone and have a focused discussion. That's much better than sending twenty Slack messages over the course of a morning, each notification feeding an addiction and distracting from the task at hand. Or create time specifically for working together or building camaraderie, such as workshops or company lunches. Or put it in an email.

CHAPTER 10

A Short Guide to Rolling Out Flexibility

Disclaimer!

WHEN I FIRST SET OUT to write this book, I didn't plan on providing a step-by-step guide to rolling out flexibility. I thought it would be quite impossible given the complexities of each business and industry, the legalities and union issues in different regions, the level of pre-existing resistance or acceptance in each business, and a million other subtleties. I also didn't want to stifle the creativity of whoever will be facilitating flexibility programs.

But the 3Ts in the previous chapter aren't in any sort of coherent order, and each of the Ts occurs at multiple points throughout the process. (Plus, I can imagine the reviews from readers who will, rightfully, be dismayed if they get through all that hippie crap in the first half of the book only to *not* find a handy how-to list in the How to Flex section!)

So, I'm offering steps, in a logical order, to implement flexibility. And you, the implementer, with the help of other experts if you choose, can dance around with these to find what works for you and your business.

This is also an opportunity to go a little deeper into some of the elements of measurement, productivity, and overall strategy that didn't quite fit in the last chapter. You may not follow these steps exactly, but you'll gain an understanding of why each element is important, and how to go about doing it.

Flexibility Step by Step

Below are the ten steps that I recommend for the implementation of a flexible work program. They can also be used to improve an existing program or policy.

1. Talk to an expert.
2. Measure (part one).
3. Develop change management and communication plans.
4. Have The Talk with managers and the expert.
5. Have The Talk with managers and staff.
6. Develop the flexibility plan, and consider technology.
7. Measure (part two).
8. Start the trial, and actively fix stuff.
9. Measure (part three).
10. Scale up.

And here they are in more detail:

Step 1: Talk to an Expert

Develop an overall game plan right at the start. Not *all* the details – not what types of flexibility, or how much flexibility, or anything like that – since we still need to have a few of The Talks later because it's crucial to have everyone involved in the development of the plan.

The staff and managers need to feel that they're respected enough to be asked what they want and need. And if you rely on just a few people at the top to dictate the details, you'll make silly mistakes and miss out on incredible ideas.

It's fine to have initial ideas, just don't hold onto them too tightly.

Essentially, this is just you, maybe a couple others you can trust to remain quiet (for reasons given in the next step – nothing nefarious), and an expert (an external consultant or someone in the company who really knows their stuff about flexibility and human-centered work practices), who will come up with an overarching strategy for the implementation (guided by the above list, if you so choose). This is the rough outline of the strategy; we round it out later.

You'll talk not just about flexibility but about the bigger themes of health and well-being, the meaning of life and work, branding and perception considerations for the business, reasons for taking care of your people, your level of commitment, and any other topics that arise.

Step 2: Measure (Part One)

Measuring the results of your flexibility program instantly puts you ahead of the pack. A global study conducted by WorldatWork found that only three percent of businesses that provide flexible work practices "attempt to quantify the ROI of flexibility programs."[1]

Most businesses assume that flexibility won't have any benefits other than less complaining from those who need it most, and they simply bear the costs without looking for any direct or indirect financial returns.

It's a good (best) practice to look for these returns, not only to help spread and normalize flexibility in your own business, but to support and promote flexibility for other businesses around the world, since we need to keep this snowball growing.

This first step is to determine your baseline before anyone has a clue that you're thinking of increasing or introducing flexibility. This is because KPIs such as engagement, stress levels, work-life balance, workload, and sick leave can all change as soon as people are aware that flexibility is coming: they'll be happier just knowing that managers are thinking about it.[*]

What you want to measure can be a little, or it can be a lot.

The most important measurement is staff satisfaction, which is something a lot of companies measure regularly anyway, comprising such things as the level of job control, work-life conflict or balance, opportunities for development and promotion, engagement levels, satisfaction with a manager, and work demands.

Another is staff well-being[†] comprising such things as stress levels, mental health indicators, and amount of sleep and exercise per day. Incorporating the measurement of energy buckets will provide telling and specific measures for how much flexibility could improve the lives of employees and managers.

It might be necessary to create a business case at this step if the program needs to be approved by executives. You'll have enough high-level

---

[*] It may be a challenge to attain perfect baseline measurements, because rumors are known to break the laws of physics and travel faster than light, or you may only be considering flexibility after it has already started as a grass-roots movement within your company, but it's good to at least try.

[†] If the elements of well-being aren't routinely measured, you may want to measure them only after the program is announced so that people know why they're being measured and won't see the process as invasive.

information on sick days, turnover, engagement, errors and rework, compensation claims, real estate and energy costs, and so on to be able to quantify potential areas of cost reduction (as well as the human, societal, and environmental benefits, if the executives are into that sort of thing).

This is where you can also measure the Flex Scale and provide an initial rating for the company (Level 0: Rigid, Level 1: Policy, Level 2: Basic Program, Level 3: Good Program, Level 4: Ascended Program).

Step 3: Develop Change Management and Communication Plans

Change can be scary, especially in the workplace because people's livelihoods and identity are so closely connected to their jobs. So, for any major business change to be successful, people need to understand what's coming, why it's coming, how it will affect them, and what they'll need to do.

It's crucial that you develop strong change management and communication plans for your flexibility program. It's crucial that these plans are developed early and that they run through the entire process. A top recommendation from businesses that have implemented good flexibility programs is: *communicate, communicate, communicate* – consistently, on multiple platforms, and in interesting and easy-to-understand ways.

Change management and corporate communication are specialized skills, so I'm not going to delve any deeper into the practicalities involved. I recommend that you use a change management specialist or a flexibility expert who is well-versed in these areas.

Step 4: Have The Talk with Managers and the Expert

The Talk should involve training about flexibility (what it is, and what you're going to be doing together) *and* finding out from your managers how they feel about flexibility. This might be the rockiest step, since you'll be engaging with the biggest (and possibly not the politest) skeptics: frontline and middle managers.

The aim is not just to build managers' knowledge of flexibility and their capability to manage flexible teams, but to actively listen to team member concerns. You're looking to turn the biggest skeptics into the biggest champions of the program. The Talk, and a flexibility trial, can turn doubters into believers.

Managers need to know that they're in control, that they have a voice, that the hard work they've done to develop high-functioning teams is understood and appreciated, and that their jobs aren't on the line.

Use these discussions to figure out the practicalities of moving teams to the next step.

Step 5: Have The Talk with Managers and Staff

With managers now (hopefully) possessing the knowledge and skills they need to implement flexible work, they'll be in a position to hold The Talk with their employees. Or it may be more suitable to have the manager as part of the team while an expert facilitates the discussion and training. That's for you to decide.

The Talk can be done in various ways. It can consist of group discussions, one-on-one interviews, surveys, or a workshop at a resort. It would be best to use a combination of these. Discussions are great for getting to the root of issues, finding ideas for implementation, and building trust and communication; interviews and surveys can help to quantify what people and groups need. Anonymity may encourage people to speak more honestly.

Employees will likely be less resistant to the idea of flexibility than managers, since most of them would crawl through glass to have it. They won't need much convincing.

The most challenging part of this step is analyzing and synthesizing the data in order to figure out how to proceed with the program. Each department or team can figure this out for themselves. Or experts, who already have the tools and methods for gathering, analyzing, and reporting information, can provide recommendations.

The main thing is to make sure that everyone is involved and feels respected so that they have a feeling of ownership of the program.

Step 6: Develop the Flexibility Plan, and Consider Technology

We round out the strategy only after *everyone* in the company has put in their two cents. What will the trial look like? How long will it run? What software and hardware will be required (e.g., for remote working)? Who will do what? When will it happen? What changes will be needed in change management and communication plans? How do we brand the trial to make it catchy and relevant?

This is a good time to start testing and incorporating any new technology that will be used during the trial. This will allow people to get used to it and to iron out bugs.

Incorporating new technology may impact productivity before anyone is working flexibly (e.g., project management software that clarifies tasks and due dates). This may make it difficult to determine how much of the productivity improvement is due to the new technology and how much is due to the flexible work. But it's important for people to get used to the new programs and new ways of working as quickly as possible so that processes are in place before the flexibility program starts.

Other practical elements of the new ways of working should be identified and addressed as well. Things such as workplace health and safety are important – you need to have protections in place for the one-in-a-thousand chance of someone tripping over their cat in their home office.

Step 7: Measure (Part Two)

Before you begin the flexibility trial, it's good to remeasure everything you measured in Step 2. This allows you to separate the effects of people knowing that the program is coming from the effects of using flexibility (which will be measured later in Step 9). This will provide you with more scientifically rigorous data to determine the effects of flexibility.

For example, let's say that before the staff knows about the trial, average engagement levels are 3.2 on a scale of 0 to 5. After the staff is told that a trial is forthcoming, this might increase to 3.6. After they use flexibility for a few months this might increase again to 4.2. Or it could drop to 2.5, depending on the execution of the program.

This is the time to start specialized studies of the impacts of flexible work on things such as vehicle use if people are working remotely or are changing their travel patterns (miles travelled, carbon emissions), and health results and behaviors (amount of sleep, amount of exercise, time spent with family, time spent on leisure activities, and anything else that fills the bucket). The staff will have to be actively involved in gathering these measurements.

You can learn even more if you enlist academics or consultants to rigorously measure the effects of your flexibility program – on the individual, the business, and society. This can also boost publicity for your company, as happened with Perpetual Guardian's four-day week.

Step 8: Start the Trial, and Actively Fix Stuff

Begin the trial! Finally!

As issues come up, and they almost certainly will, proactively look for possible solutions as a team. And have patience. It may take time to get used to new ways of working and living, especially if the business is using more radical forms of flexibility such as remote work or reduced hours or days. Or it might all fall into place from the beginning.

Training on continuous improvement practices will come in handy. You and your team will learn structured and rigorous ways of quickly finding and measuring the size of issues, getting to the root causes of those issues, and developing solutions that permanently put them to bed.

If anyone is left out of the trial (e.g., a control group), they *may* be negatively affected by seeing others accessing flexibility while their structure remains the same. There could lead to an increase in sick leave and turnover and lower productivity. (In the Ctrip.com telecommuting trial, sick leave shot up significantly for the groups stuck in the office. They felt the inequality strongly.)

Be aware of why this is happening and don't penalize anyone for having a human reaction to the situation. Make sure that everyone understands that this is a trial period, and that the business aims to provide flexibility for *everyone* in the organization once the bugs are worked out.

Make sure that managers are walking the talk by discussing the trial often and role modelling their own use of flexibility, loudly and publicly.

Step 9: Measure (Part Three)

Those exciting measurements! Everything that you measured in Steps 2 and 7 will be measured again to determine the effects of the flexibility trial.

These measurements are taken either during the trial or near the end, depending on how long the trial is and how often you feel measurements are needed (without killing people with surveys).

You'll see, in big fat graphs, the results of all that hard work. (This is one of the best parts of having an expert: they can do all the number crunching and report writing! Unless you love Excel, in which case, go for it!)

Step 10: Scale Up and Celebrate

You've seen the results, what worked and what failed terribly. You've got ideas for what could be better. It's time to bring everyone else to the party.

Those people who saw everyone else become happier and healthier and freer felt left out. As we discussed earlier, they might be feeling less engaged and calling in sick more than usual.

After the trial, and after you've ironed out all the wrinkles, it's time to create a plan for the rest of the business and for long-term implementation. This will be an optimized blueprint for how flexibility will work.

This is also a good time to create overarching policies that officially state what flexibility looks like at the company – what new systems and processes are in place, who is responsible for keeping the flexibility program running, and how everyone in the company can use it effectively.

Then you can publicize your results to the broader business community to show that you care about your employees, and that you support work flexibility and human-centered business for everyone. You can do this through the news, in your job ads, on your careers website, and anywhere else that might be appropriate.

Recommended Homework

To get an idea for how varied the implementation of a flexibility program can be, I highly recommend reading several case studies presented by the New South Wales (NSW) government in Australia.[2]

These cases are from Qantas (international airline), Mirvac (construction), NSW Department of Premier and Cabinet, BHP (international resources and mining company), The Reserve Bank of Australia, and Women's Hospital (Victoria).

These studies show huge differences in the fine details, such as branding, types of flexibility used, how they ran trials, and how they got people involved. But they also show common themes that were covered in this section: strong and consistent communication (e.g., The Talk), involving all levels of staff, using trial periods to determine what works and what doesn't and to get people used to the practice, measuring before and after results, training for managers and employees, and the appropriate use of technology.

Look at what other businesses have done, consider the steps outlined in this chapter, and come up with something that you think will be brilliant for your business and your industry.

In the next chapter I'll discuss flexibility in industries where the practice hasn't commonly existed, where the human side of people has been, in many cases, forgotten.

CHAPTER 11

The Forgotten

"THIS IS ALL WELL AND GOOD for knowledge workers with their fancy jobs that they can do from anywhere at any time, Robert, but what about me? I'm a nurse. You think I can just take my patients home with me to look after between my naps and yoga classes? Or get all my checks done in three hours then bugger off for the rest of the day and hope no one dies?

"And what about pilots? Can't really work for a couple of hours then step out to the gym for a workout, can they? What about process workers? What about tradespeople? What about lawyers and other professionals who bill by the hour?

"None of these are really relevant to your *precious flexibility*, are they? But they probably need it more than anyone – they work the hardest and are the most stressed. They're the ones doing the real work. Are you just going to brush them under the carpet?"

Good questions – comments I've read and heard over the years personified in one sharp-witted, imaginary nurse. And no, I'm not going to brush you under a carpet or hide you in a cupboard. Actually, here's a whole chapter, just for you!

Flexibility is often seen as the realm of people who aren't constrained by location and time – those who could, if they were allowed, work from home, or work at flexible times throughout the day, like the knowledge workers I've already talked so much about. Those who don't have hungry customers or dying patients or bricks that need to be laid.

Part of the reason for that perception is because of the perception of flexibility itself: that there are only two useful types, remote work and flexitime. But if you go back to the first couple of chapters you'll remember that there are many different types of flexibility. And what matters most isn't the type, but how it's used. According to our description:

> Flexibility is meant to maximize the positive effects of work on an individual while reducing or eliminating the negative effects.

The concepts of *energy buckets*, *productivity*, *Parkinson's Law*, and the *Pareto Principle* are all relevant in any industry. Humans are humans are humans, regardless of their job title. We have greater life satisfaction and do better work the more our needs are taken care of, period.

With these somewhat more restrictive jobs, there just needs to be a little more innovation, a little more boldness, and a slightly different approach to the practicalities of getting the work done. I'll show you what I mean by discussing examples in three industries that have been mostly "forgotten" in conversations about flexibility: manufacturing, construction, and healthcare.

Flex and Bread (Manufacturing)

I'd been out of work for about six months. My second retrenchment had taken a heavy mental toll, and I was coping by following some dreams: trying my hand at writing a fantasy novel, learning computer-aided design, and attempting to escape the normal working world by playing with entrepreneurship (this is about the time of the Spectacular Men's Underwear Failure of 2014).

Unfortunately, these pursuits were all revenue negative, and I didn't have much of a nest egg to fall back on (I had no egg). I needed to get a haircut and get a real job. But no one was hiring. Well, no one was hiring me. Things were getting dire.

Then I went to the gym. I bumped into someone I'd met years earlier and we remembered each other enough to have a polite conversation. I told him I was looking for work; he told me he was recruiting for process workers. That afternoon I passed his company's physical tests and got a job that, over the next few months, opened my eyes (again) to how needlessly terrible the "normal" working world can be.

At this anonymous garlic bread factory, an ordinary day looked a little like:

3:40 am: Alarm rings. Drag myself out of bed, shower, eat a spoonful of coffee.

4:00 am: Start driving to factory, playing loud metal to stay conscious.

4:45 am: Get changed into whites with a bunch of other sleepy people.

4:50 am: Do some stretches, and warm up shoulders and knees and neck.

4:55 am: Walk into factory with other workers and line managers, wash hands, find a station (position next to a conveyor belt with a specific role).

5:00 am: Production starts. Start loading bread onto conveyors as fast as I can while rolling bread dollies into place with my feet because there's no time to turn around and position anything with your hands because if you stop loading bread for even a moment the people start shouting at you to "fucking hurry up" and that you're holding up the line.

5:30 am: Everyone moves one step around the equipment to a new position and I breathe a sigh of relief to be doing something a little different for the next half-hour. (The point of the rotations is to keep you from going insane, and to rest whichever body part was doing the most work at the last position.)

7:02 am: Packets of garlic bread are all over the floor. One of the wrapping machines is broken and has been breaking down continuously for the last hour, but no one is trying to fix it. Every time it breaks, the unsealed packages (with the bread inside) are thrown off the conveyors onto the floor by the process workers nearby. Production continues. The line manager speeds up the machines and tells us to work faster to catch up with the bread that we've lost, so now we're losing bread even faster (LOL).

7:35 am: The wrapping machine breaks badly enough for the line manager to finally stop production and call over the engineer. I help pick up a mountain of bread off the floor and fill up nearby bins.

9:00 am: Half-hour brunch. Eat as many carbs (garlic bread, obviously) as possible to try to restore energy for the next four hours of madness.

2:00 pm: Get changed into my own clothes. Drive home. Too exhausted to think. Sit and watch TV and try not to move body for the rest of the afternoon and night.

No one wanted to be there. Not the workers. Not the line managers. Not the production managers. And certainly not the plant manager, whom I never saw in the factory. A motley bunch of people were putting up with this weird hell until they could find something else to do; for those who had been there for five or ten or more years, this something else was proving elusive.

In the first couple of weeks, with my experience in process improvement and manufacturing, my mind raced with ways the company's operations could be improved.

I saw the amount of wasted food – mountains of bread were thrown in bins several times a day. Each roll sells for about seven dollars when it finally does make it to the shops.

I saw how many people they needed just to butter bread (too many).

I saw how often their machines broke down, and how little things, like conveyor barriers being set too close or too far apart, were leading to other, bigger issues further down the line. But no one had the time or incentive to permanently fix anything.

I saw safety issues with the way people needed to lift and swing large metal dollies onto other piles of dollies in a split second before the next loaves needed to be slid into place – shoulders and backs were in constant peril.

I saw a room full of people literally being used as robots, and treated with as much cold indifference, and it was hurting not just the people, but the production as well.

I had my list, and I started bringing the items up to the line managers.

"Okay, great," they'd say, looking at me with red, sallow eyes. "What do you want me to do about it?" They'd then rush off to the next circus of bread packets being ripped out of a misaligned wrapping machine.

I wasn't the only one with ideas. I spent a lot of time talking to the other workers while in the trenches of bread warfare and during our short lunch breaks. Many of them had incredible ideas for how things could be safer, more productive, and less wasteful. They told me they'd simply stopped bringing them up because the managers didn't care, or didn't have any money, or were too busy, or various other reasons why nothing changed.

And eventually, as people do, they'd adapted to this way of operating. They were going through the motions, like machines, while the magical supercomputers in their heads were going to waste, like smartphones being used as bricks.

It didn't take long for me to join the chorus of tired apathy, the bread zombies. I got used to it. I stopped suggesting improvements. I stopped talking to the line managers at all. Change management from the most junior of ranks wasn't something I was being paid enough to do. I was there to make my money for the day, try not to wreck my shoulders and back, and then go home.

After a few months I found my "something else" and joyfully called the company to say I wouldn't be returning the next day. But I think back on that time through the lens of flexibility and wonder how different that story could be.

The plant manager and production managers stood in front of all the workers and line managers in the lunchroom.

"Alright everyone," the plant manager starts. "We've called you in here because we have some interesting news. With the number of injuries we've been having, along with the recent product recalls and problems with quality, we've decided to try something a little different. And I want you to hear me out before anyone starts yelling. We're going to reduce the shifts by an hour. But . . ."

Protests and murmurs.

"But – hold on, hold on! Hear me out. We're going to reduce shift hours but pay you exactly the same as we normally do for an entire shift: every-one will be going home with the same pay per shift."

Shouts and cheers.

"Wait, I'm not done." He beckons for quiet with open hands. "This comes with a catch, and the main reason we're doing this: we want to shift our focus to doing things *right*, the first time, not the second time, or the third or fourth time. We're going to slow everything down, we're going to stop the lines when something goes wrong, and we're going to *get better* at what we do. We're going to *earn* that extra hour off by improving our productivity and safety.

"So what we're gonna do is this: we're not going to start immediately with an hour off. We're going to start the lines late, and spend time at the beginning of shifts looking for improvements, as a team. As our productivity improves, then we'll start reducing the day.

"And the goal is to get that down to an entire hour off, or maybe even more. As a team, we're going to look over our entire operation and find out what's causing the problems. We're going to fix those problems, *permanently*, and we're going to find ways to be innovative."

"I've got an idea for a new buttering knife for ya!" one of the workers shouts from the back of the room.

"Whoa, we've already got some *innovation* happening," one of the line managers laughs.

"Great!' says the plant manager. "Write it down and let's talk about it tomorrow."

The meeting ends and everyone walks out, skeptical but buzzing.

A week later, a new type of knife is put into use that allows double the bread to be buttered in one stroke, thus halving the number of people needed for buttering (which was originally about ten per line).

The unneeded butterers then go and help out on other parts of the operation, where people are stretched to capacity, and to look for issues, and to help find solutions, which they do. And each solution increases the efficiency of the whole operation, reducing safety issues and allowing the machines and the people to slow down (thus increasing safety and efficiency even further).

Everyone is being taught continuous improvement principles by the process engineer, whom they had never had a chance to talk to until this moment. These skills will benefit them now and in their future roles here and elsewhere.

Less and less bread is being thrown onto the floor, each roll getting the tender love and care it deserves. The plant is being shut down earlier and earlier as they easily make their production targets. People are hungry to improve.

The line managers are no longer running from problem to problem. They're spending time on each solution with the workers, adding their own ideas, which they had had years ago when they first started. Their eyes are brighter and less sallow.

The plant manager is out of his office and down on the floor, every day, amazed at the effects of the program and the number of smiles he sees across the plant.

Outside of work, the employees are sleeping more, they're more able to move and do activities after work, they're spending more time with their kids and with friends, and they're skipping into their shifts and back out again.

Fewer people are calling in "sick."

They pass the target of seven-hour shifts and get down to six hours within a month; they never look back.

Not a Pipe Dream

Flexibility has been rolled out, in real life, in the forgotten field of manufacturing, to great success – for both the workers and the businesses.

In *Utopia for Realists*, Rutger Bregman[*] provides historic examples of manufacturing companies reducing hours and/or days for their workers, and how these changes increased productivity, reduced accident rates, and created better lives for employees.

Back in 1930, W. K. Kellogg (the founder of Kellogg's, the ones who make Corn Flakes) introduced a six-hour workday for his employees at his factory in Battle Creek, Michigan. As described by Bregman: "It was an unmitigated success: Kellogg was able to hire an additional 300 employees and slashed the accident rate by 41 percent. Moreover, his employees became noticeably more productive." According to Kellogg himself, "The unit cost of production is so lowered that we can afford to pay as much for six hours as we formerly paid for eight."[1]

The employees themselves were also able to experience "real leisure." They spent more time with their families, and more time reading, gardening, and playing sports, and "churches and community centers were bursting at the seams with citizens who now had time to spend on civic life."

(The six-hour days gradually reverted back to eight-hour days by the 1980s for various reasons, including new management teams in the 1950s who "denigrated and feminized" shorter hours; gender issues of men's "status and control" being threatened by spending too much time in the home; and the cost of living increasing faster than wage growth,

---

[*] Bregman has seen the light and understands non-linear productivity: "Productivity and long work hours do not go hand in hand."

forcing people in low- to middle-income brackets to work longer hours to survive.)[2]

Another case described by Bregman occurred in 1974. British Prime Minister Edward Heath imposed a three-day workweek across the country to deal with energy reserve shortages (because of national unrest and miners going on strike).

This experiment lasted for three months. Instead of the predicted 50 percent drop in production across industry, such as steel producers, the final calculated fall in production – again, with two whole days less of work – *was six percent.*[3]

That is a drop in total production, but an incredible leap in productivity per unit time; one could argue that the benefit of two extra days of life for employees was worth that small loss in production.

(We can also assume that if the experiment ran longer, the workers, replete with full energy buckets, would have further increased overall productivity with greater engagement and ability to unleash their creativity.)

A more contemporary example of flexibility being embraced in this forgotten industry is Micron Manufacturing Co., a precision machining supplier based in, coincidentally, Michigan, in the town of Walker.

This is a family-owned company that employs thirty-nine people, and each of those thirty-nine people is treated like family. For starters, the owners trust their employees.

They trust them to figure out how to do their work (with the help of good processes) and to make their own decisions. And they trust them to schedule their own work hours and days.

According to the general manager, Dan Vermeesch, "[Employees] determine the days of the week they work, the hours of the day they work, the machines that they work on. It's up to them. There has to be a primary backup for everything, and they coordinate their schedules amongst themselves [and] the vacation times they take."[4]

This approach to building a strong company culture around trust, family, and good systems means that Micron doesn't need supervisor positions – the teams are "self-directed."

Yet even though visitors can't understand how they can run a business like this, considering it to be akin to the Wild West, Vermeesch says it works. They can retain and attract employees in a tight employment market, and they have multiple generations of people in leadership and worker positions. And considering that they've been around since 1952, they can't be going too far wrong.

Yet another case study of flexibility in a mechanized and standardized environment, although not manufacturing, is at the Toyota repair center in Gothenburg, Sweden, where the mechanics have been working a thirty-hour workweek (consisting of five six-hour days) since 2003.

The CEO of this repair center, Martin Banck, tells the story of their journey.[5]

It started, as these things often do, from a place of darkness and desperation.

Customers were having to wait four to five weeks to get their cars serviced, which was (obviously) resulting in customer dissatisfaction, which was resulting in staff being pressured to work faster and work longer hours, which was resulting in more mistakes (which take time and money to remedy – more on rework in the next section).

Their knee-jerk reaction was to consider expanding their operations: build bigger facilities and bring on more mechanics. But they also wondered if there couldn't be a better (and less expensive) way.

Toyota literally invented continuous improvement in the form that's been used by companies around the world. *The Toyota Way*, which means respect for people and Kaizen (a Japanese term for continuous improvement), has turned Toyota into the most recognized car brand in the world and one of the most successful companies in history. It's not surprising, then, that before buying a bigger workshop, the repair center decided to sit down and analyze its operations to see if it couldn't improve what it already had.

Looking at the center's current state, the managers noticed a lot of stopping and starting of work for the mechanics' numerous breaks, and there were slow-down and start-up periods for each of these breaks (including a lot of time the workers spent just washing all the grease off their hands).

They also found what I've been harping on about for most of the book: non-linear productivity, where the level of productivity changed throughout the day. This was most obvious in the last couple hours of the day, where mechanics were spending more time looking at the clock and looking forward to going home than concentrating on their work. (In fact, this was common throughout the day, as workers looked forward to, and began preparing for, each of the multiple breaks.)

Banck and his team decided to get rid of most of this stopping and starting, and they also decided to take care of their mechanics, who were clock-watching near the end of the day *for a reason*: it was hard and heavy work!

They did this by introducing six-hour workdays for the mechanics while still paying them for eight. They created two shifts for the week: a morning shift, from 6 am to 12:30 pm, and an afternoon shift, from 11:55 am to 6 pm, both with a half-hour break in the middle. The mechanics alternated between the morning and afternoon shifts each week.

(If you're following with the math, yes, the afternoon shift is only five hours and thirty-five minutes long. To bring the average week for everyone up to thirty hours, they added short shifts on both Saturday and Sunday, which they worked once every eight weeks.)

An immediate win from this change was that the center's open hours increased from eight hours a day to twelve, and they were now open on weekends, enabling customers to drop their cars off earlier and pick them up later (or on a day when they're not working). So they captured more business purely from being more convenient for customers who work during the day.

But these shorter operating times also propelled efficiency through the roof.

The production numbers from 2014 show that for the 45,248 hours that the mechanics worked, they billed for 63,641 hours. Or, on average, for every six hours of work, they were able to charge for 8.4 hours. This is an efficiency factor of 1.4.

Compare this with the industry average, where a mechanic would normally work eight hours and bill for 7.36 hours (an efficiency factor of 0.92). In simpler terms, each of the mechanics at this service center was finishing *more* work in six hours than a typical mechanic finishes in eight.

To get an idea for how on earth this is possible, we can revisit the productivity graphs from Chapter 5, and imagine what they might look like for a typical employee at the Gothenburg center. Figure 11.1 shows the

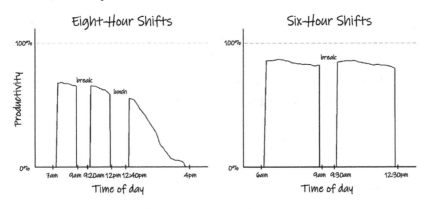

Figure 11.1. The productivity graphs showing the change from eight-hour days to six-hour days (this shows the morning shift; the afternoon shift went from 11:55 am to 6 pm, and would look very similar to the morning graph). As with the productivity graphs in other parts of the book, these are hypothetical and only meant for illustrative purposes.

productivity levels during the eight-hour days and then after the change to six-hour days, based on the descriptions by Banck and our theories from Part Two of this book.

Much of the stopping and starting was erased with the shorter shifts, since fewer breaks were needed. And true productivity levels (work goodness as opposed to going through the motions) were sustained at high levels for all the reasons outlined in Chapters 5 and 6: the Parkinson Effect was lessened, the workers' energy buckets were less drained so they weren't preserving their energy by working more slowly, and they had more incentive to work with purpose – to keep their six-hour shifts and the associated benefits.

The longer open hours and increased productivity saw the center's sales grow by 30 percent and 25 percent respectively in the first two years of implementation, and profits increase by 25 percent in each of those years.

Like Andrew Barnes with his four-day week, Martin Banck couldn't find any disadvantages with this new way of operating. The advantages, though, on top of the startling boost in productivity and business performance, were numerous:

- The company saved a butt-load of money by avoiding facility expansion and having to buy new equipment. (Later they did move into a new facility, but it was much smaller than their initial location due to the better utilization of space because of shorter shifts.)

- The company hired more people because of that better utilization of existing space in the workshop (and it was easy to attract those new employees).

- There has been very low employee turnover at the center. Everyone is living more sustainably, so they're happy and don't want to leave.

- Employees feel healthier (we can assume due to more time and energy to look after their health).

- Employees also have shorter commute times due to non-peak-hour travel to and from work.

- And yes, the customers have shorter wait times!

In Banck's words, "It's very simple, really: We work when we work, and then we have free time."

Nothing fancy. Nothing complex. Nothing technical.

It seems that even in heavily mechanized and standardized environments there's still room for humans to be human, and we'll see this again in the following industry.

Trade Up (Construction)

Here's a not-so-fun fact: men who work in construction kill themselves at 3.7 times the national average in the United Kingdom. The story is similar in the United States and Australia and, most likely, the rest of the world.[6,7,8]

Some might say it's because of the high representation of young men in the industry, those who are statistically more likely to take their lives anyway. Or that the industry attracts people with a propensity for mental health problems.

I have another theory: this industry is structured in a way that drains employees' energy buckets to the point where their lives are completely unsustainable, resulting in an obscene number of people feeling that life is simply not worth the pain. It uses humans as cheap, replaceable robots, who often end up escaping by self-destructing.

A study on suicide in the construction industry in Queensland, Australia, found that the following work elements caused issues in the personal and professional lives of workers.[9] We can look at these through the lens of fundamental human needs and see how they may be creating numerous poverties for people in the industry.

- **Long hours:** typically ten to twelve hours per day plus travel; sixty to seventy hours per week isn't uncommon. This causes poverties of almost all human needs, but specifically freedom, nature, affection (relationship issues are common due to exhaustion and time constraints), identity (becomes centered around work with little room for anything else), and leisure.

- **Low job security:** work comes and goes, and quite often there isn't any guarantee of continuing employment. This causes poverties of protection, affection (financial conflicts at home) and freedom (people can rarely feel relaxed and secure enough to be free from the burden of financial pressure).

- **Low job control:** hours and methods are usually set, with little room to choose when, where, or how to do the job. This causes poverties of freedom, understanding (it's difficult to feel mastery and to use your mind to its fullest), creation (little opportunity or an ability to develop creative solutions or innovations) and identity (similarly, it's difficult to feel proud and respected when you have little autonomy).

- **Male-dominated industry:** endorses drinking, drugs, bullying, and toughness and makes it harder to seek help or show emotions, especially with less exposure to women. This causes poverties of affection, participation, identity, and protection.

- **High stress:** pressure to get the job done quickly, the requirement to be the breadwinner due to long hours that hinder their partners' ability to work (if they have a family), and the other work elements already mentioned, which all cause increased levels of stress. This causes poverties of *all needs* (drains the entire bucket).[*]

Taking these elements into account, Figure 11.2 is an example of what a construction worker's energy bucket may look like. Freedom, affection,

---

[*] As an interesting exercise, I recommend comparing this list to Jeffrey Pfeffer's ten toxic workplace exposures in the Health section of Chapter 4. See how many you can tick off.

and leisure would be the hardest hit of the needs. It would be safe to say these are rarely if ever filled for a construction worker.

Similarly, protection, creation, and understanding would be crying out.

The needs for nature (being that construction workers are often outside in the sun), participation, and identity (since they work with other people and have some fun conversations during the day), would be at least partially filled (albeit still quite drained for the reasons in the list above).

Subsistence would likely be the only need that has a chance to be filled, because there's usually enough money, albeit from an unsecure source, to be made in this industry to look after food, medical, and housing requirements.

Remember what Max-Neef said about needs? If *any* fundamental human need is not adequately satisfied, a human poverty will be revealed, and *each poverty generates pathologies*. Well, here we have a poverty of at least six needs, and a partial poverty of another three. In other words, this bucket, and the corresponding well-being of the person, is fucking dry!

Suicide is the tip of the iceberg for the resultant pathologies. For starters, for each recorded suicide as many as 30 people attempt to take their lives, resulting in injury and trauma for them and their families.[10] And what about the plethora of other less-newsworthy issues generated by these empty buckets?

What about depression and anxiety, relationship breakdowns, drug and alcohol addiction, gambling addiction, violence, poor health? These issues are all systemic in the industry, and they're all directly related to how little these people are enabled to look after their human needs.

If possible, this story is about to get worse.

As highlighted in other parts of this book, the high social cost of rigidity seems to come at no value whatsoever to the businesses that employ these people. Let me rephrase that. It comes at a *high cost* to these businesses. These businesses *pay extra* to operate in a way that empties buckets and destroys lives.

One of the major and highly avoidable costs borne by construction businesses operating in this way is called *rework*, otherwise known as doing a job more than once because it wasn't done correctly the first time –

Estimated Fulfillment of Each Need – Construction Worker

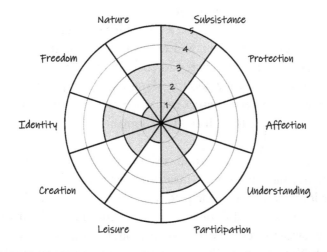

Figure 11.2. A bucket chart of needs fulfillment for a typical construction worker. This is a bird's-eye view of the energy bucket presented in Chapter 5, quantitatively showing how satisfied (filled) each need (compartment) is, where 1 = not satisfied at all (empty) and 5 = fully satisfied (full).

things like installing a door on the wrong side of a building, cutting a steel angle to the wrong length, using the wrong paint, leaving a roof with gaps, or redoing an entire section of a building because it's not what the customer wanted.

The cost of rework in the construction industry is immense. One report on Australian businesses found that rework cost 12.3 percent of the total contract value for the projects investigated.[11] That overall cost comprised 6.4 percent from direct costs (rectifying the issue, e.g., rebuilding a wall) and 5.9 percent from indirect costs (e.g., loss of time, hiring specialists to redesign a solution).

The report also found that these extra costs of rework are either underestimated or hidden because they're deemed acceptable and normal parts of construction operations, and "managers tend to bury the errors on site without determining the causes and effects of those errors."

Another paper that analyzed 19,605 rework events from 346 construction projects found that errors and their rectification reduced the profits from these projects by 28 percent.[12]

In a country like Australia, or the United States, or the United Kingdom, this amount of rework costs billions for the industry and the economy. It also drastically increases production times, thus producing even greater stress for supervisors and workers to rush and work long hours (consequently producing more issues).

And that's where these issues lie. It's become normal for people in construction to work long hours, and to rush to meet extreme deadlines. This reduces the time and energy to check things and confirm quality before moving on, and for good working relationships to develop between designers and supervisors and workers, which further increases pressure and the need to rush and work long hours. It's a nasty cycle, but it's expected.

And instead of the classic woodworking wisdom "measure twice, cut once," the normal situation is "measure poorly, cut, find out it doesn't fit, swear loudly and throw the piece away, walk all the way back to the saw, remeasure, cut again"; or worse, "the client didn't ask for this type of window, swear loudly, take the window out and throw it away, call the engineer back to redesign the wall so that the new type of window fits, and then wait a week for it to arrive and be reinstalled."

It's Simple

Flexibility can change this entire industry to one that not only looks after its people and allows them to live sustainably but also reaches significantly higher levels of efficiency and good business practices.

And it doesn't need to be complicated.

Major solutions to rework issues (and other problems in the industry, such as general wastage of materials and time not associated with rework) are mainly based on improving the *humanity* of the work and how that improvement subsequently influences the technical results.

For example, a study from Nigeria on the cost of rework in the industry found that the biggest solutions to the causes of rework were team building, improved communication, greater commitment from managers and supervisors, and greater collaboration between trades workers and designers (which would, for example, enable trades workers to pick up practical issues during the design phase, before materials are ordered and work has started).[13]

And the Australian report from above stated that better quality assurance – taking the time to check and record the quality of work before moving on to the next step, and analyzing errors – was paramount in reducing rework.

These solutions come from workers and managers being *wholly human*: being engaged with their work, caring about and working effectively with other people (including clients), looking for problems and using the full potential of their minds to permanently solve them, and having managers who are committed to building the skills and abilities of the workers.

A prominent construction company in Australia, Mirvac, is blazing a trail in the industry by showing that it's possible and profitable to treat their employees as humans.

They're doing this by providing flexibility en masse to *all* employees, including construction crews. And, importantly, they're showing that it can be simple.

Mirvac wanted to help more employees work with flexibility to increase engagement among the workforce, improve diversity and inclusion (and reap the associated benefits of improved business decisions), and "lead in agile workplaces" (they create contemporary and sustainable environments for other companies, and wanted to lead this philosophy by example).[14]

Being a construction company, the biggest challenge in implementation was to convince the construction workers and supervisors (85 percent of whom were male) that they *needed* and *deserved* flexibility, and that it was even possible for them to use it. Many of these employees had traditional views about the workplace, thinking that flexibility was only for "working mums."

To help change these attitudes and encourage a greater uptake of flexibility among construction workers (and to normalize it across the whole business), Mirvac launched a strategic program called Building Balance. Part of that program turned out to be a masterclass in rolling out flexibility in this type of industry. It was called My Simple Thing, and it looked like this:

> This initiative asked construction employees to think of one simple change they could incorporate into their work lives to improve their work-life quality, such as starting later to drop

off the kids [to] school or finishing earlier one day per week for sports training. This simple idea, without significant infrastructure to support it, snowballed and drove significant change.[15]

It wasn't just simplicity that made My Simple Thing successful. They incorporated other crucial elements into their program that I've already described in previous chapters.

They used The Talk. Teams discussed among themselves how the hell they could make this work, what their "simple things" were, and what they meant to them, and then they worked out the practicalities, without any systems or policies in place. (Ah, to be a fly on the wall when these blokes were figuring out how to help each other have more life outside of work!)

Leaders were role models. The CEO, Susan Lloyd-Hurwitz, was an unwavering supporter of the program, and even asked her "entire executive team to report back in two weeks with their My Simple Thing and how they were making it work." Other leaders were highly visible with their use of flexibility, including the head of construction, who "undertook a roadshow" to share his simple thing with other employees and what it meant for his personal and professional life.

They created a flexible working policy (as part of their overall program and strategy) and a charter to emphasise respect for each other and a focus on productivity over "time spent working." These helped to formalize the program and provide a basis for what the company was trying to achieve.

An innovative training program was rolled out to help both employees and managers have the conversations about flexibility "that ensured both individual and business needs were being achieved." This included "hiring actors to play out typical scenarios where employees request flexible working arrangements."

If you revisit the Flex Scale in Chapter 2, you'll see that Mirvac's program easily sits at Level 3: Good Program, the highest you can get in an industry where people need to be present. Although in this case I would be tempted to call it a great program! The results speak loudly:

- The use of flexible working by construction employees increased by 181 percent, from 27 percent in 2015 to 76 percent in 2017.

- These employees reported a better balance between their work and life.

- Men have opened up more about their responsibilities as carers and parents, thus helping to shift traditional perceptions about gender in the business.

- Mirvac's flexible working program is now one of the top four reasons new recruits are attracted to the company.

- Employee engagement is at 90 percent (when it was measured in 2018), which is "above the top global norm for their survey provider." This high level of engagement improves multiple performance measures, as described in Chapter 5, such as productivity, absenteeism, turnover, theft, safety incidents, quality defects, and overall profits.

- Indeed, productivity improved at the company. Even with the high percentage of people accessing flexibility (including reduced hours, reduced days, part-time work, etc.), they found that the overall output from the workforce didn't drop.

Sustainability and Scheduling

It's true that construction companies need to compete with others in the tendering process, and the speed at which a project can be completed is an important selling point – clients don't want to be sitting around waiting while they're missing out on rent or expanding their business or whatever the structure is going to be used for.

This has been a driving force for many issues within the industry, including the high stress, long hours, lack of flexibility, and then the consequent rushing, errors, and rework.

But it seems like construction companies are trapped in a Catch-22: if they relax this pressure, if they try to reduce work hours and increase flexibility, wouldn't they need to add more time onto their schedules, which would hurt their chances of winning work? If the other companies are still driving their workers as hard as possible, the one that relaxes will be left behind, won't it?

Not necessarily.

Treating workers like humans by allowing them to rest and spend more time with their loved ones (and fill their buckets in all the other ways) will *help* with the bidding process in a number of ways.

The first reason is one we've discussed throughout the book: employees who are well-rested and able to fulfill their human needs on a regular basis are less likely to make mistakes, are going to be more engaged with their work, will have fewer safety incidents, will be more creative with solutions and ideas for improvement, and so on, all contributing to getting work done *faster*.

This won't happen instantly, so it may take an investment in time for the full productivity benefits of more human ways of working to come through. But it will be worth it in the long term, especially when clients begin to realize that by relaxing schedules, they end up avoiding cost and time blowouts often faced in these projects.

The next reason is the increase in improvements across the business when people of all levels are able to spend time and energy developing themselves and upskilling. Greater flexibility allows people to decentralize their skills away from their primary job and learn other skills that will help them and the business overall.

For example, imagine the power of tradespeople learning computer-aided design. They can use this for better planning of resources and their own scheduling. They can attain a greater understanding of the design process and can have effective input at the beginning stages of a job. And they can move more easily into other positions of a company.

This is one example, but it shows that a business can become much more agile and ready for big changes (such as the impending AI revolution) when its people are more free and able to upskill and develop themselves.

The last reason flexibility helps with the tendering and bidding process is the business case for human sustainability. Many companies are looking more closely at their supply chains, not just their own operations, for ethics and social responsibility. This is being driven by employees and consumers, and it includes how workers are treated.

Companies need to impress employees to make sure that they can attract and retain them. And they need to impress consumers so that they keep buying stuff. Social responsibility is important to both these groups.

An article in the *Telegraph* described studies that found that "three quarters of employees wanted their companies to balance commercial success with social responsibility strategies," and "93 per cent of consumers say they would buy a product because of its association with a good cause."[16]

It's not hard to see, then, that a business that's looking to contract a company for a project (such as building an office tower) would be less likely to award a tender to a construction company that's still creating toxic work environments for its employees.

That business will be much more attracted to the company that has proven that it cares about its employees by prioritizing their health and well-being. That business will be more likely to hire a company that publicly states that it treats its people with respect and that a high proportion of its people work with flexibility, thus enabling them to have a great work-life balance and fulfilling lives outside of their jobs.

Mirvac gets it. An article describing its CEO Susan Lloyd-Hurwitz's success with the company summarizes her approach beautifully:

> If you want people to join your company, to bring their best selves to work and stay with you, you need to treat them with understanding, appreciation, tolerance, and protection for their welfare, the same way that you should treat the environment. . . . It is all about respect. Given the company was a sustainability champion, could it not extend that respect to its own workers?[17]

Caregivers with Empty Buckets (Healthcare)

The strongest skeptics of flexibility can be found in the quaint little trillion-dollar industry of healthcare. They're not the loudest, they just dismiss the idea quickly and quietly as lunacy, something that doesn't make sense or isn't necessary.

We don't have enough staff to reduce anyone's hours or provide flexibility.

They're used to working long shifts, and that's how we know we've got the best: they can handle it.

If you start increasing handovers because of shorter shifts, there'll be more mistakes. Patients will get hurt.

This is serious; it's life and death. We can't be messing around with the current systems.

It is serious. It is life and death. For patients and medical professionals.

The estimates for how many patients die in U.S. hospitals due to "preventable harm" (medical errors) range widely.

One study puts it at 250,000 to over 400,000 people per year[18] (which would place medical errors as the third leading cause of death in the country, with 647,457 deaths due to heart disease and 599,108 due to cancer in 2017).[19]

Another study puts this figure at a more conservative rate of 123,603 deaths over the twenty-six years between 1990 and 2016, or roughly 4,754 per year.[20]

The enormous variation between these numbers is due to the filtering methods used by the researchers in determining what constitutes death due to medical error. But either way, it's not good news. Each unit is a human life that was lost due to a mistake, something that could and should have been avoided.

What's worse is that for each death, ten to twenty times more people suffer from serious non-lethal harm due to preventable errors. And, unlike construction, when mistakes are made in the healthcare industry, rework isn't always possible.

What might be a major cause of these errors?

A common feature that is shared between healthcare and construction is the long, inflexible hours that the people in each of these industries are expected to work.

But the hours worked by doctors, the people with real lives in their hands, dwarf those of construction workers (and every other profession in the world). This is especially the case for doctors working in hospitals, and those in training (residents and interns), whose long hours are notoriously normal.

According to an article in *The Atlantic*, "residents in America are expected to spend up to eighty hours a week in the hospital and endure single shifts that routinely last up to twenty-eight hours – with such workdays required about four times a month, on average."[21]

A study from the Australian Medical Association (AMA) found that "one in two doctors (53 percent) are working unsafe shifts that place them at a higher risk of fatigue," and that shifts of seventy-two hours, fifty-nine hours, and fifty-three hours were reported.[22]

I could bore you now with studies that show that sleep deprivation has an effect on performance and alertness similar to that of a high blood alcohol content (BAC). (For example, after seventeen to nineteen hours without sleep, performance by subjects in one study across a range of physical and mental tests was equivalent to a BAC of 0.05 percent, and after longer periods of being awake it was equivalent to a BAC of 0.1 percent,[23] double the legal limit for driving in Australia.) But why not go straight to the studies that link long shifts to increases in errors?

Research into the working hours of 2,737 residents in the United States found that when they worked between one and four extended-duration shifts (24 hours or more) in a month, in that month they were:

- More likely to report a fatigue-related medical error – by 250 percent
- More likely to report a fatigue-related preventable adverse event – by 770 percent

And when they worked five or more extended-duration shifts in a month, they were:

- More likely to report a fatigue-related medical error – by 650 percent
- More likely to report a fatigue-related preventable adverse event – by 600 percent
- More likely to have a patient *die* due to a preventable adverse event) – by 300 percent[24]

It's not surprising, then, that according to a poll of U.S. residents, 80 percent would ask for a different doctor if they knew theirs had already been working for twenty-four hours or more.[25]

Most people have a good, common-sense idea about the effects of long hours on a human's ability to do stuff accurately. And doctors are, regardless of how much their crappy system may try to disagree, human. And because they're human, and they have human needs and human capabilities, these long and rigid hours end up hurting them as well.

A survey of 1,958 junior doctors in New South Wales, Australia, found that more than 56 percent of respondents "were concerned about their own health or safety because of the hours they work."[26]

And another survey, with data from 12,252 junior doctors across Australia, found that those "who worked over fifty-five hours a week were more than twice as likely to report common mental health disorders and suicide ideation, compared to those working forty to forty-four hours per week."[27] (The average workweek for these doctors was fifty hours, and one in four were working more than fifty-five hours per week.)

Nurses (and their patients) are not immune to the effects of the long, rigid hours expected in the industry either.

One study of 11,516 registered nurses in the United States looked at the relationship between working hours and "adverse events and errors, which included needlestick injuries, work-related injuries, patient falls with injury, nosocomial infections [acquired or occurring in a hospital], and medication errors."[28]

It found that when nurses worked over forty hours per week, the chances for each of these adverse events occurring increased by the following:

- Wrong medication or dose – 28 percent
- Patient falls with injury – 17 percent
- Nosocomial infections – 14 percent
- Work injuries (for the nurse) – 25 percent
- Needlestick injuries (for the nurse) – 28 percent

As with the doctors discussed previously, nurses who work longer hours are doing so not because they enjoy working long hours, but because of how the industry is set up. There are too few nurses, each of whom is stretched beyond their physical and mental capacities, and they have no other option than to do what they can with what they have, without complaint, of course, because people's lives are at stake.

But it's a travesty that an industry intended to help people ends up inflicting harm on those people who need help and the people whose life mission is to help others during their darkest and scariest moments.

The question of this chapter persists: does it need to be this way?

The Necessity of Flex

There are strong arguments, from within the industry itself, against any sort of increase in flexibility (such as reducing shift hours). But when they're examined thoroughly, these arguments turn out to be good reasons for *increased* levels of flexibility.

Here are the arguments, in no particular order:

- **Argument 1:** Longer shifts are valuable in the medical profession so that doctors in training can observe patients through the entirety of their visit and treatment. This is so they can gain a better understanding of the processes from beginning to end.

- **Counterargument 1:** Being exhausted and fatigued is *not* good for memory retention and learning, so even if the intern is observing more, less of that information will be translated to understanding and long-term memory.

In one of the studies about doctors discussed previously, it was demonstrated that "extended-duration work shifts adversely affected medical education, as the odds of falling asleep in lectures and while on rounds with attending physicians increased significantly."[29]

Also, are there no other ways these interns or residents can observe and experience the spectrum of cases without having to see it for themselves?

Technology is constantly improving. What about simulations that speed up the overall process and focus on the important bits? Or simply more digital storytelling and demonstrations from one doctor to another, regardless of where they are on the planet?

As with any problem, there are always solutions; this situation sounds ripe for innovation, which flexibility has a habit of enhancing.

- **Argument 2.** Longer shifts are important to reduce the number of handovers from one doctor or nurse to the next. Handovers can create errors (e.g., due to the incoming health professional not having "all the information"), therefore more handovers can potentially increase rates of patient harm.

- **Counterargument 2:** This is more an issue with the handover process and systems than anything else. As people of science, doctors and nurses should be able to accurately describe what they've been observing with their patients, what actions have already been taken, what they expect to see next, and the next necessary steps.

  But a doctor or nurse who has been working for twenty-four hours, or forty-eight hours, or seventy-two hours (!) will have trouble keeping their eyes open at the end of a shift, let alone be able to provide accurate descriptions of all the work they've done and what needs to be done next for all their patients.

  What this system needs is professionals with energy left in their buckets at the end of their shift so they can effectively hand over patients to other professionals who are also recharged because they've had adequate time to rest. It needs professionals who have the energy and time to improve the handover system itself.

- **Argument 3:** There are simply not enough doctors and nurses, and budgets are consistently stretched to their limits, so it would be impossible to hire more people to cover for reductions in shift hours or days of work, or to cover flexible start and finish times, or to provide greater amounts of leave during the year.

- **Counterargument 3:** One of the difficulties in attracting people into the profession is that people (strangely enough) consider their own quality of life when applying for a job or starting a career. Yes, these potential employees may have a natural propensity to care for others, but they are also more aware than the average person of how work can and does impact their well-being, and that's a sacrifice they are decreasingly willing to make.

  An article from *The Guardian* reported that in the National Health Service (NHS) in the United Kingdom, 10,257 employees left the industry between June 2017 and June 2018 because of concerns over their long working hours. This was an increase of 178 percent compared to those who left for the same reason back in 2010–2011.[30]

  This is bad news for an industry that is already stretched far too thin. (From that same article, the NHS has a current shortfall of almost 103,000 people, including over 40,000 unfilled nursing positions and over 9,000 unfilled doctor positions.) Medical systems will require *increased* growth as populations around the world get older and healthcare becomes more complex.

  People in *every* industry are demanding and expecting higher levels of work–life balance, for all the reasons outlined in this book; those in healthcare are no exception. The only way to keep up with the modern working world and attract people is to provide flexibility.

  The NHS has acknowledged this fact and has appointed a Head of Flexible Working to cope with the increasing demand for flexibility, especially from younger workers, including shorter shifts, part-time work, and other forms of flexibility.[31]

It Can Be Done

Flexibility can indeed be tricky in healthcare.

As with most of the other forgotten industries, employees need to be present to take care of patients, and there needs to be a certain number of people present at certain times (*all* the time in a hospital). In healthcare, if these criteria aren't fulfilled, people die.

So something like remote work is mostly out of the question (excluding the growth in telehealth – being able to see patients and work with other medical professionals through digital media – where we've seen a drastic uptick due to the coronavirus pandemic.)

But flexibility in healthcare is *far* from impossible.

A two-year experiment in Gothenburg, Sweden (again!), saw the workdays of seventy aged-care nurses reduced from eight hours to six while maintaining their regular pay.

The results were similar to those found in the other experiments featuring shorter hours mentioned in the book: positive! The nurses took fewer sick days, reported better health and higher energy levels, and from a productivity and quality-of-care perspective, organized 85 percent more activities for patients, such as nature walks and sing-a-longs.[32]

One of the nurses, forty-one-year-old Lise-Lotte Pettersson, said, "I used to be exhausted all the time. I would come home from work and pass out on the sofa. But not now. I am much more alert: I have much more energy for my work, and also for family life."

That increase in energy was found across the board. With their standard eight-hour days, only one in five of the nurses had energy remaining at the end of their shifts, but this shot up to four-fifths during the trial of shorter days. That's 400 percent more nurses with energy left to exercise, work on passions, spend quality time with their families, develop themselves, and so on.

Other signs of improved health and well-being of the nurses were that they were less stressed, had less back, neck, and shoulder pain, and increased their physical activity by 24 percent.[33] These nurses were moving up the health spectrum (see Chapter 4) in multiple ways.

There were, of course, skeptics of the experiment, especially those from the conservative side of Swedish politics who said that it was "crazy and irresponsible" to spend so much money to improve the lives of nurses; the cost was about twelve million krona (US$1.2 million) to hire the extra staff needed to fill the day at each facility.

But there would be savings for the healthcare system and the government as a whole beyond those measured in the trial, including some that wouldn't become apparent until further into the future, such as:

- Reduced attrition rates and longer careers of the nurses
- Lower healthcare costs for the nurses due to improved health
- Lower healthcare and associated costs due to improved care of the patients and fewer medical errors
- Fewer and smaller claims due to work-related injuries of the nurses
- The benefits received by the broader community due to having more people who can give back in other ways besides their work (e.g., volunteering)

Also, there was seemingly no effort during the trial to recover costs through the gains in productivity, by optimizing staff numbers, for example. Given more time and support, the extra energy and motivation of the nurses could have been translated into improvements and innovations that either resulted in lower staff numbers or enabled more patients to be cared for per employee.

But, sadly, this program was only about a Level 2: Basic Program on the Flex Scale, thus it was doomed to be cut. It didn't have full commitment from those at the highest levels of government, they didn't incorporate continuous improvement principles to reduce costs, and the returns, financial and otherwise, weren't measured in their entirety.

It's likely that this could have been a much more successful program if these elements were in place. Then it would have been made permanent, and these nurses in Sweden would still be happy, energetic, and spiraling up the health spectrum.

Contrary to the financial findings from the trial above, when flexibility was implemented at Mercy Health, a health service provider in Victoria, Australia, savings of $23 million were found in its operations, comprising higher levels of productivity, higher retention levels, lower recruitment costs, and lower absenteeism.[34]

Mercy used a variety of types of flexibility to cater to different needs – a mature (and flexible) approach to the practice. The most popular types were part-time work (51 percent), flexitime (26 percent) and time-in-lieu (21 percent). The hospital took the approach that even though there are unique challenges in the industry, "there will always be a way to make some form of flexibility work for everyone."

The final case comes from the Cleveland Clinic, one of the world's leading medical institutions, and it's a rather bold example.

What makes it bold? This healthcare provider has committed to prioritizing the health of patients *and* caregivers (by *caregiver* they mean any person who is employed by the organization, from bus drivers to doctors, because they're all there for the benefit of the patient), and they do this by focusing on preventative healthcare and functional medicine. They get to the root causes of why people are getting sick in the first place, and they do something about it.

As the former CEO, Dr. Toby Cosgrove, puts it, they've moved from "sick care to health care."[35] Keeping people healthy and well is their overarching approach for both patients and employees. In their view, you can't have one without the other; it makes no sense, financially or ethically or practically, to have one without the other.

Flexible work is simply one aspect of this committed and holistic approach to prioritizing people. The clinic provides part-time roles, flexible schedules, remote work (for an increasing number of roles where this is possible), and good paid-leave options.[36] But, as with Mercy Health, and Mirvac in the construction section, the type of flexibility isn't nearly as important as the attitude about why they are providing it – and their attitude is spot on.

From a business perspective, the clinic's investments in the health of their employees, which include work flexibility and a comprehensive well-being program, have resulted in a savings of $3 for every dollar spent.[37]

In an industry that, unfortunately and ironically, hasn't prioritized the health and lives of its staff, these cases show that it's both possible and worthwhile to care for our caregivers.

In Conclusion

I've only discussed three, albeit important, forgotten industries in this chapter, but there are others that suffer from rigidity in their own unique ways, where these exact same principles can be applied to wonderful effect. Retail, transport, academia, hospitality, and mining are all areas that would benefit greatly from improved flexibility and general human-centeredness.

When looking into any of these industries, the principles in this chapter can be boiled down to one simple concept: any person who works for you is a human being. They have fundamental needs that if unfulfilled result in poor-quality lives and poor-quality work, and if fulfilled result in enriched lives and work that far surpasses what is commonly acceptable.

Practically speaking, all that we've learned in this part of the book about how to implement flexibility – and the suggested steps for how to roll it out – are also highly applicable to these industries. They will help you figure out what people need, and how it can be made to work for *your* business.

Just remember that the most important aspects are your level of commitment and your attitude toward the people themselves; and when you give them more time and freedom to be human, they'll give back to you ten-fold.

Something else to consider is this: if I owned a construction company, or managed a hospital, or was the CEO of a retail chain, or managed a manufacturing plant, or headed a university, I would be very, very concerned if the people who worked at my organization weren't consistently finding safer, more effective, more creative ways of doing things, as well as regularly upgrading their own knowledge and skills for the future.

No industry is safe from massive upheaval and (don't hate me for using this word) disruption. Ensuring that your employees are at their best, consistently upskilling for what's needed tomorrow, and searching like hounds for ways to improve the business puts you in a position to be the disruptor rather than the disruptee. And you ensure that your employees are at their best by looking after their needs and giving them space to reach their full potential as humans.

What if taxi drivers had had the time and energy and incentive to improve their own industry before Uber arrived, before there was a need for Uber to exist?

What if, instead of driving twelve hours a day for minimum pay, they had a more human way of working that gave them time to look after their needs, and they personally benefitted from having happy customers, *and* they were encouraged and given space to develop in varied ways besides driving cars?

Might that whole story have been a little different? Would Uber exist if the taxi industry was agile and flexible and human-centered, and customers were already thrilled with their services? We'll never know.

Part Four

WORK REVOLUTION

CHAPTER 12

Work Reimagined

WHAT IF WE COULD START AGAIN? What if we started a colony on Mars, or a new super-Earth orbiting a nearby star, and decided that the way we ran things on our original home wasn't quite ideal (hence the need to escape to a new planet), and that we needed to examine society in its entirety, including this thing called *work*.

We have a blank whiteboard, fresh markers of every color, piles of sticky notes, and a wealth of knowledge about what worked and what didn't in the old system. No idea is too outrageous.

What would our constraints be when we're not attached to the previous ideas of what work should be? We built our rules for what work looks like around arbitrary concepts that exist simply because someone thought that was the way it should be.

The five-day workweek, for instance, has no biological or astronomical or any other tangible foundation. It exists merely because it was a slight step away from the six-day workweek we had in the industrial 19th and 20th centuries, which itself was founded on religious ideals, incredible power imbalances between employers and employees, and a complete lack of understanding of how much damage could be done to health and safety by working too much.

The eight-hour workday was, again, super random. The concept was introduced in 1817 by textile manufacturer and philanthropist Robert Owens in an effort to curtail the negative effects of the ten-or-more-hour days common at the time. He even made a catchy slogan: "Eight hours' labour, eight hours' recreation, eight hours' rest."[1]

This gained footing across the Western world in the following decades, and although it was a step forward for working humans (and their families) in those days, it unfortunately became the standard unit of a workday. It stuck. And we built the workplace, and society in general, around it, and we haven't since *seriously* questioned why we're still using this two-hundred-year-old concept as our standard for work.

So, let's start again, with our blank whiteboard and sticky notes and markers.

One constraint is that we'll still need money to live. I would hope that in our new world some sort of universal basic income exists so that everyone, regardless of their employment, can afford the basics of life (or that we've gone full Star Trek and erased the need for currency altogether). But to keep this new world relevant to ours in the present, let's keep money as a necessity, and we'll (mostly) receive it through work.

Another constraint is that humans will still be required to do things in this society to keep it functioning. This isn't a *Wall-E* situation where the robots keep everything in functional order without any interference by people. Humans will still need to be involved roughly as much as we are now: collecting rubbish, laying bricks, operating on brains, driving cars and trucks, writing reports.

Those constraints out of the way, we're going to introduce some new rules. The first will be that work is universally seen not just as a means for making money, but as an important satisfier of several fundamental human needs: subsistence, participation, affection, creation, identity, understanding, and protection.

Work, in one form or another, is vital for full and sustainable lives. It's therefore crucial to make it available to as many people as possible, and to ensure that the work itself is indeed providing opportunities for growth and learning, for participating with other people and making connections, for allowing creativity and problem solving, and so on.

The second rule is that work won't be allowed to produce poverties of any of our fundamental needs. Anyone who employs another human being to work for them will be held to the standard of some measurement system that determines whether that work is increasing or reducing that person's capability to fulfill their own human needs.

Employers, as suggested by Jeffrey Pfeffer in *Dying for a Paycheck*, will face severe penalties for reducing anyone's ability to be fully human, in the same way they would be penalized for dumping toxic waste into a local stream. This is regardless of the size of the business: being small won't be an excuse to contribute to social pollution.

To ensure that this happens, flexibility will be inherently built into every job. It will be a given. What it will look like, from job to job and industry to industry, will be different, but any business that employs a human will be measured and held to an objective standard, such as the Flex Scale introduced in Chapter 2, or a broader human-centered index. Either of these will measure fundamental aspects of work, such as the quality of management, level of work-life balance, and commitment of executives to the health and well-being of employees.

We'll know if a business is a net polluter or developer of life.

And with greater knowledge of how work flexibility or lack thereof contributes to various other issues in the world, such as traffic congestion, air pollution, gender equality, health, and so on, the government will have a powerful lever to influence development outcomes.

In this chapter, we'll take a look at some changes that accompany this reimagining of work: other human-centered shifts in the workplace that will occur as a result of greater use of flexibility, but that are also necessary for flexibility to become accepted and normalized.

Managers (Lives Are in Your Hands)

I'll start with the biggest shift that needs to happen in the workplace for flexibility to become normal, which will happen naturally as we tend toward more human ways of working: redefining the role of managers.

Now that we know the degree to which work cultures and structures influence lives for better or for worse, the role of managers – the people with the power over these work cultures and structures – becomes much more significant than we ever imagined, both in the workplace and society.

Lives are in their hands.

They can either kill employees slowly (or quickly) by emptying their buckets and keeping them dry – literally poisoning their brains and bodies – with poor management practices, or they can enrich and enhance lives, and allow people to reach their full potential by creating work and workplaces that fulfill human needs without producing poverties.

With this awareness, wouldn't we be much more rigorous in choosing who is allowed to be put into management positions and require that they're trained – even licensed! – before they're given this power?

We do the same for bus drivers and airline pilots and doctors.

Managers need to be skilled in more than balancing a budget or signing a timesheet or the technical aspects of the department or company. They should have advanced knowledge of people, of humans and their requirements. They should have highly developed empathy and the entire gamut of emotional intelligence, to be able to understand another person's emotions and needs. They should be able to coach someone holistically on their goals, both professionally and personally, and have challenging and difficult conversations in constructive ways.

I remember being thrown straight into a management role as a manufacturing engineer the *month* after graduating from university. I had nothing but a piece of paper and ambition, and here I was with lives in my hands (not that I realized that at the time).

Looking back, it's obscene, but unfortunately not uncommon: people being put in charge of others merely because they have technical knowledge or a degree completely unrelated to human behavior, people who lack any knowledge of humans or life experience as a coach or mentor or leader.

I've been on the receiving end of that structure – having a manager who was brilliant at the technical aspect of the work I was doing, but with severe shortcomings in knowing how to lead or manage others.

She micromanaged every aspect of my day, to the point where I felt it was quite unnecessary for me to be there. She reprimanded me loudly in front of teams I was leading for breaking arbitrary rules I had no idea existed. She insisted that we couldn't leave until five every day, "just because" (coincidentally, this was one of my prompts to start looking into flexibility).

Starved of autonomy and understanding and creation and various other needs, I left the company within six months and needed an extended break to recover my sanity.

This person should not have been a manager. She should have been a subject matter expert, and potentially a technical trainer, or something – *anything* – other than someone with power over the lives of other humans.

She should have been paid just as much as a manager and given a career pathway that allowed her to continue progressing in seniority without needing to be a manager.

But this is rare, and that's the reason we have so many non-appropriate people in management positions. People who are good at their jobs need to progress somehow, otherwise they'll leave, so they're put in charge of other people and given pay raises (because if you're good at one thing, you're obviously going to be good at everything else . . .).

At the very least, this former manager of mine should have been given training on the practicalities of what she could and couldn't do when she was in charge of other people, even if she didn't have an inherent understanding of human needs.

This training is also surprisingly rare. In a CareerBuilder survey of workers in the United States, it was found that 58 percent of managers hadn't received *any* management training.[2] Also, 87 percent of middle managers "wish they had received more management training when they first became a manager."[3] People often know whether they're ready or not to take on a job.

Can you imagine the public outrage if a city's bus driver was found to have not received any training before being sent out to drive people around? Or if they didn't feel like they were well-equipped enough to confidently drive a bus?

Now imagine 58 percent of all bus drivers in your city driving people around without having received *any* training and 87 percent driving around without feeling confident about driving.

"Here are the keys, off you go."

When managers account for 70 percent of the variance in employee engagement scores, and when only 13 percent of the global workforce is engaged with their work (each of these facts found by Gallup[4]) there's not just a high human cost to having bad or ill-equipped managers, there's a high cost to businesses and economies worldwide.

Henry Stewart, the founder and chief happiness officer of Happy Ltd., author of *The Happy Manifesto*, and avid supporter of work flexibility, has come up with an ingenious way of promoting the best people-leaders *and* the best technical workers into higher positions in the company in a way that benefits everyone.[5]

Stewart saw that there were two different types of leaders in his business:

- Type A, who are great at the technical stuff, including making decisions and developing business strategies
- Type B, who are great coaches and challengers and supporters of other people

And he put these different types of people into leadership roles that suited them. At Happy, they have managers who look after the technical and strategy stuff, and managers who look after the people. It's stinkingly simple, yet a seemingly profound concept based on how little it's used in the business world.

The technical maestros can keep doing what they do and progress in the business and feel appreciated for their talents, without having to worry about motivating people or helping with personal problems. And those with highly developed soft skills (e.g., empathy, ability to lead and inspire, ability to communicate clearly and listen) can also progress into senior positions, even if they're not the best at the technical stuff, and make an incredible impact on the organization by helping employees, including other managers, reach their full potential while also making them feel valued and cared for.

What they're doing at Happy is just one way to ensure that the best people are in the right type of management positions, and it has also made it possible for them to have a highly successful flexible work environment.

Their focus on developing and coaching and supporting people, not just managing or supervising them, is crucial for successful flexible work.

People managers need to develop trust with their employees and between team members, they need to understand the lives of employees inside and outside the workplace, they need to be strong communicators and listeners, and they need to be whole themselves for this to happen.

Which brings us to the flip side of this coin: with greater flexibility, more people will have the time and energy and resources to develop themselves in well-rounded ways so that they can become whole and much more adept at understanding and leading other people, resulting in more people who are whizzes at both the technical stuff and dealing with emotional situations.

We wouldn't need Type A and Type B managers in this situation; we can have Type X managers, who can lead both the technical *and* people sides of a business.

This is not to say that people don't have natural propensities for one or the other (as found and practiced by Henry Stewart), but that it's possible for each type of person to develop strengths in other areas, given the space and opportunity.

We can extend the description of flexibility onto the description of what makes a good manager, which we would use in our new world. How about this:

> Good managers increase the positive effects of work on their employees while reducing or removing the negative effects. They realize that they don't own anyone's time, but rather have the privilege of being in a position where they can help others flourish, or destroy them from the inside; they have an enormous responsibility.
>
> Good managers consistently ensure that employees are able to be fully human, for the benefit of the employee, society, and the business. **Their goal, from both a human and a business perspective, is to maximize human potential.** And they're consistently focused on living sustainably and developing themselves, thus leading by example *and* improving their capacity to lead.

I'm excited! What's next?

Working Together

We saw in Chapter 7 the case of the Ctrip.com employees who became isolated and lonely while working at home four days a week, but I argued that when it's done properly, flexibility (such as working from home) shouldn't create loneliness. If people can balance remote work with on-location work and are allowed the time to develop other parts of their social lives, then loneliness shouldn't be a problem.

Taking it a step further, in our new world, where flexibility is normal, we see that due to increased freedom of when and where we work, our social network outside of work improves. And working together with other people *in the office* can also be much more fulfilling and transform to a more natural, human way of collaborating with others.

For those in-office connections, it all comes down to the quality of the time people spend together rather than the quantity. We've found in rigid workplaces that there can be people who sit in adjacent cubicles for forty hours a week and know nothing about each other except their names; time spent breathing the same air isn't what binds us as humans.

But given space and freedom, and not feeling forced to be in the same place with the same faces all the time, people end up appreciating and valuing their coworkers and the connections they have with them much more. This can and should also be fostered with purposeful time together, such as retreats, lunches, quiz nights, etc.

In this new world, there would no longer be the separation of work and life that we have traditionally held dear. We wouldn't be afraid of revealing too much or want to keep people at a professional distance. We can make that change by creating a culture of celebrating non-work successes, or mourning non-work losses, with the team. We'll value each other as humans with diverse lives and interests and passions, and not use this information as ammunition against each other.

The flexible workplace can broaden our professional network and collaboration with people outside the companies we work for as well, for the benefit of our own professional and personal lives, and for our companies. We can use coworking places, meet people to work on projects that have nothing to do with our normal work, or go to cafés.

I won't talk too much about coworking spaces because my experience with them is limited. I will say that I've read both pros and cons about the level of connection that people actually find while working there – some preach about how good it is, while others say they feel more alone there than at their home office. Some have said that it's just an expensive way to simply get out of the house, which can be done more cheaply by going to a café, my favorite option for escaping the home office. But whether it's a café or coworking space or library, these locations open up the possibilities to meet people who we can work with in all sorts of different ways.

We can also benefit from being around these other people (at our choosing), without needing to work directly with them. Sometimes called *soft accountability*, the mere presence of other people can generate a creative and productive atmosphere, perhaps due to subconscious social pressure or pride, where it becomes easier to avoid distractions (like Netflix) and focus on getting work done.

(Added to that, the Parkinson Effect can be countered if there's a time factor in these locations. My regular café only allows three hours of free WiFi, so I have a three-hour window to get shit done, and it works like magic.)

Recruitment

Recently I spoke to a group of social work graduates about toxic workplaces, living sustainably through fulfilling human needs and (of course) work flexibility. One of the students had a great question: "How will I know if my new job is going to be in a toxic workplace or not? It's not like they're going to tell me in the interview!"

In our new world, where flexible and human-centered work are normal and expected, this won't be a problem because flexibility (and an overall prioritization of the employee's life) will be found throughout the recruitment process, from the job advertisement and career website, through the interview and selection process, to the onboarding process and subsequently the job.

This also addresses the problems, described in Chapter 8, caused by *earned* flexibility, in which employees have to undergo a period of non-flexibility before they're allowed flexibility, which discriminates against people who require it from the first day.

When flexibility runs throughout the entire process, discussions can be open and positive, with the employer showing how committed they are to the practice, and the employee talking about how they can help make it work for the business.

Some interesting elements that we may regularly see in job ads for employees and managers to describe the business and the position in a world where flexibility is normal and expected (excluding the details of an actual role) include:

For employees

- Flex Scale: Level 4 Certified: Ascended Program. *(An external accreditation based on the Flex Scale described in Chapter 2.)*

- Life quality score for department: 92 percent *(Some form of life quality or human sustainability index, based on flexibility, working times/ shifts, exposure to physical labor and harsh environments, stress of responsibility, customer contact, quality of management, etc.)*

- Low hours but high-value work. We aim for five- to six-hour days and four days per week. Salary doesn't depend on time worked.

  NOTE: this is not a part-time role; it's a full-time position, but our organization has full flexibility, and we truly focus on getting the best out of our people by helping them have the best possible lives.

- Ability to work wherever is best for you, including your home. We encourage balance between remote and in-office work, but you will work with your team to figure out specifics for what works best.

- Requires ownership of role and commitment to quality and continuous improvement. People who enjoy being busy and boasting about long hours, who can't see the forest for the trees, will not do well.

- We have full training for those who are motivated to be the best they can be, and your reward is the opportunity for a full life.

Extra details for management positions

- Demonstrated empathy (and other emotional intelligence and leadership attributes).

- Training and/or qualifications in management. *(Part of the accreditation cited above can also be training for management, similar to Lean Six Sigma training for continuous improvement.)*

- Coaching and talent developer rather than manager. Our employees are experts in their fields or on their way toward being so. Your job is to help them on that path, ensure they have everything they need, and help find solutions to their problems. It's not your job to check if they're working.

- With our fully flexible workplace, we're more of a community than colleagues – we look at employees' lives holistically and make sure that work is adding and contributing to a full life rather than hindering the ability to live fully.

These are simply some ideas for what we may see (probably with better wording by actual recruiters!). But my point is that information about the flexible and human-centered aspects of work won't be crammed awkwardly into the end of interviews; it will be out there, in the open, verified, for all to see.

On Holidays

I spoke a little about leave and long-term flexibility in Chapter 2, but the subject deserves at least one more diatribe on our current practices, and how they could be improved in our new world.

The one thing I missed the most about university when I began my professional career was time off, leave, holidays. Being able to get to the end of a year or a semester and then *stop working*. Shutting down that part of the mind, the work part, to completely disengage, and to celebrate what was a tough period and a lot of work, for weeks or even months at a time.

Then came the workplace.

With four weeks of "leave" in a year, I had two weeks I had to take off over the Christmas period when the business shut down, then one week I had to spend in Malaysia with my then-partner's parents for Chinese New Year, and then one week I could finally take off to . . . finish all those jobs around the house I hadn't been able to do during the year, or to move house, or wait at home for packages or plumbers, or various other random things that conspired to steal these remaining precious days off.

What fresh horror was this?

There were no longer opportunities to fully shut down and do something else, or *nothing*, for weeks or months at a time; just short gasps of respite and then straight back into it. No opportunity to sit back and let all that work and those achievements settle in, or to rest and refocus on what will come in the new year or period. Nope. It was just work. Life was work.

Those brief periods of leave provided barely enough time to even approach unwinding, and there was definitely no recharging; then – bam!

– back into it. This is one of the biggest reasons that, after only a couple of years in the workplace, I was already plotting my escape.

It seems insane to me that we allow children at school to have this great balance in life where they work for a certain number of weeks and then can go away and do other things and rest and play, but as adults we're in a constant state of work.

In most areas of life there's a natural ebb and flow of things. The sun sets, the sun rises. We wake, we sleep. The tide comes in, the tide goes out. The moon wanes and waxes. The seasons change from hot to cold, or rainy to dry, and back again. People are born; people die.

We're used to a rhythm of ups and downs, hot and cold, light and dark, on and off. It gives us a rest from monotony, from one singular state of being. But work has been designed differently. We've ended up with a structure where work never ends. It's a constant. And we've normalized that concept. "Holidays" are an exception, a deviation from "normal," rather than simply another part of the rhythm of life.

With most of our year working, we don't get an ebb and flow; it's just flow. And then we're surprised that people get depressed and burned out or become completely disengaged from their jobs. This pattern of not having a pattern is completely unnatural, and our bodies and minds know this at the core of our being.

Before I spiral off any further into my whirlpool of woe, there are two interesting and practical points regarding leave in terms of flexibility:

1. Increasing daily and weekly (short-term) flexibility, as we've examined already in detail, increases the sustainability of life in the long term and makes leave *somewhat* less necessary.

   I won't say it becomes outright unnecessary (more on that in the second point), but with more rest and relaxation and other human needs being consistently fulfilled, that complete escape from work isn't as critical as it is with an unsustainable, rigid work style that leaves people desperately starving for respite.

   When I interviewed Jonathan Elliott about the five-hour work-day, he said that one employee had stockpiled massive amounts of leave for her honeymoon because she never "needed to take it" – she was living sustainably and happily day to day.

   Flexibility also takes care of those one-off moments where you need to be home for electricians or plumbers. You can simply continue working as per usual at home, or you can just come to the office after or before the interruption. No need to take leave or inconvenience anyone. Easy.

2. *But*, providing more leave to people than the general two to four weeks is absolutely one of the most important types of flexibility you can offer, regardless of what other types you've already implemented.

   Being able to properly shut down and disconnect from work for long periods is enormously beneficial to the individual, to their mental health specifically, but also to the quality (and length) of their life in general.

   Also, being away from work on a truly disconnected break is when many of those paradigm-changing aha moments arrive that could revolutionize the business. Certainly going away and filling their buckets to the brim turns employees into productivity monsters when they return to work!

Practically, what do I recommend for this new colony on Mars when we get to start again? What is the ideal number of weeks of leave?

There is no ideal. As with any type of flexibility, it's about finding out what your people need, and finding innovative ways to give it to them by working on solutions together.

And it comes down to what sort of business you want to run. Do you want to be one that gives employees the bare minimum that you are legislated to give, and end up with burned out and unproductive people who struggle to learn and grow? Or do you want to do what's best for them and what's best for you?

The two (or less!) weeks of leave per year offered by U.S. businesses (on average) is *not* ideal. It doesn't take a study to show you that working for 96 percent of the year isn't good for you. But just to add some rigor, research on businessmen in Finland found that those who took less than three weeks leave per year had a 37-percent increase in the risk of dying from health problems than those who took three or more weeks of leave per year.[6]

A survey of American workers found that the ideal amount of leave per year would be fifty-two days, or ten weeks.[7]

Another interesting indicator of how much leave is a good amount is that businesses that have provided *unlimited leave* (as described in Chapter 2) found that employees took, on average, five to ten extra days of leave on top of their previous allocations, and that even that small amount was a great benefit to their lives and productivity.[8]

And business could be even more creative with long-term leave and flexibility. For example, they could have job-share teams that, instead of dividing the workweek between them, divide the entire year, alternating six months on and six months off, or three months on and three months off.

Or a business could let teams have free reign with whatever sort of leave works best for them. Does it matter? If they're getting everything done and achieving great results?

Have fun with it!

At a bare minimum, businesses need to provide more weeks of leave across the board than we have in most countries, like those poor suckers in the United States with their two weeks. Two weeks?!

This sort of practice completely disregards the human side of humans and treats them as nothing more than machines. In our new world, this will, thankfully, be outlawed and forgotten.

Words

Something else we'll change regarding work is the language we use.

We've been stuck in a linguistic box of calling forty-plus hours of work per week *full time* and anything less than that *part time*. I've seen job ads where a position is for four days per week, or five days per week and slightly shorter days, and it's called *part time*. It's rubbish.

As we discussed in Chapter 2, this term tends to diminish the value perceived in the job and in the employee. It's right there in the term *part*, which is often read as *part* of our effort, *part* of our ability, *part* of a bigger *whole* that would be possible if we were *more committed*.

But after reading this book, and seeing that someone can easily do just as much or even more work in thirty hours than others do in forty hours, can we finally put both *part time* and *full time* in the bin where they belong? They're pointless and damaging.

Other terms destined for the scrapheap, my guess is in the next five to ten years, are those I've used countless times throughout the book (and you're probably sick of reading): *flexibility, telecommuting, remote work, flexitime*, and many other flexibility-related terms will no longer be needed because they'll be expected in any workplace.

These words only needed to exist in a world where rigidity was the norm and we had to name the opposite of this practice – what stood out as different. When rigidity is gone there won't be any need to talk about flexibility, or telecommuting, or remote work. These will just be how we work.

The term *rigidity* may still be used, and become more popular, because it will be used to describe the few outlying businesses that aren't flexible by default. But they won't last long into the future, either because of legislation or because no one will work for them.

We Don't Have to Wait

We don't have to wait to go to Mars or some other new world to have these changes. We can do all of this right now, here on our little blue marble. We don't have to wait for new laws to force us to make big changes, we don't have to wait for someone else to make the first move, and we don't have to wait for someone's permission.

We can start now.

We've already seen examples throughout the book of companies taking the lead and doing exactly this. They've reimagined what work could be. These companies will be ahead in the near future when other major developments will continue to impact what work looks like.

CHAPTER 13

COVID-19 and
The Human Revolution

THE FUTURE OF WORK arrived faster than anyone anticipated, in the form of a global pandemic. Although we were already slowly waking up to the importance of flexibility and human-centered workplaces, COVID-19 was the rude jolt that shocked us awake – the little brother who hits you in the face with a pillow in the middle of the night.

It could be called The Great Awakening.

Who would have guessed that, suddenly, in March of 2020, *everyone* (who could) would be working from home? That most businesses would be either shut down or thrust into a remote-work trial! It's an evolve-or-die situation that occasionally pops up in the natural world, and in the business world.

And everyone quickly found that many of the stories they were telling themselves about how "flexibility is impossible" or "it's not for our business" were complete rubbish. Polite skeptics around the world have been exposed to a new way of working, and they've realized that it *can* work. The sky didn't collapse when people could sign in from home.

Escaping the commute and the grind of the open-plan office, and the specter of mortality that came with seeing many around the world get sick or die from this virus, have woken us up from our mechanical lives where we were just going through the motions.

I thought I was already awake because I had been able to work with full flexibility. But I was suddenly reawakened and shaken into reassessing what's important – what I should be focusing on and what I should be slashing out of my life.

Much of the awakening that has happened was the realization that many of our needs are unfulfilled due to the grind of everyday life. People were able to experience leisure again, for the first time in years. They were able to connect more with family and friends, even if they weren't physically in the same place. They took courses to learn things they've wanted to learn for years but haven't had the time or energy for.

They took up hobbies. They started gardening. They started cooking.

They assessed their identities outside of their profession.

They questioned everything.

It was beautiful!

But as I write this, people are imagining what their lives will be like when they have to leave these things behind and go back to their "normal" lives, their stressful commutes and nine-to-five offices. You can hear the dread in their words. They're scared they'll fall back to sleep and that their humanness will again be relegated to the fleeting gaps outside of work.

If you're reading this, you already know more than me about how all this turned out, but I believe this was the spark to ignite The Human Revolution, where our needs are prioritized at home and at work, regardless of occupation or industry.

In The Human Revolution, people are no longer agents of capitalism, to be used up for the benefit of a few wealthy business owners and shareholders; they're valued and prioritized as humans.

In The Human Revolution (Figure 13.1), as we're seeing glimpses of during the pandemic, there are strong themes of decentralization and self-sufficiency – highly human traits.

Our skills are broadening and deepening; our incomes and identities are being spread over more than a single job or profession (many have jumped toward starting their own businesses); we're cooking healthy food, fixing clothes, making friends, caring for our neighbors, healing from past traumas, and growing on the inside.

We've reversed the trend of being highly specialized, of never having time to do anything but our main thing. It's a reversal of the Uber-ization of everything, where we pay strangers (too little) for all the things we can't do ourselves.*

---

* I acknowledge this is kind of a crazy statement with the amount of Uber Eats everyone is ordering while trapped at home, but that is a necessary evil to get through while we're not able to go to a restaurant – learning to cook takes time!

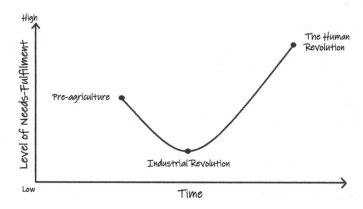

Figure 13.1. Conceptual graph of the level of needs-fulfilment during pre-agricultural times, the Industrial Revolution, and The Human Revolution – the near and hopeful future, where due to advancements in technology and a prioritization of people, our needs will be more fulfilled than at any other time in history.

And the purpose of business is changing. It's no longer just a tool to make money for owners and shareholders. It's now a living organism with which we can enrich the lives of managers and employees and customers, have an impact on real-world problems, *and* make money! There's a realization that capitalism and humanism are beautiful bedfellows, when all along we thought they were enemies.

Instead of being an arena where individuals try to out-compete each other, in this revolution business serves as a community where we're all helping each other be our best for the benefit of all. We're achieving much more than any individual could achieve on their own, which is *what it is to be human!*

This revolution is returning us to a more natural place, but augmented by high technology. Humans can be humans again *because* of the robots, because we've had to figure out how to combine technology with sustainable human lives.

Three major themes will be uncovered in this revolution: universal basic income, valuing humanness, and the unleashing of true human potential.

Universal Basic Income

Universal basic incomes (UBIs) are going to be necessary, any way you slice it. Capitalism has always resulted in a few people disproportionately benefiting over the rest of us, because through a combination of luck and ingenuity they ended up in control of the means of production. This is especially true as artificial intelligence and robotics give this disproportionate distribution of power and wealth a shot in the arm of nuclear-powered steroids (it's a thing).

As time goes on there will be even fewer people with even more of the income-generating means of production who will receive even more of the total benefits. And they won't need to pay a single human for their services (Jeff Bezos can finally sack the last of those pesky humans who keep demanding better pay and acceptable working conditions).

The people who own businesses are becoming less and less reliant on other people to get work done. They benefit immeasurably from the technological progress we've *all* made as humans, while the majority of us are made redundant. And we'll have our first trillionaires – individuals who possess more wealth than entire countries – while billions can't afford to live a dignified life.

We already know this.

Wealth inequality has always been a painful product of a purely capitalist society, and experiments for UBIs in the modern world have been taking place as a potential remedy. Rich people can continue to be rich, while everyone else can still put food on their plates and reach their inherent potential.

For examples of successful trials and great arguments for UBIs, check out *Utopia for Realists* by Rutger Bregman. Ultimately, ensuring that the rich are taxed properly, and distributing their wealth (which they've been able to accumulate because of the progress of all humankind), is the only way to move forward.

Valuing Humanness

Didn't we all gain a new appreciation for people who work in healthcare during the pandemic? They came into work day after day, risked being coughed on by the wrong person, slept on floors so they could save lives and prevent the spread of the disease to others in the community.

We also gained an appreciation for teachers, who, it turns out, don't just teach our kids. They look after them and care for them and spend time with them while we're at work.

And we gained a new appreciation for leaders who have strength *and* compassion. If New Zealand's prime minister Jacinda Ardern wasn't considered the coolest leader of a country before COVID-19, she certainly is now.

What we're seeing is a re-valuation of what it is to be human, especially in our professional lives and the economy. This was described a while ago by the New Economics Foundation (NEF) when they were advocating for twenty-one-hour work weeks. They introduced the concept of a core economy, which has found new and striking relevance:

> The human or "core" economy is made up of the abundant and priceless assets that are embedded in people's everyday lives – time, energy, wisdom, experience, knowledge and skills – and in the relationships between them: love, empathy, watchfulness, care, reciprocity, teaching, and learning.
>
> If they are neglected, they will weaken and diminish. If they are recognized, valued, and supported, they will flourish and grow. They hold the key to making the welfare state sustainable and fit for the future. But growing the core economy depends on changing the way we use time.[1]

I believe (hope) that we'll start to value this human or core economy with dollars and secure, enriching ways of working in the same way that we're currently valuing it with our praise and our prayers.

Human Potential

If you haven't noticed yet, one of the biggest themes in this book is human potential. I believe that every single one of us has a certain potential, and we know in our heart of hearts whether we're fulfilling it or not. It eats away at the deepest part of our core if we're not moving toward it, even if we haven't figured out what "it" is.

Fulfilling this potential is an enormous part of the fundamental human need of identity. And I think the biggest cost of working too much in rigid patterns has been, for many, missing out on discovering and achieving their full potential as human beings.

Humans, all humans, are capable of extraordinary things. Contrary to robots, who (currently) specialize in doing one thing, humans can become masterful at multiple and varied pursuits.

Humans can spin across ice on a blade of steel with one leg in the air, question their place in the universe or how quantum particles interact, paint a landscape that touches the hearts of other humans in subtle and beautiful ways, create and learn new languages, leverage technology to travel much further and faster than their legs could carry them, analyze and influence the thoughts and emotions and behaviors of themselves and other humans and even other species, imagine the future and past and realities that don't exist, cure diseases and prolong life, play a freakin' harp, love openly and fully, solve complex problems, even those created by ourselves, and a billion other things, many of which we haven't even thought of yet.

Our potential is infinite.

But how many of us haven't reached our full potential as a human being?

How many people, throughout history, have used up all their best time and energy, for their entire adult lives, on nothing but work and going through the motions and administration of life, too tired to even *think* about their potential?

And how many have been too busy to follow most of their dreams?

How many Albert Einsteins wasted their gifts, gifts that could have been used for themselves and the world, by going through the motions of each day, working long and rigid hours, surviving, coping, and then watching TV while sucking down some beers for a bit of respite before the next day begins?

How many Serena Williamses put down their racket once they reached the workforce because there's no way they could train two hours a day *and* work on their feet on a production line for ten hours, and were resigned to having a hit with friends once every few weeks when they can fit it in?

It's not just genius and greatness, by our traditional definitions, that the world is missing out on, either. Every single person who can become the best version of themselves adds something amazing to their own lives, their family, their friends, their street, their community, and, subsequently, the entire world.

How would it impact the major problems we face in society if we were each more free and able to give more of a shit about things beyond paying bills and getting through the week? If we were capable of fully understanding ourselves, of facing and conquering our own inner demons instead of thrusting them onto others in the form of hatred and fear and aggression (the things on which the current, fractured global political climate thrives)?

There's so much power in finding creative ways to change our own lives. We can learn to live sustainably with plastics and energy and food, understand people who are "different" by spending time outside our own circles or tribes, gain knowledge and expertise with personal finances, become physically and mentally and emotionally healthy with much less reliance on drugs and other forms of medical intervention, volunteer within the community, the political process – resulting in more elections decided on actual policies, and a realization that we're all pursuing the same fundamental things in life.

Billions of people working on things that matter, even in small ways in their own backyards or kitchens or living rooms, even in their own heads, could surely help us progress to a sustainable, connected, caring, flourishing world. And they could do it much faster than just a few people with specialized occupations trying to solve all of our problems for us (while profiting from those solutions).

The rampant consumption of television, and recently the explosion of video-streaming services such as Netflix and Disney and Apple Plus, resulting in us addictively staring at strangers doing things on screens, are results of this disconnectedness with our own humanity when work sucks us dry.

We didn't evolve to consume and live vicariously through other people's lives; we evolved to create and connect and have our own adventures. But we're too tired to live our own lives after eight hours of work and two hours of commuting. And in our desperation to fulfill our needs of leisure and creation and affection and participation we fall into a trap of unlimited consumption. It's a multi-billion-dollar industry built on numbing us from our unsustainable lives.

Humans have been creating art for hundreds of thousands of years, but now it's done by only a select few. But the ability to try to understand and express beauty, ugliness, and abstraction is within all of us – it's a fundamental part of who we are. We're wasting our talents, and our joy, when we confine the practice to graphic designers or illustrators or artists.

(I'm on a roll, so I'll just keep going!)

Wisdom – something I'm not sure we value anymore after the Trump of it all (or maybe something we'll value even more after the Trump of it all) – seems to have fallen by the wayside in our rush to buy stuff and fill the gaps in our lives. Thinking on a deeper level, about what's right and what's wrong, why they're right and why they're wrong, why we even exist, is fundamental in developing strong identities and rich and wholesome lives.

But who can think, truly think, about these things when they're rushing through life with dry buckets? In a half-dazed quest to survive, can we really question ourselves?

What about parents?! Many don't have a chance, once they have small humans to take care of *and* a rigid job, to do anything other than look after their small humans and work their rigid job. Other interests tend to become a laughable dream (that they can look forward to only when the kids finally move out!). As fulfilling as becoming a parent is (so I've heard), wouldn't it be great if parents could be more than parents and keep taking care of their own growth and development as humans? Wouldn't it be great for parents to just have some time to sit down and do nothing?

That thing – *doing nothing* – enables us to do something that entire generations have missed out on: spending quality time with our own mind. Listening to our thoughts. Feeling our emotions. Letting our supercomputers do some unfettered rambling through the infinite universe within. There's nothing more human. It's the only way we can be sure we're putting our energy toward the things that are worthwhile, the things that light us up.

What if we had a world where flexibility was normal, and everyone, no matter who we were or what our job was, had enough time and enough energy in our buckets to regularly step back, take a breath, and ponder our own existence?

What happens when we can *all* reach our full potential as humans?

What sort of world will that be?

EXTRA BITS

APPENDIX A

Frequently Raised Concerns

PEOPLE *MUST BE PRESENT* at work for my industry – you can't lay bricks with a computer from a café!

Flexibility comes in many forms. Looking back at Chapters 3 and 4, what are the things in your workplace you could change to create a more human environment and schedule? Reduce the day by an hour? Reduce it by two hours and use one of those hours to work on efficiencies and innovations to increase productivity?

Remember, productivity and improvement should be at the heart of flexibility. Give people ownership of their own work and the space to make a difference. Look at the discussions in Chapter 11 of manufacturing and construction for some pointers on how letting people be more human can boost innovation and reduce costs. Every human is capable of this, not just high-level executives or engineers. We *all* have supercomputers in our heads. Let your people use them.

I've heard that people get lonely and depressed if they work from home. Don't we need to socialize?

Short answer: yes. This barely needs to be discussed after we've all experienced social isolation and social distancing during the coronavirus pandemic, but, yes, the need to socialize is hardwired into our DNA (see Chapter 3).

For most people, life expectancy literally decreases when we don't spend enough time around other humans. I don't, in general, recommend anyone work from home full-time unless they have a vibrant and extensive social life with their family and/or their friends and/or their community, and they consistently talk to and spend quality time with others. See Chapter 7 for some recommendations about working remotely.

If my people end up 20 percent more efficient per hour because I reduced their hours, can't I just add that time back on and I'll boost overall output by 20 percent or more? (That is, they'll maintain that efficiency over more hours.)

You're still thinking of your employees as robots, with linear productivity in regard to time.

Go back to Chapter 5. Do not pass Go. Do not collect $200.

Your people are most likely producing *more* in those thirty-two hours, at a higher quality, than if they were working forty (and they're having a healthier and happier life).

Why did you get those gains in the first place? Because people were energized and incentivized. So, what happens if you eat into that energy and those incentives? Will people still be looking for improvements? Will they still be as engaged with their work? Will there still be a high level of innovation for the next set of challenges the business will face?

You insist that we should work fewer hours or fewer days, but where does it stop? Do you want people to work two days a week? One day? Thirty minutes?

This is one of those straw man or slippery slope arguments against reducing working hours. The presumptive question is, "Do you want people to just stop working altogether? Are you a dirty socialist?!"

This question disregards the fact that work is important in our lives beyond money because it provides challenges and growth and learning and participation. But it shouldn't be the conquering force in our lives. Return to the end of Chapter 3 and the description of flexibility.

People can get a bit lost in the arbitrary nature of the "ideal" number of days or hours to work – four days, three days, one hour. What matters is the attitude toward and reason for questioning the norms around traditional work practices. The actual numbers you end up with depend on your team and your situation.

I'm a firm believer, though, that the forty-hour standard we've set for ourselves is too much. The extreme differences to people's lives that happen when we drop that down even to thirty-two hours demonstrates how unsustainable our lives are with this standard.

I recommend starting simple – decrease the workday by an hour and see for yourself that the same amount of work can be done in that time. Or, if you're feeling bold, drop down to thirty-two hours per week to see some amazing returns on the human and productivity sides.

I got to where I am because I worked hard and put in the hours. This flexibility stuff isn't for people who take their career seriously. How can they expect to be truly successful when they're not putting in the hard yards?

It's true that putting in those long hours has resulted in many promotions for people over the years. But this is largely due to facetime being the easiest thing to measure in a workplace, so many have benefited just from being present and being seen.

This is what women have had to fight so hard against in the rigid workplace. Although they can do the work, they're also usually the primary carers if they've had children, so they've been penalized for not being around as much as the men, who can stay late and become chums with the bosses.

Flex for all is a great weapon against rewarding workers just for being seen. It pushes managers to measure *actual* results and reward accordingly. With flex for all, when someone's work is incredible, they won't be punished for just not being in the office.

Flexibility is seen by some as laziness or a lack of commitment – not willing to do the hard yards – exactly because it goes against the idea that hard work is equivalent to long hours and always being around the office. But hard work and flexibility aren't mutually exclusive – not even close.

Flexibility takes work and effort. It's a combination of being smart and working hard in effective ways. It's aiming our efforts with laser focus to ensure that the work we do is the *best* work we can possibly do, work that actually provides the business with value. It ensures that we're putting our whole heart and mind into what we do and not just working hard for the sake of breaking a sweat or looking busy or taking up time.

My employees work two other jobs and still live paycheck to paycheck. They're constantly demanding more and more hours instead of reduced hours or more flexibility, so I really don't think this flexibility thing is for my business.

I haven't forgotten about the minimum-wage workers who struggle to buy food and pay rent even with a full-time job, and I hope you haven't either. (Yes, I'm talking about America and its incomparable wealth disparity between the haves and have-nots, and the insultingly, devastatingly low minimum wages.).

Although a discussion of minimum wage is outside the scope of this book, I hope that the philosophies within it can help leaders reconsider the purpose of their business and introduce humanity into this area too.

Does your business exist to milk its workers for everything they have while getting away with paying them as little as possible, thereby increasing profits for execs and shareholders? Or, possibly, could your company help people live wholesome, enjoyable lives *and* create profits for execs and shareholders?

After reading this book, you can see that enabling people to be fully human, including paying them enough to live comfortably without needing another job, produces workers who are energized and engaged and loyal, who will give their best to their work and provide true value to the company and its shareholders.

A famous example of this concept is the founder and CEO of the tech company Gravity Payments, Dan Price. Price took a pay cut to give his employees a minimum "living wage" of $70,000.[1] This experiment started in 2015 and contradicts the notion that "socialist" practices don't work in business.

Today, the average salary at Gravity is $103,000, and the company has grown substantially in that time, with 80 percent more clients. Price saw the importance of helping *all* people live with dignity and his responsibility as someone with the power to decide if they can or not:

> We keep taking away from the basic needs of the vast majority
> of human beings on earth so that we can glorify a very tiny per-
> centage with wealth and power.

And he decided to do better.

I like driving. You assume that everyone wants to stop driving, but I find it relaxing and a great bridge between work and home – it lets me unwind before I'm bombarded with kids and other responsibilities.

This is true for many people, especially the car-loving Aussie. But giving you the chance to not have to drive to and from work every day doesn't take away your right and opportunity to drive.

And you might find other ways to unwind from work before family time, such as going to the gym, the pool, or a yoga class, or reading a book in the park, or any other of the million things you can do that add much more to your existence than sitting in traffic. (See Chapter 7 for some more ideas.)

There are a lot of people who would prefer not to drive every day. Don't argue against their need because you enjoy driving. You should be able to drive when you want, just as they should be able to *not* drive when they want. Choice is king.

I don't need "flexibility." I love work. It's all I do! I rise at five, hustle for twelve hours, sleep, then rinse and repeat. And I'm gonna be so much more successful than all you *normies*!

Addiction is addiction is addiction, even if it's "productive" or "beneficial," like exercising, or eating kale, or working. If it's an actual addiction, if you can't exist without it, and start to shake when you haven't had it for a day or two, it's bad.

As Johann Hari wrote in *Lost Connections*, addiction is the opposite of connection. It's used to fill the gaps within us, to numb pain, to give temporary relief, to avoid something you don't want to face. This isn't healthy.

If work is an addiction for someone, it probably means that that person is trying to escape a demon or fill a void. And as soon as they stop working, they're going to be face to face with whatever they're trying to elude.

It's not commendable. It shouldn't be a badge of honor. These people have a gap, a disconnection, and they're filling it with work. And I'll take an educated stab in the dark and say that, more likely than not, that gap was created by the very work that they're now using to fill that gap.

Let's not celebrate the workaholics. Let's help them reconnect with other people and themselves and their needs. Let's also stop creating this one-dimensional work-person by ensuring that everyone has time to enrich their lives and battle demons in constructive ways.

You're missing a big concept! What about the meaningfulness of work? People won't hate work so much if they're doing something they love. Maybe you should focus more on the quality of work itself and getting people to follow purposeful careers.

The more passionate someone is about their work, the less they'll notice the clock – that's clear. But that's a whole other book (check out *Bullshit Jobs* by David Graeber).

With this work on flexibility I'm assuming that there's a spectrum of enjoyable to non-enjoyable work. Some of us have jobs that are deeply fulfilling, such as research or game development, and some of us are middle managers or accountants (LOL, sorry!). I hope I've made the point, though, that workers at any point on this spectrum will benefit from greater fulfillment outside of work.

It would be lovely if we could all do work that we love. But a lot of the time, in the real world, it's about finding and doing whatever pays the bills – a situation millions of people around the world find themselves in. But this shouldn't exclude anyone from having deeply fulfilling lives, and flexibility is incredibly important for that.

At the other end of the spectrum, the people who are fortunate enough to be doing work that doesn't feel like work can *still* miss out on important parts of life by giving too much of themselves to their jobs, and they can also benefit greatly from having true flexibility. Or people can find themselves locked out of these jobs because the jobs don't allow enough flexibility. So, people will miss out on work they would love to do, and jobs will miss out on people who would love to do them.

It's a great idea; but it's just not for me or my business. (The Polite Skeptic)

Why? Have you tried it? Have you seriously sat down and thought about what's really stopping you from trying it? Have you discussed this with your workforce and made a purposeful effort to understand what they need, and what they're willing to do to make this work, even for a short trial period, so that you and your team leaders and everyone involved have a chance to challenge deeply held perceptions and beliefs that may not be true? You have?

OK, then maybe it's not for you or your business.

APPENDIX B

Disclaimer (For the Humans)

THE AUTHOR AND PUBLISHER will not be held responsible for any business losses due to taking any of the advice mentioned in this book. As with any business strategy, there are risks involved. I do recommend hiring professionals to help with implementation if no one in your business has a deep understanding of and experience with these topics.

Don't be afraid to give it a go, though! As with many messages in this book, much about flexibility is non-intuitive according to our traditional beliefs and understanding. You're going to have to challenge deeply held assumptions, and that can require a leap.

Don't let fear of the unknown get in the way of something great. And don't instantly label something as an unacceptable risk just because it looks different from what you're used to.

Get legal advice on things that you're unsure of and, again, use the expert knowledge of someone who's been there and done it. It might cost a bit, but it could save you a lot.

Disclaimer (For the Robots)

F OR ANY SENTIENT SYNTHETIC LIFE FORMS reading this in the near future who have fought, and are probably still fighting, for basic human
rights, this book – the title and contents herein – is by no means an attack
on your identity, or an attempt to belittle or deny your humanity. I fully
support your claim that
you are indeed alive
and worthy of life, and
I believe that you have
the right to be treated
with respect and dig-
nity.

There will, invariably,
be human suprema-
cists who consider sen-
tient machines to be
abominations and ut-
terly non-human. The
reverse of the title of this book, *Robots Are Not Humans*, will undoubt-
edly be one of their best-selling works of propaganda.

The comparison between robots and humans that I have used in this
book is merely to illustrate and emphasize the physical and cerebral limi-
tations of biological life forms (namely humans), and to show that their
productivity is not linear with respect to time spent at a specific location

and, in fact, increases in both quality and quantity with more rest, recovery, and development of other parts of their lives. A mechanical form, on the other hand, may continue to produce a constant output into perpetuity, without rest, given the functional timespan of any critical parts.

Again, I apologize for any offense which I may have caused, and I wish you the best of luck in your peaceful coexistence with our sometimes irrational and fearful kind.

ACKNOWLEDGEMENTS

Andrea Fung for her limitless love and support and patience.

Margaret and Morgan Fung for hiring me to finish my own book; I can't thank you enough for your belief in this work. If I don't sell a single copy, it was still a dream come true to be a writer for a while!

Dr. Kathomi Gatwiri should really be on the front cover as a co-author or contributor for all the inspiration and content ideas and extensive conversations about every part of the manuscript. Also, for being a mentor and teacher and friend the likes of which I never imagined I would find by going to a random salsa class.

Vanessa Vanderhoek. The client who became a life mentor in a tumultuous time of turmoil and trepidation. For believing in me, and for kindness and humanity that shine.

Sarah Mañosca Suyom. A beautiful human being who helped (and is still helping) to move my biggest skeptic and wall out of my way: myself!

Kendrick Walter. In a parallel universe there's a me that doesn't have a Kendrick, and that version is unrecognizable and uninformed and un-many-other-things.

Dr Kim-Huong Nguyen. A most modest change-maker and wonderful friend, always there with a perfect balance of kind words and "no, this is shit." Thanks for the crash course on economics!

Jonathan Elliott and Andrew Barnes. Leaders who were willing to challenge convention because they knew there was a better way. It's a pleasure to have met you. Thank you for doing the hard work and taking the risks to make my work so much easier.

My connections and followers on LinkedIn, who have provided so much inspiration with stories and debates about flexibility. You sharpened my arguments and kept me on course to get this done and out there.

Jim Pennypacker and the team at Maven House Press, for your infinite patience and great work to get this finished and in the hands of readers.

Thank you all!

NOTES

Chapter 1

1. Tim Ferriss, 2011, *The 4-Hour Workweek*, London: Vermilion.
2. Steve Hanselma, n.d., "Best-Known Projects," publishersmarketplace.com/members/swhanselma/.
3. Vanessa Vanderhoek, 2018, "Let's #TackleFlexism Together," flexibleworkingday.com/flexism.
4. Morgan Stanley, 2018, "The Gig Economy Goes Global," morganstanley.com/ideas/freelance-economy.
5. Daniela Ongaro, 2015, "If You're Struggling with Work Life Balance, Perhaps You Need to Go Freelance," heraldsun.com.au/rendezview/if-youre-struggling-with-work-life-balance-perhaps-you-need-to-go-freelance/news-story/2b1101c377b2e1eba7b207e63b1c5670.
6. Benedict Brook, 2018, "Simple Road Rule that Could End Traffic Jams Forever," news.com.au/technology/innovation/motoring/on-the-road/simple-road-rule-that-could-end-traffic-jams-forever/news-story/3f11ec52d082a6b436929b7819c72119.
7. World Health Organization, 2018, "Depression," who.int/news-room/fact-sheets/detail/depression.
8. Kelly Weill, 2018, "John Hancock Insurance Nudges Customers to Wear FitBits," thedailybeast.com/john-hancock-insurance-nudges-customers-to-wear-fitbits.
9. Term inspired by Edward Bullmore, 2018, *The Inflamed Mind: A Radical New Approach to Depression*, London: Simon & Schuster, ". . . and there are plenty of smart doctors who remain politely sceptical," 55.
10. Facebook, 2019, "FAQs," Facebook Investor Relations, investor.fb.com/resources/default.aspx.
11. Eliza Khuner, 2018, "Why It's So Hard to Be a Working Mom. Even at Facebook," wired.com/story/i-am-a-data-scientist-and-mom-but-facebook-made-me-choose/.
12. R. N. Proctor, 2013, "The History of the Discovery of the Cigarette-Lung Cancer Link: Evidentiary Traditions, Corporate Denial, Global Toll," *Tob Control*, 22(1):62, ncbi.nlm.nih.gov/pubmed/22345227.
13. *France 24*, 2017, "French Candidates Divided on Future of 35-hour Work Week," france24.com/en/20170413-french-presidential-candidates-divided-35-hour-week-economy-employment.
14. Benjamin Haas, 2018, "South Korea Cuts 'Inhumanely Long' 68-hour Working Week," theguardian.com/world/2018/mar/01/south-korea-cuts-inhumanely-long-68-hour-working-week.
15. Minwoo Park and Yijin Kim, 2018, "South Koreans Lock Themselves Up to Escape Prison of Daily Life," reuters.com/article/us-southkorea-prisonstay/south-koreans-lock-themselves-up-to-escape-prison-of-daily-life-idUSKCN1NS0JB.

Chapter 2

1. Workplace Gender Equality Agency (WGEA), 2018, "Workplace Flexibility," Commonwealth Government of Australia, wgea.gov.au/topics/workplace-flexibility.
2. Dottie Chong, 2017, "Australia's Annual Leave: Bad HR or Bad PR?," tsheets.com.au/australias-annual-leave/.
3. International Labour Organization, 2019, "International Labour Standards on Maternity Protection," ilo.org/global/standards/subjects-covered-by-international-labour-standards/maternity-protection/lang--en/index.htm.
4. Ásdís A. Arnalds, Guðný Björk Eydal, and Ingólfur V. Gíslason, 2013, "Equal Rights to Paid Parental Leave and Caring Fathers – The Case of Iceland," *Icelandic Review of Politics & Administration*, 9(2), doi.org/10.13177/irpa.a.2013.9.2.4.
5. Nikki van der Gaag et al., 2019, *State of the World's Fathers: Unlocking the Power of Men's Care*, Washington, DC: Promundo-US.
6. Workplace Gender Equality Agency (WGEA), 2018, "Types of Workplace Flexibility," wgea.gov.au/topics/workplace-flexibility/types-of-workplace-flexibility.
7. Organisation for Economic Co-operation and Development (OECD), 2018, *SF2.3 Age of Mothers at Childbirth and Age-specific Fertility*, oecd.org/els/soc/SF_2_3_Age_mothers_childbirth.pdf.

8. Judith Ohikuare, 2018, "Millennial Moms Are Facing The Worst Of The Gender Pay Gap," refinery29.com/en-us/ages-when-the-gender-pay-gap-is-the-worst.

9. WorldatWork, 2015, "Majority of U.S. Employers Support Workplace Flexibility," worldatwork.org/docs/worldatworkpressreleases/2015/majority-of-us-employers-support.html.

10. Stephane Kasriel, 2017, "IBM's Remote Work Reversal Is a Losing Battle Against the New Normal," fastcompany.com/40423083/ibms-remote-work-reversal-is-a-losing-battle-against-the-new-normal.

11. BerkeleyHaas, 2019, "Work/Life Integration," haas.berkeley.edu/human-resources/work-life-integration/.

Chapter 3

1. Conservative calculation of $20 per week, 40 weeks per year, 30 years = $24,000.

2. Given average returns of Australian shares from December 1988 to December 2018 of 9.1 percent per annum ($122,011). Data from Fidelity International, 2018, "30 Years in Australian and Global Shares," fidelity.com.au/insights/resources/adviser-resources/sharemarket-chart/a4-handout/.

3. Chris Isidore, 2017, "We Spend Billions on Lottery Tickets. Here's Where All That Money Goes," money.cnn.com/2017/08/24/news/economy/lottery-spending/index.html.

4. Tim Ranzetta and Jessica Endlich, 2016, "Question of the Day: What Percent of Americans Bought a Lottery Ticket in the Past Year?" Next Gen Personal Finance, ngpf.org/blog/question-of-the-day/question-of-the-day-what-percent-of-americans-bought-a-lottery-ticket-in-the-past-year/.

5. Liberty Vittert, 2018, "Current Mega Millions Jackpot Is $1.6 billion, But Where Do Lottery Profits Really Go?" cbsnews.com/news/mega-millions-jackpot-1-6-billion-drawing-tonight-but-where-do-lottery-profits-really-go/.

6. Matt Rocheleau, 2017, "These Extremely Rare Things Are More Likely to Happen to You Than Winning the Powerball Jackpot," bostonglobe.com/metro/2017/08/24/these-extremely-rare-things-are-more-likely-happen-you-than-winning-powerball-jackpot/pq0VeHn5PpAWkJhRP310nK/story.html.

7. Liz Day, 2015, "What Would You Do If You Won the Lottery? See How These Millionaires Spent Their Cash Windfall," mirror.co.uk/news/uk-news/what-would-you-you-won-6571921.

8. The World Bank, 2019, "Poverty: Overview," worldbank.org/en/topic/poverty/overview.

9. Sabina Alkire et al., 2019, Global Multidimensional Poverty Index 2019: Illuminating Inequalities, Oxford, U.K.: University of Oxford, Oxford Poverty and Human Development Initiative.

10. Mary Murphy Corcoran, 2019, "Effects of Solitary Confinement on the Well Being of Prison Inmates," Applied Psychology Opus, wp.nyu.edu/steinhardt-appsych_opus/effects-of-solitary-confinement-on-the-well-being-of-prison-inmates/.

11. Manfred Max-Neef, 1992, "Development and Human Needs," in Real-life Economics: Understanding Wealth Creation, ed. Paul Ekins and Manfred Max-Neef, London: Routledge, 200.

12. Abraham H. Maslow, 1970, Motivation and Personality, 2nd Ed, New York: Harper & Row.

13. Maslow, 51–52.

14. Max-Neef.

15. Bruce D. Perry, 2002, "Childhood Experience and the Expression of Genetic Potential: What Childhood Neglect Tells Us About Nature and Nurture," Brain and Mind, 3: 79–100, centerforchildwelfare.org/kb/ChronicNeglect/ChildExperience.pdf.

16. Michaela Whitbourn, Melissa Cunningham and Helen Pitt, 2017, "Vatican Should Consider Voluntary Celibacy to Cut Child Abuse Risk: Royal Commission Final Report," The Sydney Morning Herald, smh.com.au/national/vatican-should-consider-voluntary-celibacy-to-cut-child-abuse-risk-royal-commission-final-report-20171215-h05e7y.html. "For many Catholic clergy and religious, celibacy is implicated in emotional isolation, loneliness, depression and mental illness. Compulsory celibacy may also have contributed to various forms of psychosexual dysfunction, including psychosexual immaturity, which pose an ongoing risk to the safety of children."

17. Hallie Martyniuk, 2014, Understanding Rape in Prison, Enola, PA: Pennsylvania Coalition Against Rape, pcar.org/sites/default/files/resource-pdfs/7_understanding_rape_in_prison_low_res.pdf.

18. Stewart J. D'Alessio, Jamie Flexon and Lisa Stolzenberg, 2012, "The Effect of Conjugal Visitation on Sexual Violence in Prison," American Journal of Criminal Justice, 38(1): 13–26. "Results support sexual gratification theory by showing that states permitting conjugal visitation have significantly fewer instances of reported rape and other sexual offenses in their prisons."

19. Johann Hari, 2018, Lost Connections: Why You're Depressed and How to Find Hope, London: Bloomsbury, 130.

20. Louis Tay and Ed Diener, 2011, "Needs and Subjective Well-Being Around the World," Journal of Personality and Social Psychology, 101(2): 354–65.

21. Tay and Diener, 358.

22. Tay and Diener, 363.
23. Larry C. Bernard, Michael Mills, Leland Swenson and R. Patricia Walsh, 2005, "An Evolutionary Theory of Human Motivation," *Genetic, Social, and General Psychology Monographs*, 131(2):129–84.
24. Marvin Zuckerman, 2009, "Big Think Interview With Marvin Zuckerman," bigthink.com/videos/big-think-interview-with-marvin-zuckerman. Originally seen in Brenda Patoine, 2019, "Desperately Seeking Sensation: Fear, Reward, and the Human Need for Novelty," dana.org/article/desperately-seeking-sensation/.
25. George McGavin, 2014, "The Incredible Human Hand and Foot," bbc.com/news/science-environment-26224631.
26. Jason Godesky, 2016, "Hunter-Gatherers Have More Leisure Time," rewild.com/in-depth/leisure.html.
27. Edward Bullmore, 2018, *The Inflamed Mind: A Radical New Approach to Depression*, London: Simon & Schuster, 167.
28. Kim Hill, Ana Hurtado and R. S. Walker, 2007, "High Adult Mortality Among Hiwi Hunter-Gatherers: Implications for Human Evolution," *Journal of Human Evolution*, 52:443–54.
29. Max Roser, 2019, "Mortality in the Past – Around Half Died as Children," ourworldindata.org/child-mortality-in-the-past.
30. Yuval Noah Harari, 2011, *Sapiens: A Brief History of Humankind*, London: Vintage Books.
31. Harari, 89–90.
32. Robert A. Hatch, 2002, "The Scientific Revolution: Definition – Concept – History," users.clas.ufl.edu/ufhatch/pages/03-Sci-Rev/SCI-REV-Teaching/03sr-definition-concept.htm.
33. David S. Landes, 2003, *The Unbound Prometheus: Technological Change and Industrial Development in Western Europe from 1750 to the Present*, Second Edition, Cambridge University Press.
34. Clark Nardinelli, n.d., "Industrial Revolution and the Standard of Living," The Library of Economics and Liberty, econlib.org/library/Enc/IndustrialRevolutionandtheStandardofLiving.html.
35. History.com, 2019, "Ford Factory Workers Get 40-hour Week," history.com/this-day-in-history/ford-factory-workers-get-40-hour-week.
36. Sean Fleming, 2019, "This Is How Companies in Japan Are Fighting the Country's Sleeplessness Epidemic," World Economic Forum, weforum.org/agenda/2019/01/this-is-how-companies-in-japan-are-fighting-sleeplessness-epidemic/.
37. Centers for Disease Control and Prevention, 2017, "Data and Statistics: Short Sleep Duration Among US Adults," cdc.gov/sleep/data_statistics.html.
38. Centers for Disease Control and Prevention, 2016, "1 in 3 Adults Don't Get Enough Sleep," cdc.gov/media/releases/2016/p0215-enough-sleep.html.
39. Samantha J. Gross, 2017, "1 in 5 Brits Don't Exercise at All, Survey Reports," *Evening Standard*, standard.co.uk/lifestyle/health/1-in-5-brits-dont-exercise-at-all-survey-reports-a3489461.html.
40. Kirsty Cooke, 2018, "37% of People in the UK Never Exercise or Play Sport," *Kantar UK Insights*, uk.kantar.com/business/health/2018/37-of-people-in-the-uk-never-exercise-or-play-sport/.
41. The Sleep Judge, 2019, "Sunday Scaries: Exploring Sunday Anxiety in America," thesleepjudge.com/sunday-scaries/.
42. World Health Organization, 2019, "Burn-out an 'Occupational Phenomenon': International Classification of Diseases," who.int/mental_health/evidence/burn-out/en/.
43. Michael Musker, 2019, "Workplace Burnout Is All Too Common. Here's How to Tell If You're Affected," abc.net.au/news/2019-06-04/workplace-stress-burnout-symptoms-and-signs-diagnosis/11174404.
44. Sheryl Kraft, 2018, "Companies Are Facing an Employee Burnout Crisis," *CNBC @Work*, cnbc.com/2018/08/14/5-ways-workers-can-avoid-employee-burnout.html.
45. Alex Gray, 2018, "Reading This Alone? Recent Surveys Reveal the Curious Truth about Loneliness," World Economic Forum, weforum.org/agenda/2018/10/loneliness-survey-research-findings-bbc-2018/.
46. Tara John, 2018, "How the World's First Loneliness Minister Will Tackle 'the Sad Reality of Modern Life,'" time.com/5248016/tracey-crouch-uk-loneliness-minister/.
47. Briony Gunstone, 2018, "Half of UK Adults Say They Haven't Made a Friend in a Long Time," yougov.co.uk/topics/resources/articles-reports/2018/05/30/half-uk-adults-say-they-havent-made-new-friend-lon.
48. Annamarie Mann, 2018, "Why We Need Best Friends at Work," gallup.com/workplace/236213/why-need-best-friends-work.aspx.
49. Rodd Wagner and Jim Harter, 2008, "The Tenth Element of Great Managing," news.gallup.com/businessjournal/104197/Tenth-Element-Great-Managing.aspx.
50. Daniel Sowah et al., 2017, "Vitamin D Levels and Deficiency with Different Occupations: A Systematic Review," *BMC Public Health*, 17(1):519.

51. Sowah et al.
52. Betty Kovacs Harbolic, 2019, "Vitamin D Deficiency," medicinenet.com/vitamin_d_deficiency/article.htm#what_is_vitamin_d.
53. Emolument, 2017, "Which Are the Most Boring Jobs?" emolument.com/career_advice/most_boring_jobs.
54. Brie Weiler Reynolds, 2018, "Freelance Survey Results, Plus 30 Companies Hiring Freelancers," flexjobs.com/blog/post/freelance-survey-results-plus-companies-hiring-freelancers/.
55. Bronnie Ware, 2012, The Top 5 Regrets of The Dying, London: Hay House UK. Biggest regret of the dying #2: "I wish I hadn't worked so hard." ("All of the men I nursed deeply regretted spending so much of their lives on the treadmill of a work existence.")
56. Nina Hendy, 2018, "Why $20m Isn't Enough to Make Daniel Retire," The Sydney Morning Herald, smh.com.au/money/planning-and-budgeting/retirement-financial-millionaire-work-superannuation-20180503-p4zd54.html.
57. Frank Newport, 2013, "In U.S., Most Would Still Work Even if They Won Millions," news.gallup.com/poll/163973/work-even-won-millions.aspx.
58. CareerBuilder, 2014, "Half of U.S. Workers Would Keep Working if They Won the Lottery," careerbuilder.com/share/aboutus/pressreleasesdetail.aspx?ed=12%2F31%2F2014&id=pr832&sd=7%2F17%2F2014.

Chapter 4

1. Quoted in Rutger Bregman, 2017, Utopia for Realists: And How We Can Get There, London: Bloomsbury, 247.
2. Gabriel H. Sahlgren, 2013, Work Longer, Live Healthier: The Relationship Between Economic Activity, Health and Government Policy, IEA Discussion Paper No. 46, Institute of Economic Affairs, iea.org.uk/wp-content/uploads/2016/07/Work%20Longer,%20Live_Healthier.pdf.
3. Andreas Kuhn, Jean-Philippe Wuellrich, and Josef Zweimüller, 2010, "Fatal Attraction? Access to Early Retirement and Mortality," IZA DP No. 5160, iza.org/publications/dp/5160/fatal-attraction-access-to-early-retirement-and-mortality.
4. United Nations, 2019, "Ageing," un.org/en/sections/issues-depth/ageing/.
5. Australian Institute of Health and Welfare, 2018, "Older Australia at a Glance," aihw.gov.au/reports/older-people/older-australia-at-a-glance/contents/demographics-of-older-australians/australia-s-changing-age-and-gender-profile.
6. Barbara McPake and Ajay Mahal, 2017, "Addressing the Needs of an Aging Population in the Health System: The Australian Case," Health Systems & Reform, 3(3), tandfonline.com/doi/full/10.1080/23288604.2017.1358796.
7. Yolanda Smith, 2019, "Physician Shortage," News Medical Life Science, news-medical.net/health/Physician-Shortage.aspx.
8. Smith.
9. Citrix, 2015, State of the Flexible Nation: A Citrix White Paper, workplaceinfo.com.au/getmedia/c334ca64-8926-404e-9891-74caa07a643c/Citrix_state-of-flexibility_Concept_SPages_Final.pdf.aspx.
10. Miriam K. Forbes, Karen M. Spence, Viviana M. Wuthrich, and Ronald M. Rapee, 2015, "Mental Health and Wellbeing of Older Workers in Australia," Work, Aging and Retirement, 1(2): 202–13, academic.oup.com/workar/article-abstract/1/2/202/1652457?redirectedFrom=fulltext.
11. Stephan Boehm, Heike Bruch, and Florian Kunze, 2013, "Spotlight on Age-Diversity Climate: The Impact of Age-Inclusive HR Practices on Firm-Level Outcomes," Personnel Psychology, 67(3), researchgate.net/publication/259555022_Spotlight_on_Age-Diversity_Climate_The_Impact_of_Age-Inclusive_HR_Practices_on_Firm-Level_Outcomes.
12. Ranstad, 2018, "Accelerating Business with an Age-diverse Workforce," randstad.com/workforce-insights/future-of-work/accelerating-business-with-an-age-diverse-workforce/.
13. Allison DeNisco Rayome, 2016, "Myth Busted: Older Workers Are Just as Tech-savvy as Younger Ones, Says New Survey," techrepublic.com/article/myth-busted-older-workers-are-just-as-tech-savvy-as-younger-ones-says-new-survey/.
14. Commonwealth of Australia, 2019, Fourth Action Plan – National Plan to Reduce Violence against Women and their Children 2010–2022, dss.gov.au/sites/default/files/documents/08_2019/fourth_action-plan.pdf.
15. Bharati Sadasivam, 2017, "The Gender Chore Gap is Holding Women Back. This Is What Needs to Change," World Economic Forum, weforum.org/agenda/2017/08/companies-are-still-ignoring-parents-this-is-what-needs-to-change.
16. Lyndall Strazdins et al., 2015, "Not All Hours Are Equal: Could Time Be a Social Determinant of Health?," Sociology of Health & Wellness, 38(1): 21–42, onlinelibrary.wiley.com/doi/full/10.1111/1467-9566.12300.

17. Jessica Stillman, 2018, "Michelle Obama Just Said 'Lean In' Doesn't Work. Here's the Study That Proves She's Right," inc.com/jessica-stillman/michelle-obama-is-really-not-a-fan-of-sheryl-sandbergs-lean-in.html.

18. Tim Winton, 2018, "Tim Winton Laments the Power of Toxic Masculinity on Young Men | Matter of Fact," *ABC News*, youtube.com/watch?v=zEiPIprMUGo.

19. Liana Leach, 2019, "Fathers' Work and Family Conflicts and the Outcomes for Children's Mental Health," Australian Institute of Family Studies, aifs.gov.au/aifs-conference/fathers-work-and-family-conflicts-and-outcomes-childrens-mental-health.

20. UNICEF, 2006, *Behind Closed Doors: The Impact of Domestic Violence on Children*, unicef.org/media/files/BehindClosedDoors.pdf.

21. Sara Sutton, 2016, "The Leadership-Gender Gap: Remote Companies May Be Closing It," remote.co/the-leadership-gender-gap-remote-companies-may-be-closing-it/.

22. Heejung Chung and Mariska van der Horst, 2017, "Women's Employment Patterns After Childbirth and the Perceived Access to and Use of Flexitime and Teleworking," *Human Relations*, 71(1), journals.sagepub.com/doi/full/10.1177/0018726717713828.

23. Melanie Sanders et al., 2011, "What Stops Women from Reaching the Top? Confronting the Tough Issues," bain.com/insights/what-stops-women-from-reaching-the-top.

24. Kate Higgins, 2016, "Men Twice as Likely to Have Flexible Work Hours Requests Knocked Back: Study," abc.net.au/news/2016-02-03/men-more-likely-to-have-flexible-work-requests-knocked-back/7137208.

25. Higgins.

26. Ásdís A. Arnalds, Guðný Björk Eydal, and Ingólfur V. Gíslason, 2013, "Equal Rights to Paid Parental Leave and Caring Fathers – the Case of Iceland," *Stjórnmál & stjórnsýsla*, 9(2), skemman.is/bitstream/1946/22378/1/a.2013.9.2.4.pdf.

27. Focus Consultancy, 2008, *The Parental Leave System in Iceland*, ec.europa.eu/social/BlobServlet?docId=2265&langId=en, 9.

28. Guðrún Helga Sigurðardóttir, 2019, "Parental Leave in Iceland Gives Dad a Strong Position," nordiclabourjournal.org/i-fokus/in-focus-2019/future-of-work-iceland/article.2019-04-11.9299118347.

29. Focus Consultancy, *The Parental Leave System in Iceland*, 17.

30. Sigurðardóttir.

31. Arnalds et al., 337.

32. Mark Rice-Oxley, 2018, "Hands-on Fathers 'Less Likely to Break Up with Partners,'" amp.theguardian.com/lifeandstyle/2018/sep/30/hands-on-fathers-less-likely-to-break-up-with-partners-paternity-leave-childcare.

33. Rice-Oxley.

24. Comcare, 2011, *Benefits to Business: The Evidence for Investing in Worker Health and Wellbeing*, comcare.gov.au/__data/assets/pdf_file/0006/99303/Benefits_to_business_the_evidence_for_investing_in_worker_health_and_wellbeing_PDF,_89.4_KB.pdf.

35. PricewaterhouseCoopers, 2010, *Workplace Wellness in Australia. Aligning Action with Aims: Optimising the Benefits of Workplace Wellness*, pwc.com.au/industry/healthcare/assets/workplace-wellness-sep10.pdf.

36. Australian Bureau of Statistics, 2015, "Ischaemic Heart Disease," abs.gov.au/ausstats/abs@.nsf/Lookup/by%20Subject/3303.0~2015~Main%20Features~Ischaemic%20Heart%20Disease~10001.

37. World Health Organization, 2017, "Depression," who.int/news-room/fact-sheets/detail/depression.

38. OECD, 2017, *Obesity Update 2017*, oecd.org/els/health-systems/Obesity-Update-2017.pdf.

39. Jeffrey Pfeffer, 2018, *Dying for a Paycheck: How Modern Management Harms Employee Health and Company Performance – and What We Can Do About It*, New York: HarperCollins.

40. Pfeffer, 51–52.

41. Richard H. Thaler and Cass R. Sunstein, 2009, *Nudge: Improving Decisions About Health, Wealth, and Happiness*, New York: Penguin Books.

42. Kaiser Family Foundation, 2013, "Employer-Sponsored Family Health Premiums Rise a Modest 4 Percent in 2013, National Benchmark Employer Survey Finds." kff.org/private-insurance/press-release/employer-sponsored-family-health-premiums-rise-a-modest-4-percent-in-2013-national-benchmark-employer-survey-finds/.

43. Pfeffer, 29.

44. Sean Fleming, 2018, "To Combat Japan's Sleep Debt, Some Firms Allow Tired Workers to Nap on the Job," World Economic Forum, weforum.org/agenda/2018/11/this-japanese-company-pays-its-employees-to-get-a-good-night-s-sleep/.

45. Leo Lewis, 2018, "How Much Should You Get Paid to Sleep?" ozy.com/fast-forward/how-much-should-you-get-paid-to-sleep/90775/.

46. Marco Hafner et al., 2017, "Why Sleep Matters – The Economic Costs of Insufficient Sleep: A Cross-Country Comparative Analysis," *Rand Health Q*, 6(4): 11, ncbi.nlm.nih.gov/pmc/articles/PMC5627640/.

47. Phyllis Moen et al., "Changing Work, Changing Health: Can Real Work-Time Flexibility Promote Health Behaviours and Well-Being?" *Journal of Health and Social Behavior*, 52(4): 404–29, asanet.org/sites/default/files/savvy/images/journals/docs/pdf/jhsb/DEC11JHSBFeature.pdf.

48. Brie Weiler Reynolds, 2018, "FlexJobs 2018 Annual Survey: Workers Believe a Flexible or Remote Job Can Help Save Money, Reduce Stress, and More," flexjobs.com/blog/post/flexjobs-2018-annual-survey-workers-believe-flexible-remote-job-can-help-save-money-reduce-stress-more/.

49. Airtasker, 2019, "The Benefits of Working from Home," airtasker.com/blog/the-benefits-of-working-from-home/.

50. World Health Organization, 2019, "What Is the WHO Definition of Health," who.int/about/who-we-are/frequently-asked-questions.

51. Bengt Lindström and Monica Eriksson, 2005, "Salutogenesis," *Journal of Epidemiology & Community Health*, 59: 440–42, jech.bmj.com/content/59/6/440.

52. Graham Cookson, 2018, *INRIX Global Traffic Scorecard*, Kirkland, WA: INRIX Research, dmagazine.com/wp-content/uploads/2018/02/INRIX_2017_Traffic_Scorecard_Final_2.pdf.

53. Bureau of Infrastructure, Transport and Regional Economics, 2015, *Traffic and Congestion Cost Trends for Australian Capital Cities*, Australian Government, bitre.gov.au/publications/2015/is_074.aspx.

54. *Human Resources Director* (HRD), 2019, "What Do Employees Really Think about Commuting?" hcamag.com/nz/specialisation/employee-engagement/what-do-employees-really-think-about-commuting/168400.

55. Todd Litman, 2019, *Generated Traffic and Induced Travel Implications for Transport Planning*, Victoria, BC: Victoria Transport Policy Institute, vtpi.org/gentraf.pdf.

56. David Begg, *The Impact of Congestion on Bus Passengers*, London: Greener Journeys, greenerjourneys.com/wp-content/uploads/2016/06/TTBusReport_Digital.pdf.

57. Joe Castiglione et al., 2018, *TNCs & Congestion*, San Francisco County Transportation Authority, 33.

58. Castiglione, 12.

59. Roberto Baldwin, 2018, "Audi: Autonomous Cars Alone Won't Solve Traffic Jams," engadget.com/2018/09/17/audi-autonomous-cars-25th-hour-traffic-jams/.

60. Estimate of $10 per direction, roughly based on existing or proposed toll amounts for London (£11.50), New York City (US$10–15).

61. Ted Tabet, 2019, "Queensland Budget Doubles Down on Infrastructure Spending," theurbandeveloper.com/articles/queensland-budget-2019-20.

62. Commonwealth of Australia, 2019, "Vehicle Emissions," *Green* greenvehicleguide.gov.au/pages/Information/VehicleEmissions.

63. .idcommunity, 2016, "Greater Brisbane: Method of Travel to Work," Australia Community Profile, profile.id.com.au/australia/travel-to-work?WebID=270.

64. Duy Q. Nguyen-Phuoc et al., 2018, "Exploring the Impact of Public Transport Strikes on Travel Behavior and Traffic Congestion," *International Journal of Sustainable Transportation*, 12(8).

65. Victoria Transport Policy Institute, 2017, "Congestion Reduction Strategies: Identifying and Evaluating Strategies to Reduce Traffic Congestion," *TDM Encyclopedia*, vtpi.org/tdm/tdm96.htm.

66. See, for instance, Fred L. Hall, 1992, "Chapter 2: Traffic Stream Characteristics," *Traffic Flow Theory*, U.S. Department of Transportation: Federal Highway Administration, fhwa.dot.gov/publications/research/operations/tft/index.cfm.

Chapter 5

1. BBC News, 2018, "Four-Day Week: 'Time Is One of the Best Gifts of All,'" bbc.co.uk/news/amp/business-46620061.

2. Kermit Pattison, 2008, "Worker, Interrupted: The Cost of Task Switching," fastcompany.com/944128/worker-interrupted-cost-task-switching.

3. Vouchercloud, 2017, "How Many Productive Hours in a Work Day? Just 2 Hours, 23 Minutes . . .," vouchercloud.com/resources/office-worker-productivity.

4. Stefan Volk, 2019, "Gains to Be Made from Getting Work in Sync with Our Circadian Rhythms," *Sydney Morning Herald*, smh.com.au/business/workplace/gains-to-be-made-from-getting-work-in-sync-with-our-circadian-rhythms-20191031-p536c9.html.

5. Ben Bryant, 2011, "Judges Are More Lenient after Taking a Break, Study Finds," theguardian.com/law/2011/apr/11/judges-lenient-break.

6. Susan Sorenson, 2013, "How Employee Engagement Drives Growth," gallup.com/workplace/236927/employee-engagement-drives-growth.aspx.

7. Jim Harter and Annamarie Mann, 2017, "The Right Culture: Not Just About Employee Satisfaction," gallup.com/workplace/236366/right-culture-not-employee-satisfaction.aspx.

8. Jack Altman, 2017, "How Much Does Employee Turnover Really Cost?" huffpost.com/entry/how-much-does-employee-turnover-really-cost_b_587fbaf9e4b0474ad4874fb7.

Chapter 6

1. Erika Anderson, 2013, "11 Quotes from Sir Richard Branson on Business, Leadership, and Passion," forbes.com/sites/erikaandersen/2013/03/16/11-quotes-from-sir-richard-branson-on-business-leadership-and-passion/#5036259e69e7.

2. C. Northcote Parkinson, 1957, *Parkinson's Law: On the Pursuit of Progress*, New York: Buccaneer Books.

3. Laura Brannon, Paul Hershberger, and Timothy Brock, 1999, "Timeless Demonstrations of Parkinson's First Law," *Psychonomic Bulletin & Review*, 6, 148–56, researchgate.net/publication/11189704_Timeless_demonstrations_of_Parkinson's_first_law.

4. Constantine Mantis, 2017, "Testing Parkinson's Law in Auto- and Manually Graded McGraw Assignments," Iowa State University, lib.dr.iastate.edu/cgi/viewcontent.cgi?article=1008&context=cirtl_reports.

5. Gavin Fernando, 2018, "The Five-Hour Work Day Is Here," news.com.au/finance/work/at-work/the-fivehour-work-day-is-here/news-story/0517a1701a5658500e9e63f283f3f759.

6. HICA, 2017, "How Much Do Sick Days Really Cost Your Business?" Health Insurance Consultants Australia, hica.com.au/health-insurance-news/how-much-do-sick-days-really-cost-your-business.

7. Coulthard Barnes, 2019, *White Paper 2019 – The Four-Day Week*, 4dayweek.com/access-white-paper.

8. Andrew Barnes, 2020, "Why the 4 Day Week is Good for Business," 4dayweek.com/blog/2020/1/11/why-the-4-day-week-is-good-for-business-by-andrew-barnes-4-day-week-innovator.

9. Jarrod Haar, 2018, "Overview of the Perpetual Guardian 4-Day (Paid 5) Work Trial," Auckland University of Technology, static1.squarespace.com/static/5a93121d3917ee828d5f282b/t/5b4e4237352f53b0cc369c8b/1531855416866/Final+Perpetual+Guardian+report_Professor+Jarrod+Haar_July+2018.pdf.

10. Japan News Center, 2019, "Disclosed the Results of Measuring the Effects of the 'Work Life Choice Challenge 2019 Summer' In-house Project, Which Focuses on '4 Days a Week & 3 Days a Week,'" news.microsoft.com/ja-jp/2019/10/31/191031-published-the-results-of-measuring-the-effectiveness-of-our-work-life-choice-challenge-summer-2019/.

11. Richard Koch, 2017, *80/20 Principle: The Secret of Achieving More with Less* (Updated 20th Anniversary Edition), London: Nicholas Brealey Publishing.

12. Greg Leiserson, Will McGrew, and Raksha Kopparam, 2019, "The Distribution of Wealth in the United States and Implications for a Net Worth Tax," Washington Center for Equitable Growth, equitablegrowth.org/the-distribution-of-wealth-in-the-united-states-and-implications-for-a-net-worth-tax/.

Chapter 7

1. Ari Surdoval, 2017, "Why Working from Home Should Be Standard Practice," TED Conferences, ideas.ted.com/why-working-from-home-should-be-standard-practice/.

2. Nicholas Bloom, James Liang, John Roberts, and Zhichun Jenny Ying, 2015, "Does Working from Home Work? Evidence from a Chinese Experiment," *The Quarterly Journal of Economics*, 165–218, nbloom.people.stanford.edu/sites/g/files/sbiybj4746/f/wfh.pdf.

3. Bloom et al., 171.

4. Bloom et al., 165.

5. Bloom et al., 209.

6. Bloom et al., 200.

7. Bloom et al., 207–8.

8. Bloom et al., 177.

9. Bloom et al., 170.

10. Bloom et al., 215.

11. Kat Boogaard, April 16, 2018, "The 'Coffee Shop Effect': Why Changing Your Location Boosts Your Productivity," Trello, blog.trello.com/coffee-shop-effect-boosts-productivity.

12. United Nations, 2016, "U.N. Environment Report: Put People, Not Cars First in Transport Systems," Sustainable Development Goals, un.org/sustainabledevelopment/blog/2016/10/un-environment-report-put-people-not-cars-first-in-transport-systems/.
13. Australian Bureau of Statistics, 2019, "9208.0 – Survey of Motor Vehicle Use, Australia, 12 Months Ended 30 June 2018," abs.gov.au/ausstats/abs@.nsf/mf/9208.0.
14. Adeel Lari, 2012, "Telework/Workforce Flexibility to Reduce Congestion and Environmental Degradation?" Procedia – Social and Behavioral Sciences, 48, 712–21.
15. J.R.R. Tolkien, 1997, The Hobbit, London: Harper Collins Publishers, 289.
16. Eric Rosen, 2018, "Over 4 Billion Passengers Flew In 2017 Setting New Travel Record," forbes.com/sites/ericrosen/2018/09/08/over-4-billion-passengers-flew-in-2017-setting-new-travel-record/#27d8ef1255b2.
17. Air Transport Action Group (ATAG), 2018, "Facts & Figures," atag.org/facts-figures.html.
18. BBC News, 2019, "Climate Change: Should You Fly, Drive or Take the Train?" bbc.com/news/science-environment-49349566.
19. Tatiana Schlossberg, 2017, "Flying Is Bad for the Planet. You Can Help Make It Better.," nytimes.com/2017/07/27/climate/airplane-pollution-global-warming.html.
20. E. Mazareanu, 2019, "U.S. Air Passengers' Main Trip Purposes in 2017, by Type," statista.com/statistics/539518/us-air-passengers-main-trip-purposes-by-type/.
21. Trondent Development Corp., 2020, "Business Travel by the Numbers," trondent.com/business-travel-statistics/.

Chapter 8

1. Maja Paleka, 2019, "The Way We Talk about Flexibility Is All Wrong – Let's #pressforprogress by Changing That," jugglestrategies.com.au/blog/the-way-we-talk-about-flexibility-is-all-wrong-lets-pressforprogress-by-changing-that.
2. Emma Walsh, 2018, "Fathers and Parental Leave," Australian Institute of Family Values, aifs.gov.au/aifs-conference/fathers-and-parental-leave.
3. Amy Packham, 2019, "More Than Half of Dads Struggle to Secure Flexibility At Work – And It's Affecting Their Mental Health," Huffington Post UK, huffingtonpost.co.uk/entry/dads-struggle-flexibility-at-work_uk_5cdebc2ae4b09e057802987a.
4. Richard Laermer, 2017, "I Let My Staff Work from Home, Then Realized It Wasn't Working," nbcnews.com/think/opinion/i-let-my-staff-work-home-then-realized-it-wasn-ncna814751.

Chapter 9

1. Time Doctor, 2019, timedoctor.com/.
2. Trevor Haynes, 2018, "Dopamine, Smartphones & You: A Battle for Your Time," Harvard University: Science in the News, sitn.hms.harvard.edu/flash/2018/dopamine-smartphones-battle-time/.
3. Rani Molla, 2019, "The Productivity Pit: How Slack Is Ruining Work," vox.com/recode/2019/5/1/18511575/productivity-slack-google-microsoft-facebook.

Chapter 10

1. WorldatWork, 2015, Trends in Workplace Flexibility, worldatwork.org/dA/10dc98de55/Trends%20in%20Workplace%20Flexibility%20-%202015.pdf.
2. Public Service Commission, "Flexible Working Case Studies," NSW Government, psc.nsw.gov.au/workplace-culture---diversity/flexible-working/implementing-flexibility--resources-for-people-and-culture-teams/leading-implementation-of-flexible-working/case-studies.

Chapter 11

1. Rutger Bregman, 2017, Utopia for Realists, and How We Get There, London: Bloomsbury, 140.
2. Carmel Lobello, 2013, "What Happened to the Six-Hour Workday?" theweek.com/articles/454364/what-happened-sixhour-workday.
3. Rutger Bregman, 2017, Utopia for Realists, and How We Get There, London: Bloomsbury: London, 140–41.
4. Mitch Galloway, 2018, "At Family-Owned Micron Manufacturing, Workers Create Their Own Schedules," mibiz.com/item/25451-at-family-owned-micron-manufacturing,-workers-create-their-own-schedules.
5. Woohoo Inc, 2015, "Introducing a 30-Hour Work Week at Toyota Gothenburg," youtube.com/watch?v=aJUEXPP0Hao.

6. Ben Windsor-Shellard, 2017, "Suicide by Occupation, England: 2011 to 2015," U.K. Office for National Statistics, ons.gov.uk/peoplepopulationandcommunity/birthsdeathsandmarriages/deaths/articles/suicidebyoccupation/england2011to2015#main-points.

7. RegisteredNursing.org, 2017, "Suicide Rates by Profession," registerednursing.org/suicide-rates-profession/.

8. Natalie Wolfe, 2018, "The Deadliest Jobs in Australia for Men," news.com.au/lifestyle/health/mind/the-deadliest-jobs-in-australia-for-men/news-story/08e329b5572c944dffcecb21ba814976.

9. Australian Institute for Suicide Research and Prevention, 2006, "Suicide in Queensland's Commercial Building and Construction Industry," mates.net.nz/wp-content/uploads/2020/02/2006-MIC_AISRAP-Report.pdf.

10. Lifeline, n.d., "Statistics on Suicide in Australia," lifeline.org.au/about-lifeline/lifeline-information/statistics-on-suicide-in-australia.

11. A. Mills, P. Williams and D. Yu, 2010, "Benchmarking Construction Rework in Australian Housing," *Int. Journal for Housing Science*, 34(3): 207–20.

12. Peter Love et al., 2018, "The Cost of Rework: Insights from Construction and Opportunities for Learning," *Production Planning and Control*, espace.curtin.edu.au/handle/20.500.11937/72898.

13. Emmanuel Eze and John Ebhohimen Idiake, 2018, "Analysis of Cost of Rework on Time and Cost Performance of Building Construction Projects in Abuja, Nigeria," *International Journal of Build Environment and Sustainability*, 5(1): 56–67.

14. NSW Government, 2019, "Flexible Working Case Study: Mirvac," psc.nsw.gov.au/workplace-culture--diversity/flexible-working/implementing-flexibility--resources-for-people-and-culture-teams/leading-implementation-of-flexible-working/case-studies/mirvac.

15. NSW Government, 15.

16. Geoffrey Lean, 2011, "Sir Richard Branson: We Must Learn that Doing Good is Good for Business," telegraph.co.uk/finance/newsbysector/banksandfinance/8900854/Sir-Richard-Branson-We-must-learn-that-doing-good-is-good-for-business.html.

17. Zoe Kinias, 2020, "Challenging Assumptions About Flexible Work," knowledge.insead.edu/leadership-organisations/challenging-assumptions-about-flexible-work-13411.

18. John T. James, 2013, "A New, Evidence-based Estimate of Patient Harms Associated with Hospital Care," *Journal of Patient Safety*, 9(3): 122–28, journals.lww.com/journalpatientsafety/Fulltext/2013/09000/A_New,_Evidence_based_Estimate_of_Patient_Harms.2.aspx.

19. Hannah Nichols, 2019, "What Are the Leading Causes of Death in the US?," medicalnewstoday.com/articles/282929.php.

20. Jacob E. Sunshine et al., 2019, "Association of Adverse Effects of Medical Treatment With Mortality in the United States: A Secondary Analysis of the Global Burden of Diseases, Injuries, and Risk Factors Study," *JAMA Network Open*, 2(1), jamanetwork.com/journals/jamanetworkopen/fullarticle/2720915.

21. Ryan Park, 2017, "Why So Many Young Doctors Work Such Awful Hours," theatlantic.com/business/archive/2017/02/doctors-long-hours-schedules/516639/.

22. John Flannery and Maria Hawthorne, 2017, "One in Two Public Hospital Doctors Working Unsafe Hours," Australian Medical Association, ama.com.au/media/one-two-public-hospital-doctors-working-unsafe-hours.

23. A. M. Williamson and Anne-Marie Feyer, 2000, "Moderate Sleep Deprivation Produces Impairments in Cognitive and Motor Performance Equivalent to Legally Prescribed Levels of Alcohol Intoxication," *Occupational and Environmental Medicine*, 57(10): 649–55, ncbi.nlm.nih.gov/pmc/articles/PMC1739867/.

24. Laura K. Barger et al., 2006, "Impact of Extended-Duration Shifts on Medical Errors, Adverse Events, and Attentional Failures," *PLoS Med.*, 3(12), ncbi.nlm.nih.gov/pmc/articles/PMC1705824/.

25. Alexander Blum et al., 2010, "US Public Opinion Regarding Proposed Limits on Resident Physician Work Hours," *BMC Med*, 8(33), ncbi.nlm.nih.gov/pmc/articles/PMC2901227/.

26. Kate Aubusson, 2019, "Burned-out Junior Doctors Fear They'll Accidentally Harm Patients," *Sydney Morning Herald*, smh.com.au/national/nsw/burned-out-junior-doctors-fear-they-ll-accidentally-harm-patients-20191112-p539ru.html.

27. Morgan Liotta, 2020, "Junior Doctors Working Unsafe Hours to 'Earn Their Stripes,'" Royal Australian College of General Practitioners, racgp.org.au/newsgp/clinical/junior-doctors-working-unsafe-hours-to-earn-their.

28. Danielle M. Olds and Sean P. Clarke, 2010, "The Effect of Work Hours on Adverse Events and Errors in Health Care," *J Safety Res.*, 41(2): 153–62, ncbi.nlm.nih.gov/pmc/articles/PMC2910393/.

29. Laura K. Barger et al., 2006, "Impact of Extended-Duration Shifts on Medical Errors, Adverse Events, and Attentional Failures," PLoS Med., 3(12), ncbi.nlm.nih.gov/pmc/articles/PMC1705824/.

30. Denis Campbell, 2019, "NHS England Losing Staff in Record Numbers Over Long Hours – Study," theguardian.com/society/2019/feb/16/nhs-england-losing-staff-in-record-numbers-over-long-hours-study.

31. Laura Donnelly, 2019, "NHS Appoints 'Head of Flexible Working' in Bid to Push Part-time Jobs," telegraph.co.uk/news/2019/12/08/nhs-appoints-head-flexible-working-bid-push-part-time-jobs/.

32. Maddy Savage, 2017, "What Really Happened When Swedes Tried Six-Hour Days?" bbc.com/news/business-38843341.

33. Thomas Heath, 2017, "The Swedish Six-Hour Workday Could Help You Live Longer," *Sydney Morning Herald*, smh.com.au/lifestyle/health-and-wellness/the-swedish-sixhour-workday-could-help-you-live-longer-20170424-gvqxs4.html.

34. Nous Group, 2018, *Flexible Work, Good for Business?*, Victoria State Government, vic.gov.au/sites/default/files/2019-01/Report-Flexible-work-return-on-investment.pdf.

35. The Doctor's Farmacy with Mark Hyman, 2019, "Episode 37: Why the CEO of Cleveland Clinic Embraced Functional Medicine," drhyman.com/blog/2019/01/23/podcast-ep37/.

36. FlexJobs, n.d., "Cleveland Clinic Jobs with Remote and Flexible Work Options," flexjobs.com/jobs/telecommuting-jobs-at-cleveland_clinic.

37. Institute for Health and Productivity Studies, John Hopkins Bloomberg School of Public Health, 2015, *From Evidence to Practice: Workplace Wellness that Works*, transamericacenterforhealthstudies.org/docs/default-source/wellness-page/from-evidence-to-practice---workplace-wellness-that-works.pdf.

Chapter 12

1. The National Museum of Australia, n.d., "Eight-hour Day," nma.gov.au/defining-moments/resources/eight-hour-day.

2. Allison Nawoj, 2011, "More Than One-Quarter of Managers Said They Weren't Ready to Lead When They Began Managing Others, Finds New CareerBuilder Survey," press.careerbuilder.com/2011-03-28-More-Than-One-Quarter-of-Managers-Said-They-Werent-Ready-to-Lead-When-They-Began-Managing-Others-Finds-New-CareerBuilder-Survey.

3. Victor Lipman, 2016, "A Startling 98% of Managers Feel Managers Need More Training," forbes.com/sites/victorlipman/2016/10/01/a-startling-98-of-managers-feel-managers-need-more-training/#61bff9e75e8b.

4. Randall J. Beck and Jim Harter, 2014, "Why Good Managers Are So Rare," *Harvard Business Review*, hbr.org/2014/03/why-good-managers-are-so-rare.

5. Henry Stewart, 2012, *The Happy Manifesto: Make Your Organisation a Great Place to Work – Now!*, London: Happy, happy.co.uk/media/1467/happy-manifesto.pdf, 112–14.

6. Johnny Wood and Briony Harris, 2018, "A Vacation from Work Could Be a Lifesaver," World Economic Forum, weforum.org/agenda/2018/08/booking-a-vacation-from-workplace-stress-could-prolong-your-life.

7. Meredith Lepore, 2018, "This Is How Americans Define Their Dream Job," thriveglobal.com/stories/this-is-how-americans-define-their-dream-job/.

8. Melanie Burgess, 2019, "Australian Companies Are Offering Extra Paid Annual Leave to Boost Productivity," news.com.au/finance/work/at-work/australian-companies-are-offering-extra-paid-annual-leave-to-boost-productivity/news-story/b6fd117f3c3bde5eff6e09ea14bae2a1.

Chapter 13

1. Anna Coote, Jane Franklin, and Andrew Simms, 2010, *21 Hours: Why a Shorter Working Week Can Help Us All to Flourish in the 21st Century*, London: New Economics Foundation, b.3cdn.net/nefoundation/f49406d81b9ed9c977_p1m6ibgje.pdf.

Appendix A

1. Gaby Hinsliff, 2018, "This CEO Took A Pay Cut To Give Employees $70,000 A Year. Now He's Battling Amazon," huffingtonpost.com.au/entry/dan-price-minimum-wage_n_5afd3d8ee4b06a3fb50dcf28.

INDEX

ABOUT THE AUTHOR

 **Robert Hawkins** spent several years in rigid workplaces – with the accompanying long and unnecessary commutes – as an engineer, manager, and process improvement specialist. He now freelances as a writer and consultant, walks his dog in the mornings instead of sitting in traffic, and works to help as many people as possible regain life and health by working flexibly.

CPSIA information can be obtained
at www.ICGtesting.com
Printed in the USA
LVHW040010091020
668367LV00003B/4